Postcard History Series

Fresno

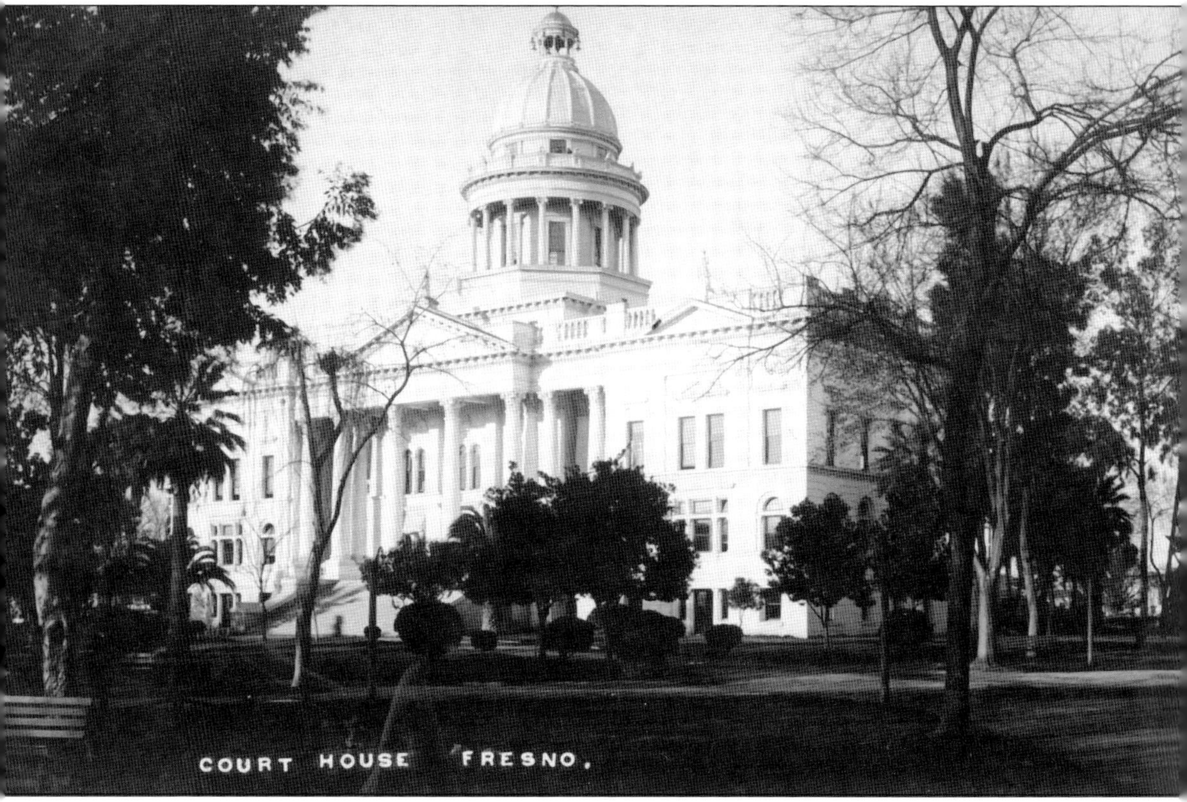

Fresno County Courthouse is pictured about 1907.

On the Cover: This image was reproduced as a colorized postcard by the Pacific Novelty Company of San Francisco. The image shown here is the actual proof that was used to create the card. It shows the front of the courthouse in Courthouse Park. (Fresno County Library.)

POSTCARD HISTORY SERIES

Fresno

John Reynolds and Michael J. Semas

ARCADIA
PUBLISHING

ISBN 978-0-7385-9620-4

Published by Arcadia Publishing
Charleston, South Carolina

Printed in the United States of America

Library of Congress Control Number: 2012941141

For all general information contact Arcadia Publishing at:
Telephone 843-853-2070
Fax 843-853-0044
E-mail sales@arcadiapublishing.com
For customer service and orders:
Toll-Free 1-888-313-2665

Visit us on the Internet at www.arcadiapublishing.com

The book is dedicated to my lovely wife of 54 years, Karen, whose understanding of spelling, grammar, and sentence structure made this entire book readable. –JR

This book is dedicated to my wife, Christine, who feigns a modicum of interest in my hobby and to my daughters Katherine and Sarah, who are always asking how much their postcard collection is worth. –MJS

Contents

ACKNOWLEDGMENTS

This book represents a labor of love for both of us. Learning local history has been a passion of ours for most of our lives and we strive to share our knowledge with all who ask. We wish to thank the staff of the Fresno County Library California History and Genealogy Room who tirelessly assisted us in this book, including Nance Espinosa, Bill Secrest Jr., Melissa Scroggins, Lois Bakar, and Chris Her. We would also like to thank John Walker of the *Fresno Bee* for his assistance in our research. The Fresno County Library and Mark Jost provided several key images that helped perfect the content of this book. Images not receiving credit are from our personal collections. Finally, we would like to extend a special thank-you to Karen Reynolds, who proofed the captions and pointed out where all the commas, hyphens, and apostrophes needed to go. We hope you will enjoy reading this book as much as we did writing it.

INTRODUCTION

Fresno was originally established in early 1872 when the Central Pacific Railroad was constructing its rail line south through the San Joaquin Valley. The site was selected in 1871 when a group of railroad officials led by Leland Stanford visited the A.Y. Easterby Ranch, which was located directly east of the current town site. Leland Stanford commented on how productive the farm appeared and insisted that a local town be situated in the same area.

Based upon Stanford's wishes, the company built a small depot in the sinks of Dry Creek and named the stop Fresno Station. The original town was nothing more than a depot building and a series of tents erected by the railroad construction workers. James F. Faber established Fresno's first general store from one of those tents. On March 1, 1872, a post office was established with Russell H. Fleming as its first postmaster. Around that same time, telegraph service also began. In December 1873, a site map for the "Town of Fresno" was filed with the Fresno County recorder at the original courthouse in Millerton. In March 1874, a countywide election was held to determine which community should become the county seat. Fresno won the election in a landslide with 417 votes, with Lisbon, Centerville, and Millerton receiving 124, 123, and 93 votes respectively. Rumor has it that it was Fresno's offering of free liquor that attracted a large number of railroad employees to the town on election day and skewed the vote.

In 1885, the town incorporated, and the City of Fresno was born. The first town leaders were Thomas E. Hughes, Arthur Tombs, J.M. Brady, Dr. W.L. Graves, and William Faymonville as the first mayor. The city conducted its business at several different rented locations until the first city hall was built in 1888 on the 1200 block of J Street.

Fresno was fortunate to come into existence when the natural bounty of the county was first being discovered. Early on, cattle were shipped from the Fresno railhead to the slaughterhouses of south San Francisco. Abundant wheat harvests were sent nationwide from the same location. However, it was not until the waters of the San Joaquin and Kings Rivers were diverted through newly dug canals that the true worth of the area was discovered.

The climate of Central California coupled with the fertile soil created a true Garden of Eden. Almost overnight, large crops of alfalfa and wheat were grown. Vast tracts of fruit trees and vines were planted and their abundance was immediately realized. Francis T. Eisen established Fresno County's wine industry in 1875 by producing 200 gallons of wine. To compound nature's wealth, the Sierra Nevada Mountains to the east were filled with virgin timber. Massive lumber operations were established to develop the use of that resource. Oil was discovered on the west side of the county, and an entire new industry was born. Through it all, Fresno enjoyed the prosperity that accompanied the exploitation of all these resources.

During the 20th century, Fresno developed into an economic and political powerhouse. Being situated in the center of California was a distinct advantage for the city. Many national fruit, nut, and vineyard operations claimed Fresno as home. Local banks were formed, and they grew into statewide lending institutions. Industries that supported agriculture also grew into some of the largest businesses of their kind in the world. All these enterprises employed thousands, and these people made their homes in Fresno.

As the seat of the county, the city also enjoyed the benefits of an expanding and stable tax base. Large public buildings were constructed to house the various county operations. The US government established a federal courthouse in Fresno. The US Treasury located one of the largest tax return processing centers in Fresno, which employed thousands of federal employees.

The City of Fresno also enjoyed the generosity of many individuals. In 1903, Frederick and Marianne Roeding gave 118 acres for the establishment of Roeding Park. In 1905, Martin Theodore Kearney bequeathed his 5,400-acre estate to the University of California where Kearney Park is located today. In 1912, Wilber Chandler donated the land where Chandler Airport is now located. In 1968, Ralph Woodward bequeathed 235 acres on the south bank of the San Joaquin River for the establishment of Woodward Park.

Today, Fresno is the fifth largest city in California, with over 510,000 residents. Agriculture still dominates the city's economy, and much of the industry and job base are still connected with it. However, Fresno has a large industrial and service-based economy that extends throughout the San Joaquin Valley. Furthermore, because of its proximity to Yosemite, Sequoia, and Kings Canyon National Parks, there is a burgeoning tourist industry. Being centrally located is an advantage that Fresno has over many other cities in California.

Fresno is the Spanish word for ash tree. The name was originally used in connection with an earlier settlement, Fresno City, near where the town of Tranquility is currently located. Surrounding that settlement were several ash trees. It is rather ironic that Fresno once had no trees anywhere in sight. It was described at one time as a barren, desert-like plain with only elk, antelope, and jackrabbits inhabiting the area. Fresno has come a long way since 1872.

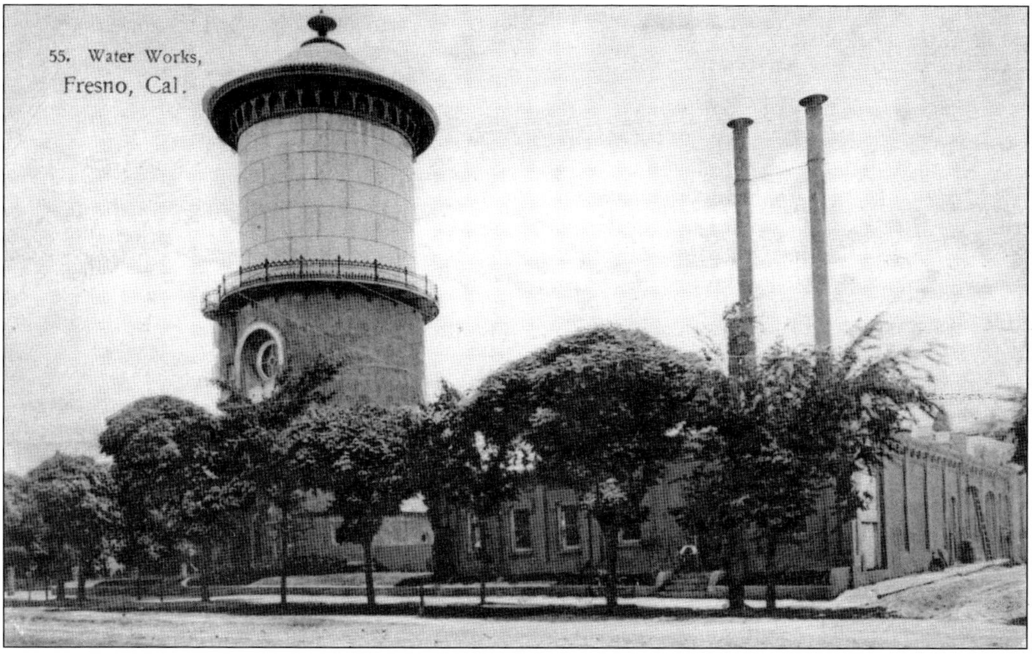

One of Fresno's most iconic buildings is the Fresno Water Tower, which is located on the southwest corner of O and Fresno Streets. It was built in 1894 at a cost of $20,000 and was designed by George Washington Meher in the American Romanesque style. In this image, the water tower is shown next to the San Joaquin Electric Power substation, which was located on the southeast corner of N and Fresno Streets.

One

Fresno on the Go

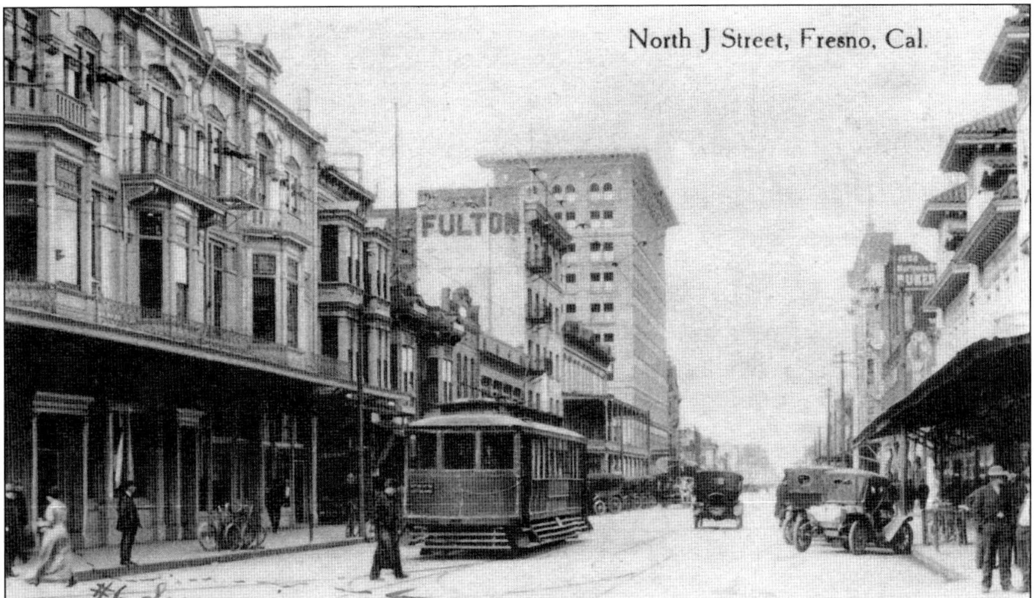

This view is looking up Fulton Street from the corner of Tulare and shows a streetcar in operation. On the far right is the Patterson Block, with its turrets and dark covers. The Owl Drug Store was located in this building. The tall building in the center was originally named the Griffith-McKenzie Building but is now known as the Helm Building. (Fresno County Library.)

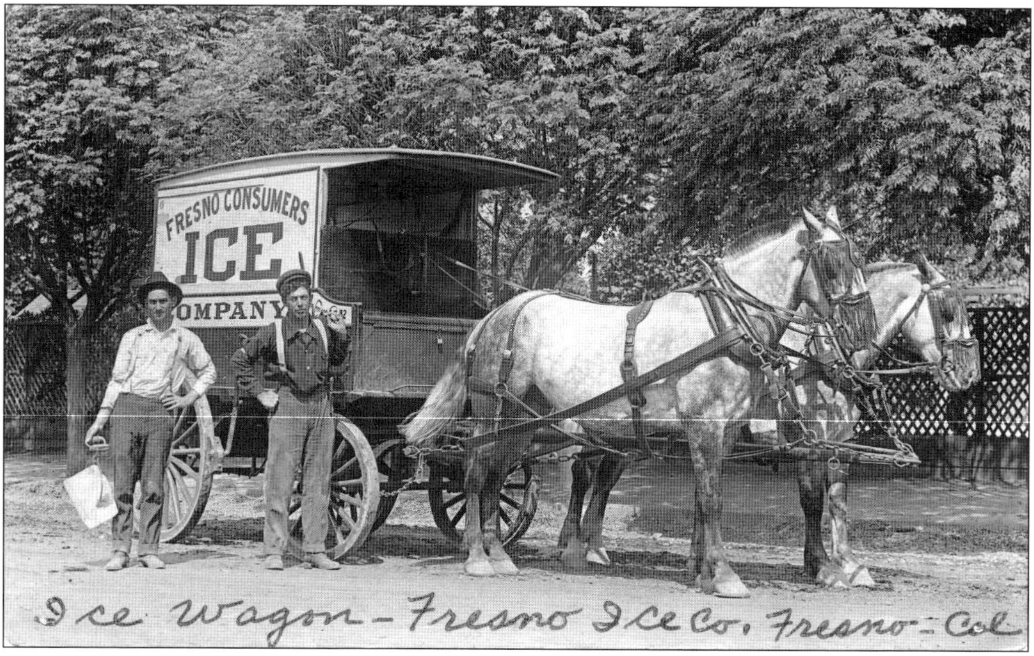

This image shows a Fresno Consumers Ice Company wagon on a delivery run. Note the man holding a block of ice using tongs.

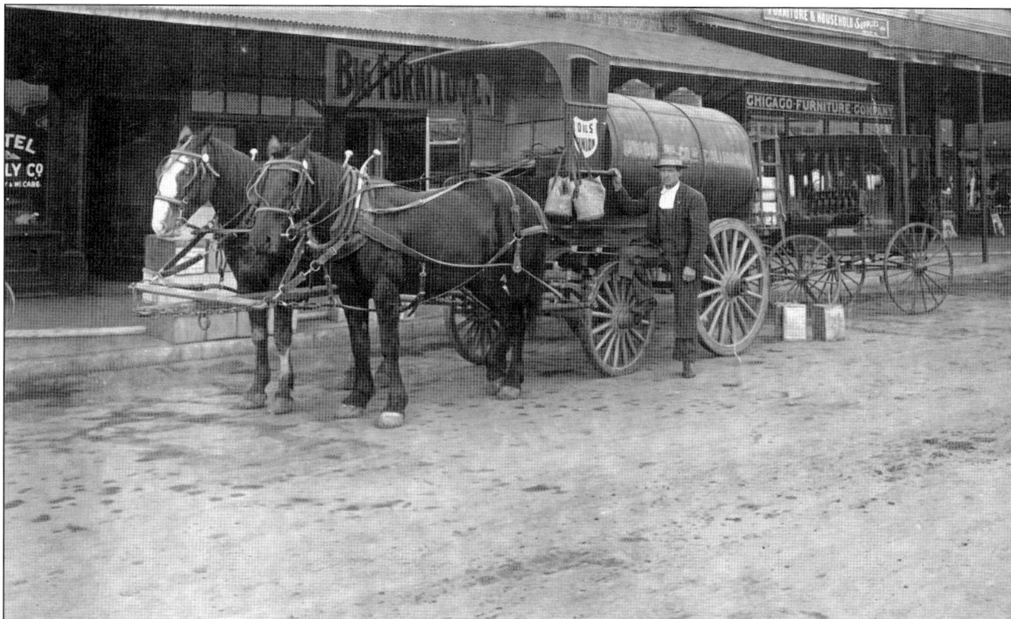

This horse-drawn tank wagon of the Union Oil Co. delivered oil products such as gasoline (motor fuel), kerosene (lamp oil), benzene (cleaning liquid), or distillate (heating oil) to homes and businesses in Fresno. The Union Oil Co. plant was at Nielson and West Avenues. (Fresno County Library.)

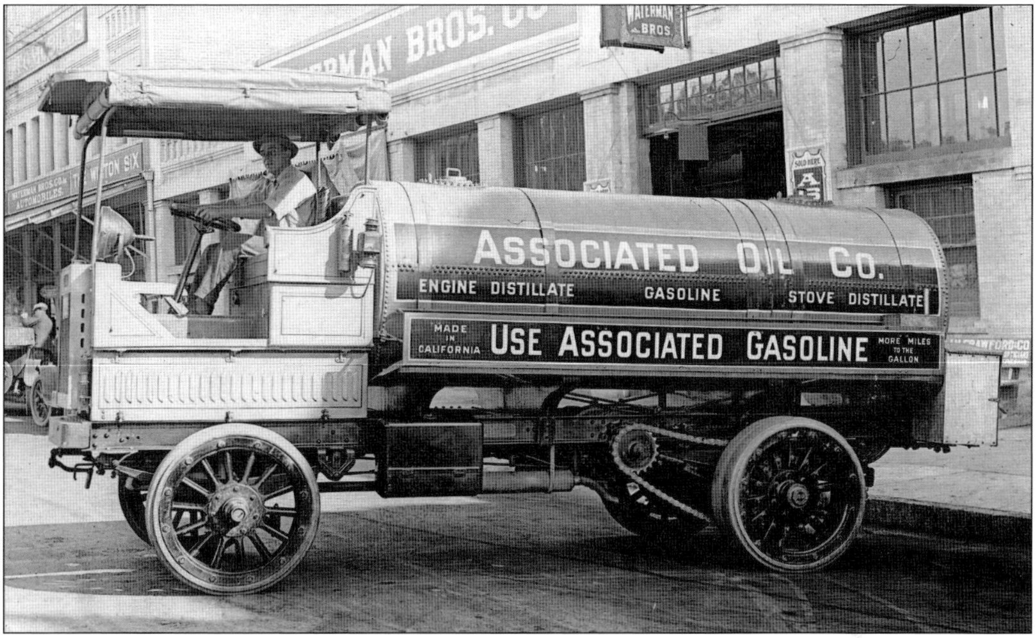

Shown on this card is an Associated Oil Company chain-driven oil delivery truck, which is parked in front of the Waterman Bros. Buick shop in Fresno. Associated Oil was formed in 1901, and its logo was an "A" with flying wings. The tank lists three oil products: engine distillate, gasoline, and stove distillate.

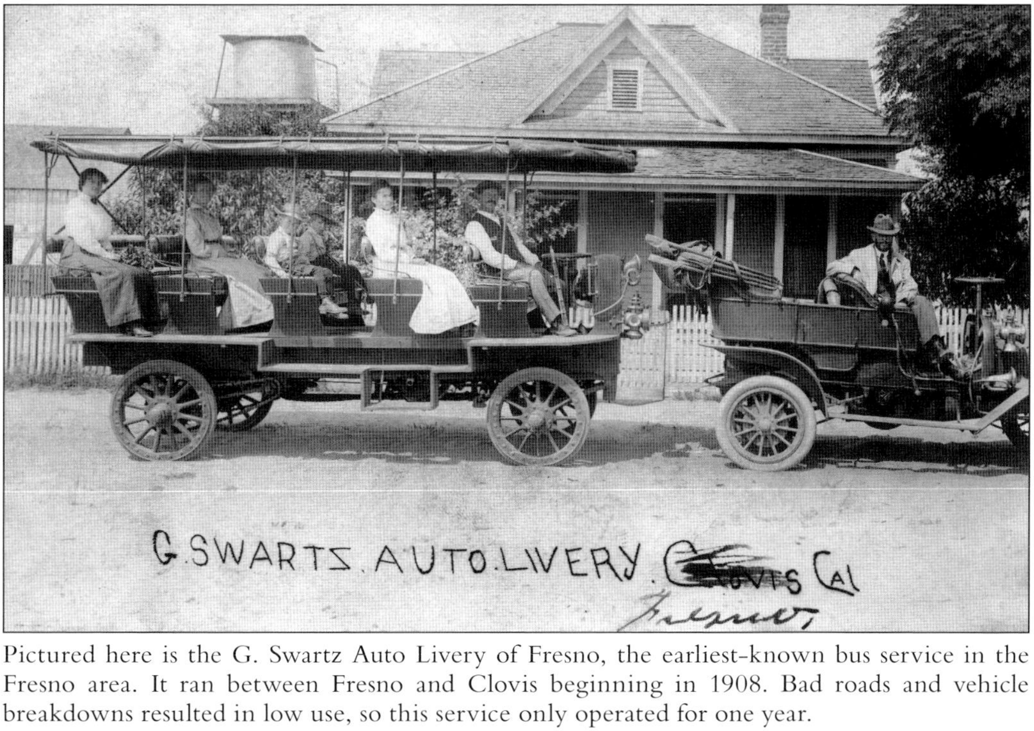

Pictured here is the G. Swartz Auto Livery of Fresno, the earliest-known bus service in the Fresno area. It ran between Fresno and Clovis beginning in 1908. Bad roads and vehicle breakdowns resulted in low use, so this service only operated for one year.

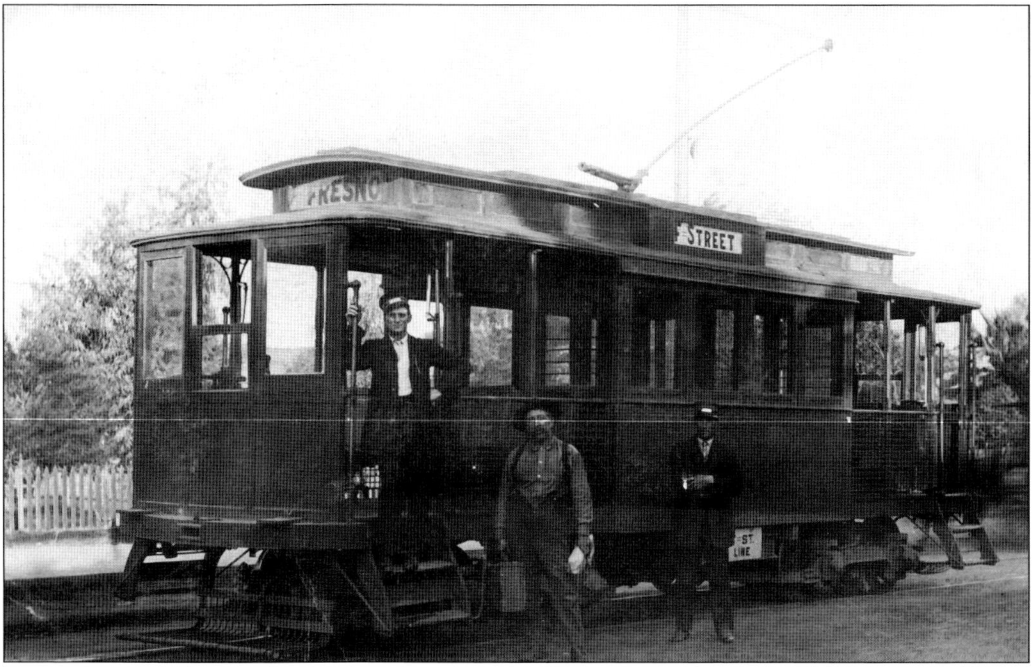

This Fresno streetcar is marked as the "F Street" line. Two motormen ran the car, one for each end. The third man shown could have been a line mechanic. Streetcar motormen wore distinctive uniforms with hats.

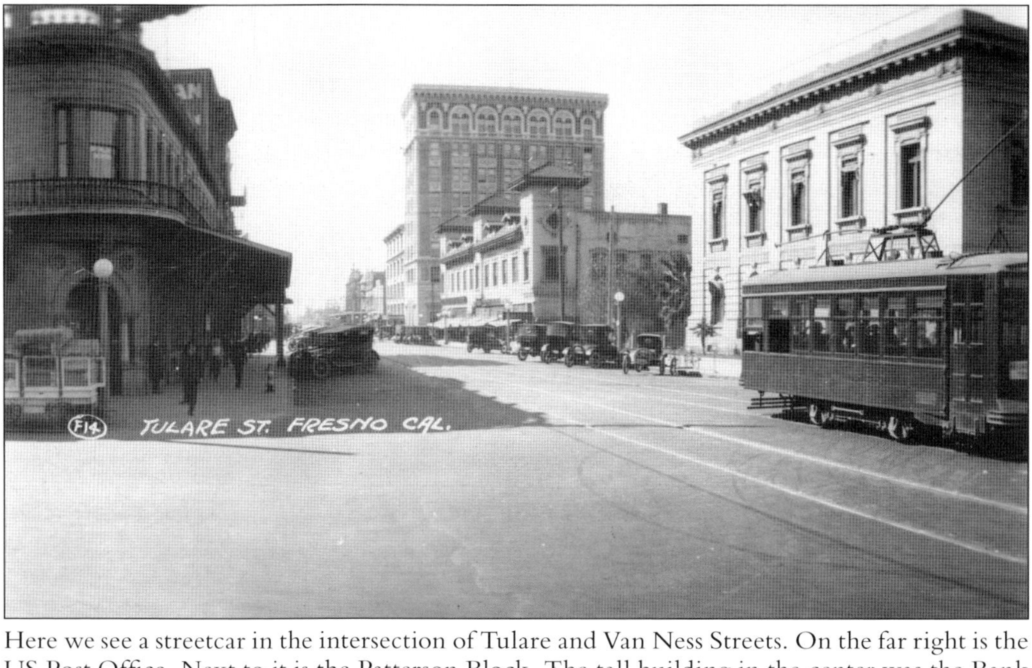

Here we see a streetcar in the intersection of Tulare and Van Ness Streets. On the far right is the US Post Office. Next to it is the Patterson Block. The tall building in the center was the Bank of Italy Building, later known as Bank of America. Located in the building on the left was the *Fresno Morning Republican* newspaper (1876–1922).

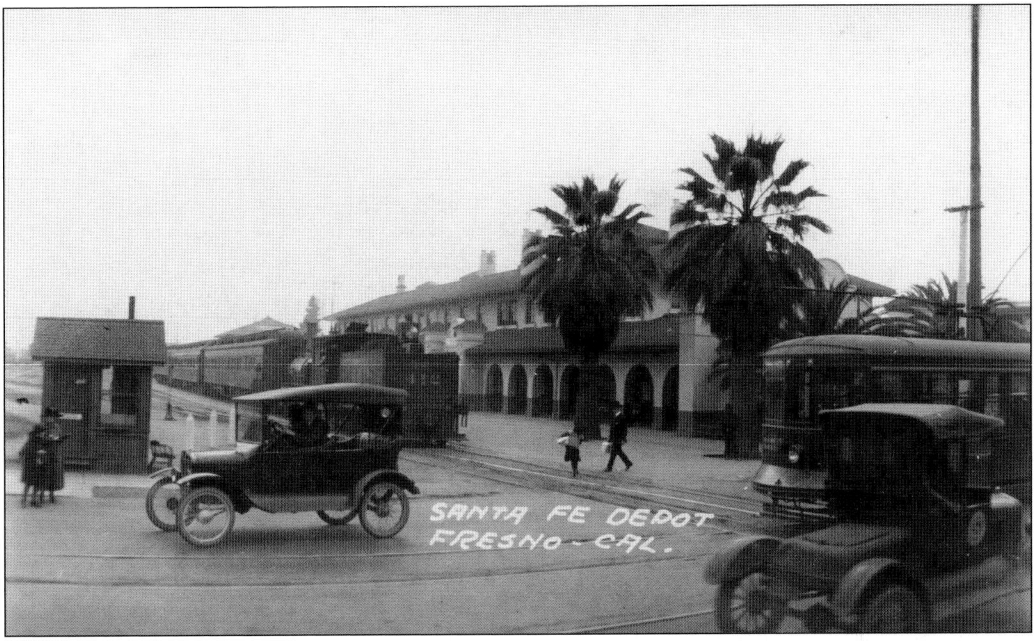

Autos, streetcars, and trains later served Fresno. In 1899, the Santa Fe Depot was built in the Mission Revival style. In 1966, passenger service stopped, and the depot was used for the district communication center and then stood vacant. In 2005, the building was restored and is now used by Amtrak as a passenger depot.

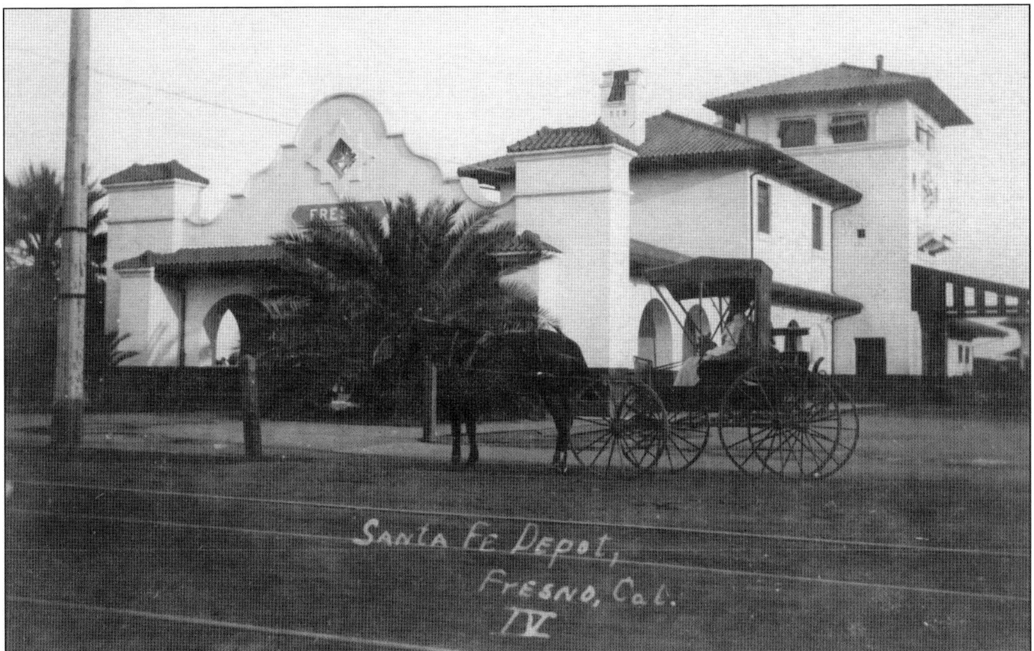

The tracks of the San Francisco and San Joaquin Valley Railroad reached Fresno on October 5, 1896. The rail line, which ran from Point Richmond to Bakersfield, was sold to the Santa Fe Railroad in 1901. Pictured here is the Santa Fe Depot in the horse and buggy era. This depot is still located west of the tracks on Tulare Street.

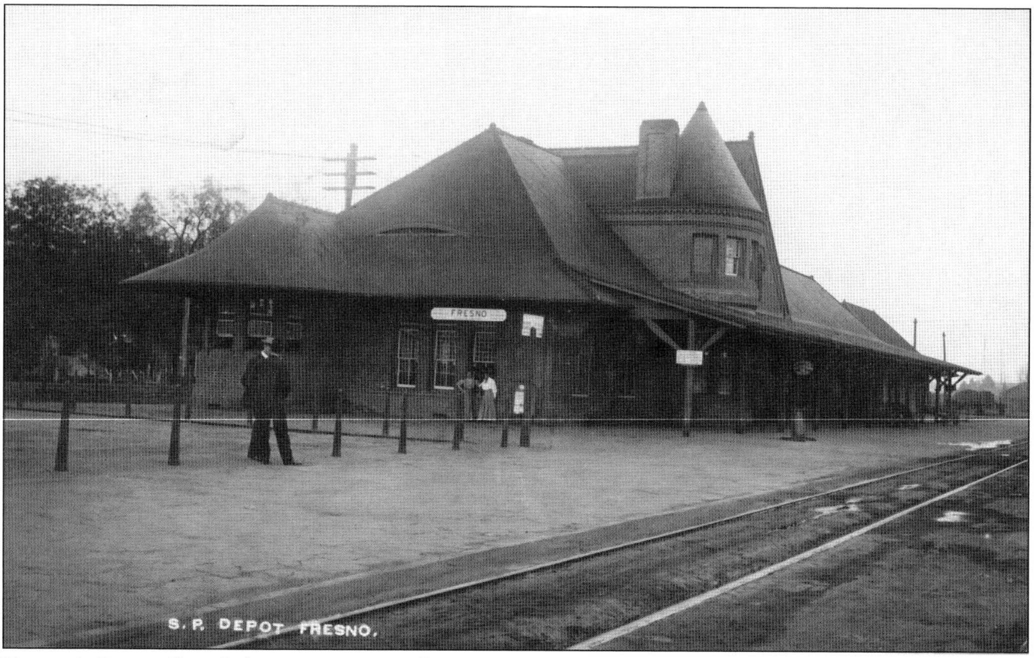

Fresno's first railroad depot was a small wooden structure built in 1872. Because of increased rail traffic in both passengers and freight, Southern Pacific decided to build a spacious, brick, Queen Anne–style depot. This depot is still located where Tulare Street crosses the SP tracks. In 1971, passenger service was discontinued, and the depot was remodeled into a modern, upscale office building.

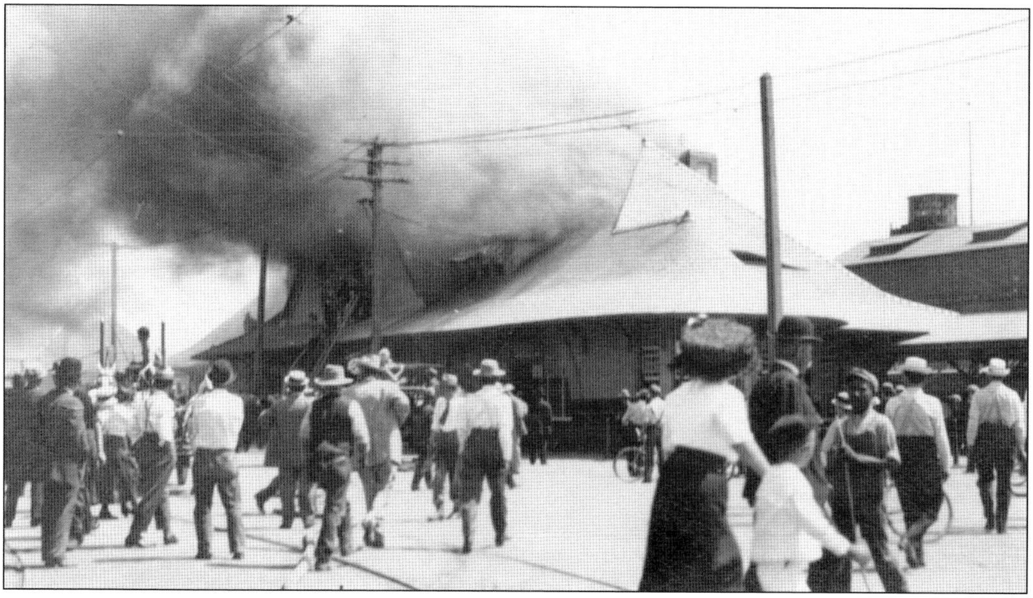

In 1911, Fresno residents ran to watch the Southern Pacific Depot burn. The fire destroyed the second floor offices, but the building was saved. (Fresno County Library.)

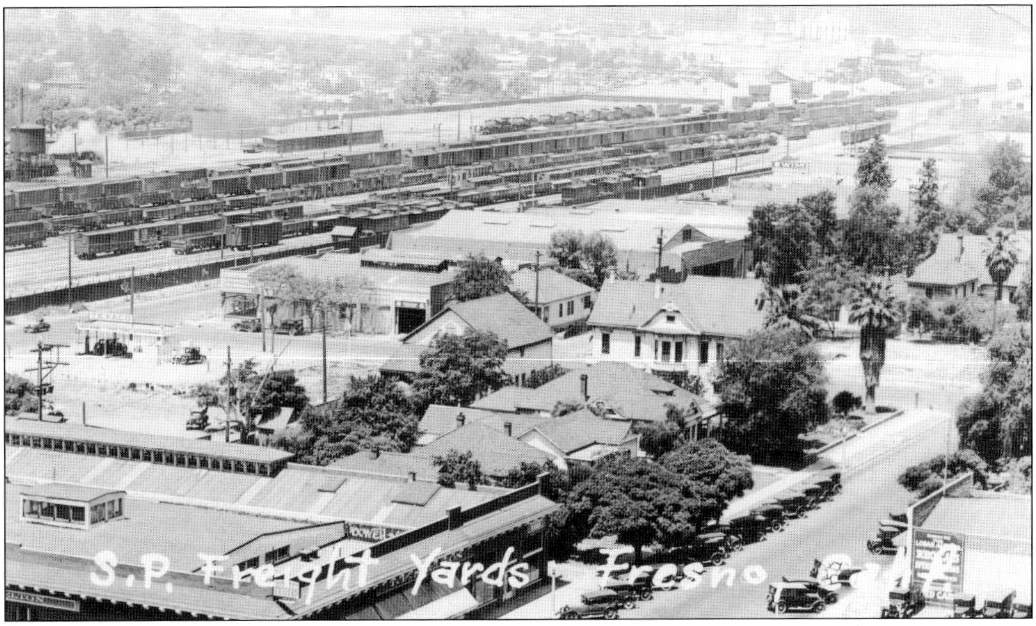

The Southern Pacific Railroad freight yard is located north of downtown Fresno, off the main line. Shields Avenue stops at the east side of the tracks and resumes on the west side of the freight yard.

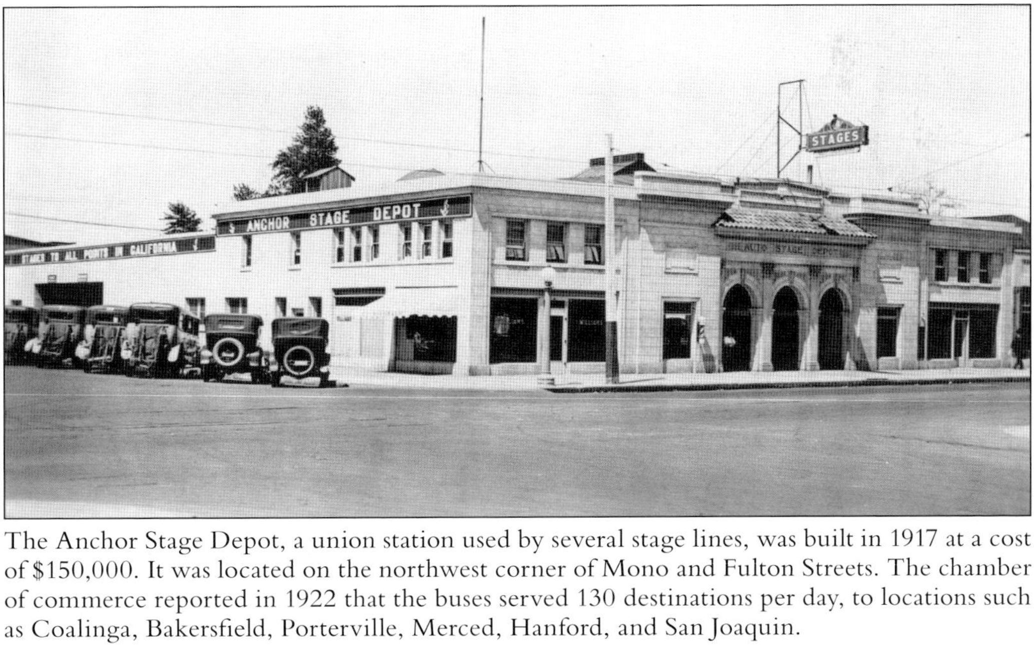

The Anchor Stage Depot, a union station used by several stage lines, was built in 1917 at a cost of $150,000. It was located on the northwest corner of Mono and Fulton Streets. The chamber of commerce reported in 1922 that the buses served 130 destinations per day, to locations such as Coalinga, Bakersfield, Porterville, Merced, Hanford, and San Joaquin.

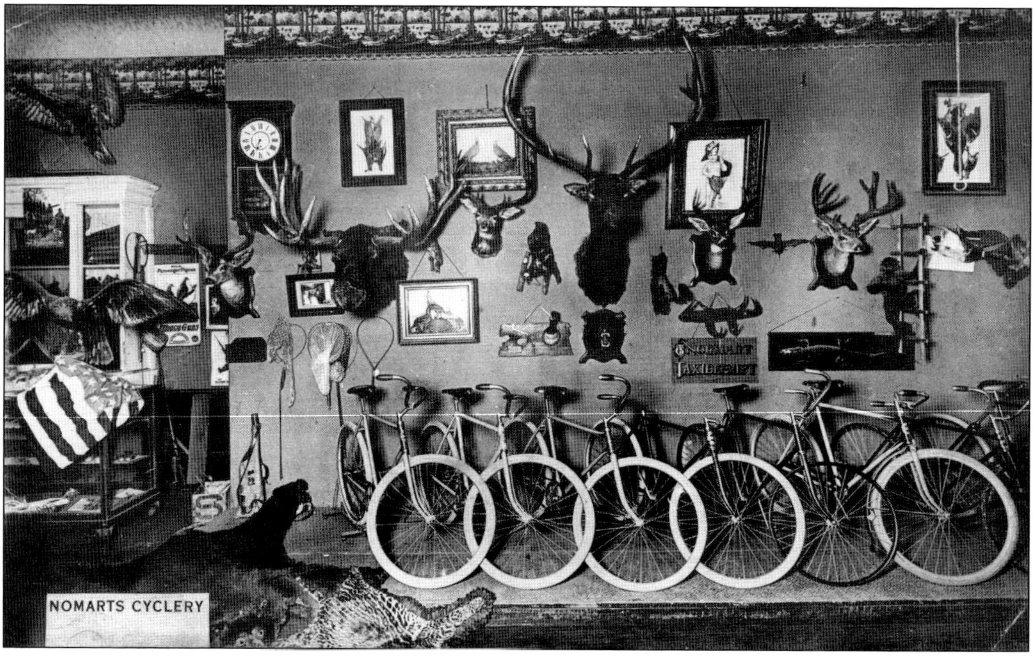

This image shows Nomart's Cyclery, which was located at 2025 Fresno Street. In addition to bicycles, this business sold a curious combination of items including guns, keys, and fishing tackle, and provided leather tanning and taxidermy services as well.

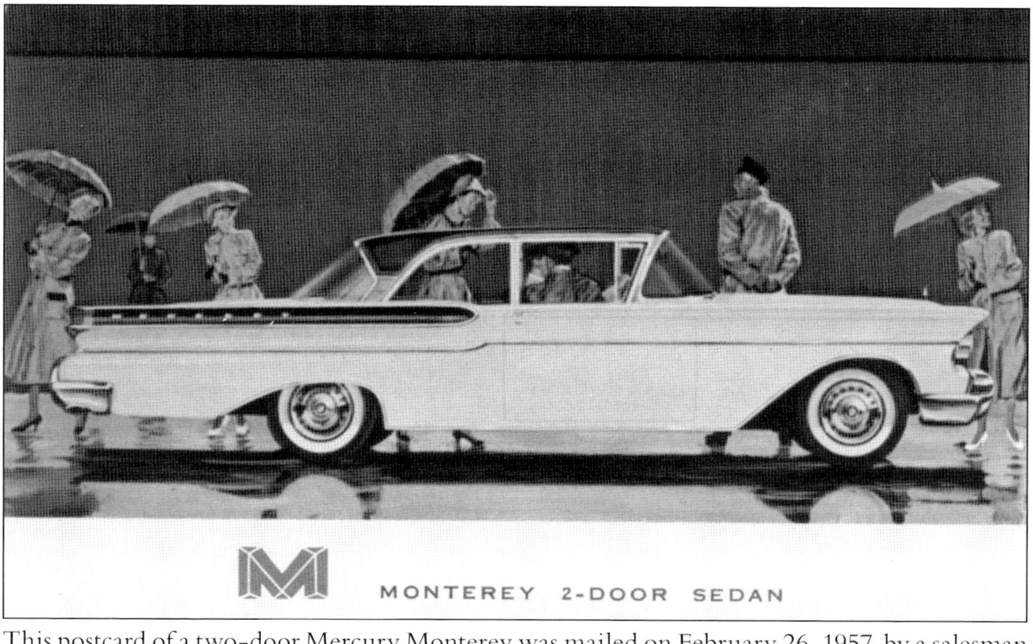

This postcard of a two-door Mercury Monterey was mailed on February 26, 1957, by a salesman at Frank J. Sanders Lincoln-Mercury of Fresno. Every Christmas season, Sanders hosted a free movie (and free candy) for children at either Hardy's or Warner's Theatre. Sanders passed away in August 2011 at the age of 99.

This is an advertising corner card on an envelope from Standard Oil Company of Fresno, postmarked October 1, 1915. The service station on the front displays signage for Red Crown Gasoline and Zerolene Motor Oil.

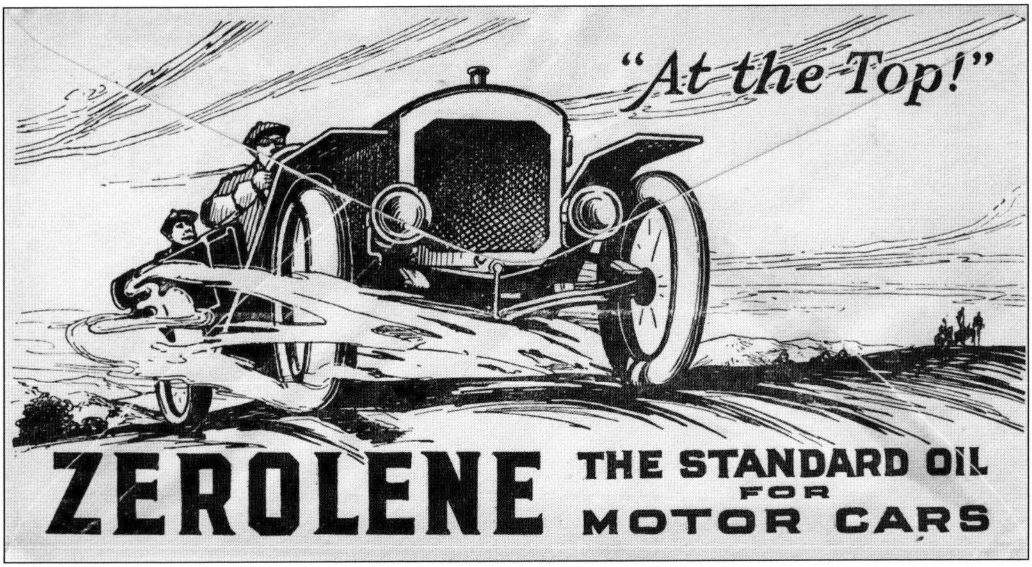

Here is the back of the Zerolene Motor Oil card, which shows an open car running at full speed, with the driver wearing goggles.

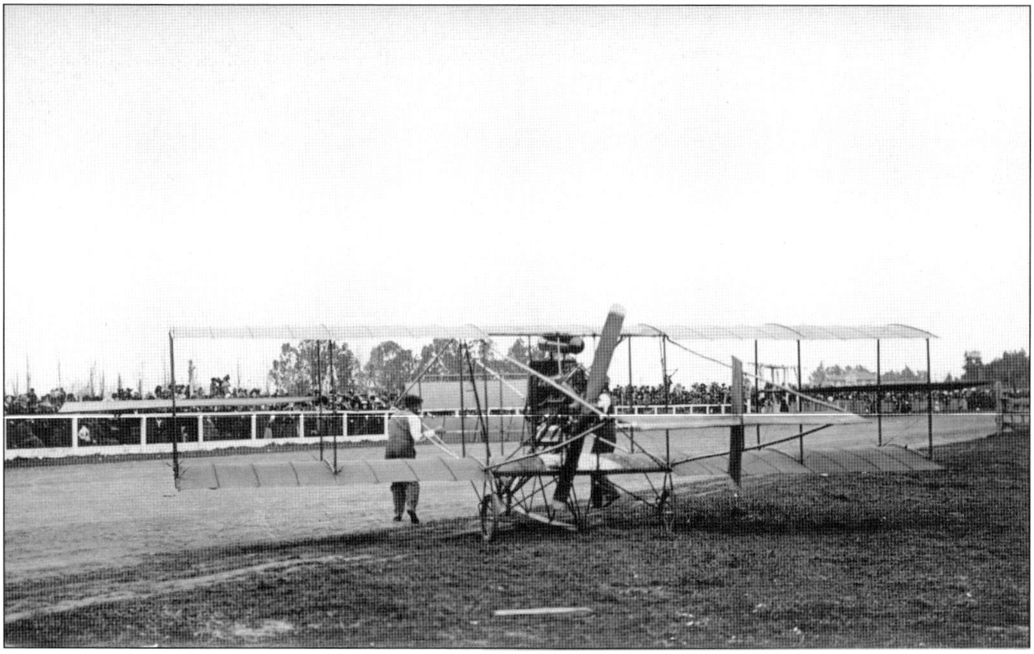

One of the most famous early 20th century events of Fresno was the Fresno Air Meet. It was held at the Fresno Fairgrounds on February 4–6, 1910. The two pilots who arrived were Charles K. Hamilton, flying a G. Curtiss biplane with an eight-cylinder engine, and Charles F. Willard, flying a second Curtiss. Pictured here is Hamilton's biplane at the Fresno Fairgrounds.

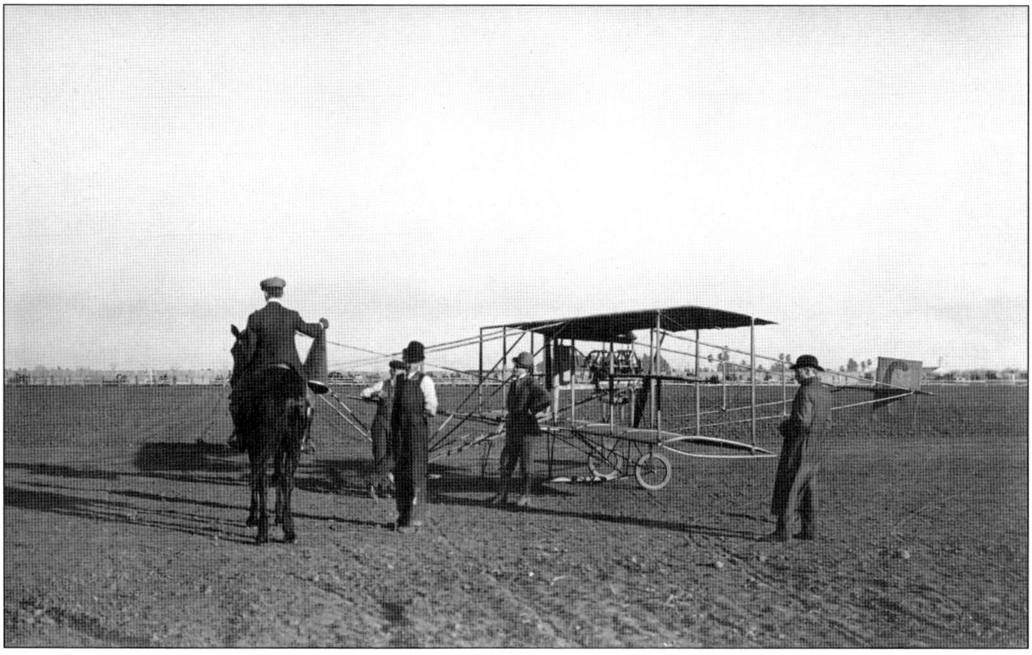

Shown here is a postcard of Charles Willard's Curtiss biplane at the Fresno Fairgrounds. Willard was the fourth person to fly in the Unites States, preceded by both Wright Brothers and Glen Curtiss. He was also the first person to start "barnstorming," daredevil flying that was popular in the mid-1920s.

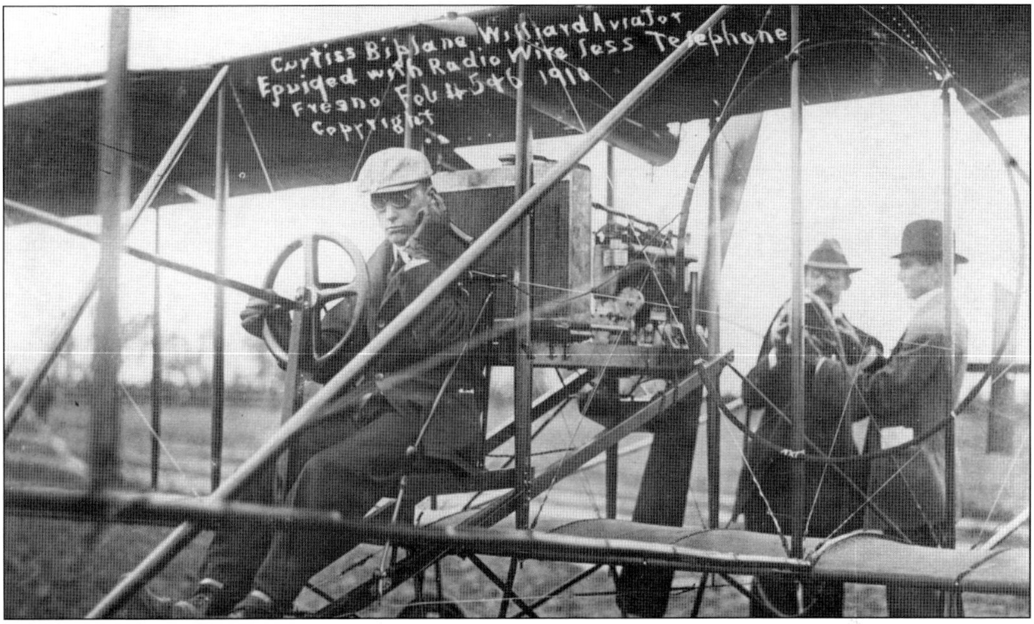

This postcard shows Charles F. Willard at the controls of his Curtiss biplane while attending the Fresno Aviation Meet. As a special treat, his airplane was equipped with a wireless telephone and he communicated with the spectators while flying. Both Willard and Hamilton were members of the Curtiss Flying Team and had the support of ground personnel and spare parts from the Curtiss Company.

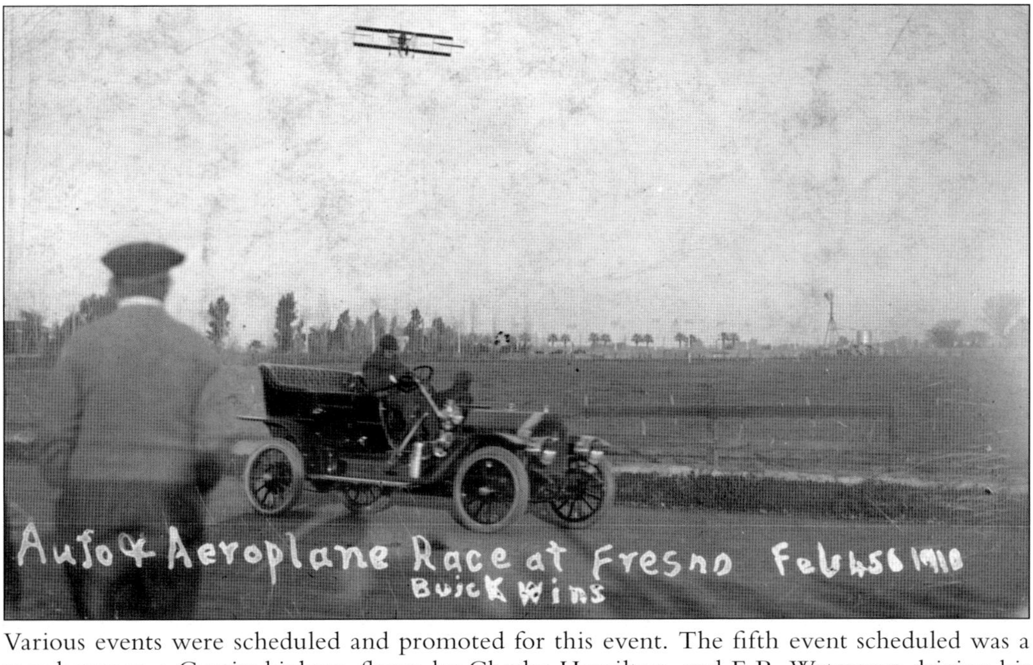

Various events were scheduled and promoted for this event. The fifth event scheduled was a race between a Curtiss biplane, flown by Charles Hamilton, and E.B. Waterman driving his new Buick. The race was around the Fresno Fairgrounds track. Waterman beat Hamilton in the one-mile race while Hamilton beat Waterman in the four-mile race, his biplane crossing the finish line 30 feet in front of the car.

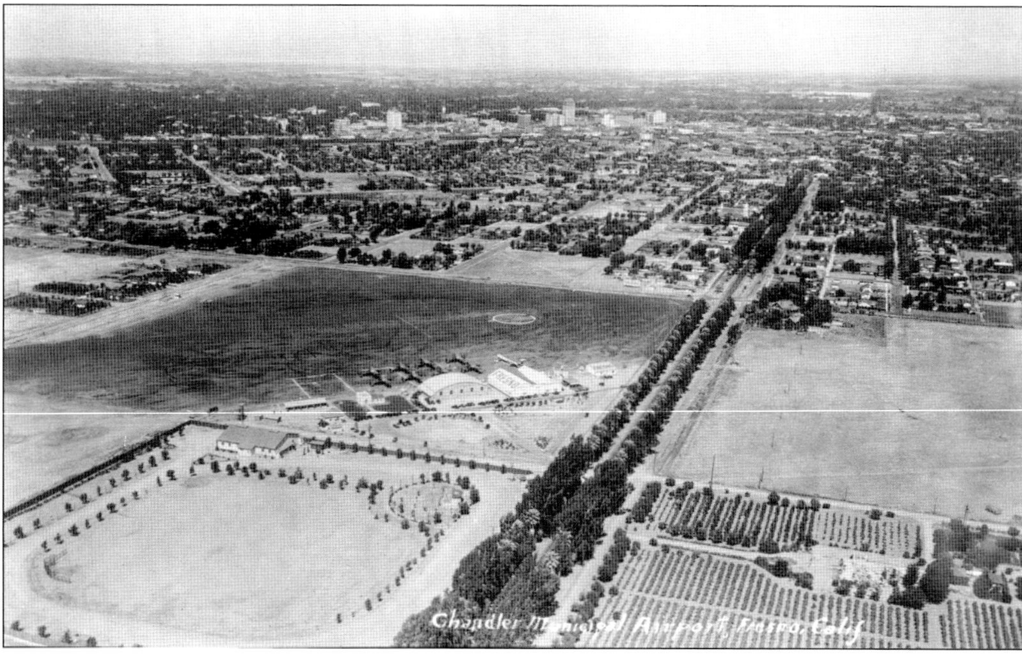

Fresno's first real airport was Chandler Field, located along Kearney Boulevard at Thorne. It was the first 2,000-foot oiled runway in Fresno and cost $50,000 to construct. The airport was dedicated on November 2, 1929.

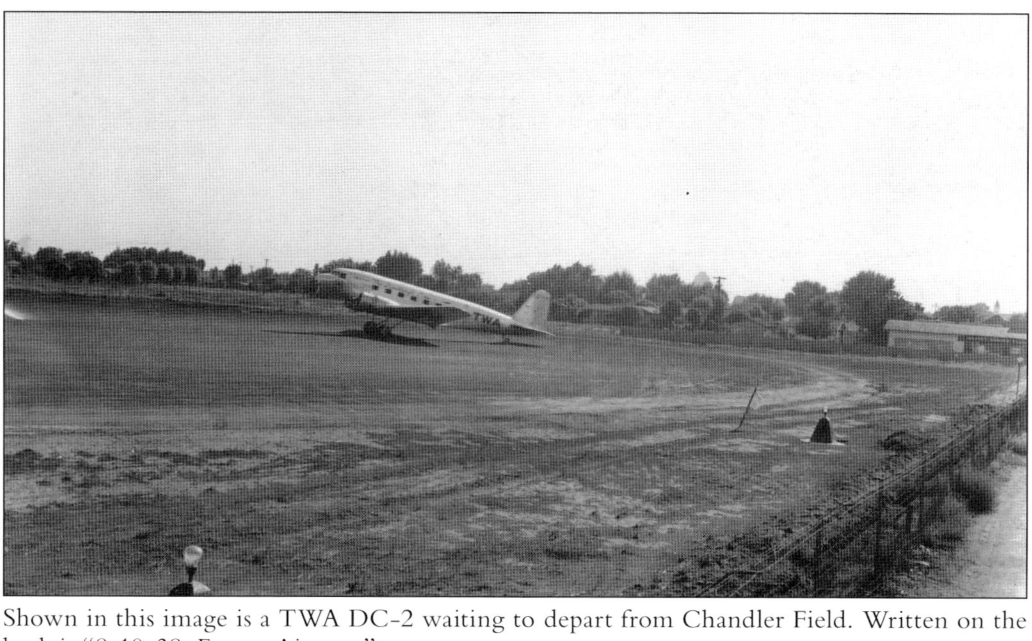

Shown in this image is a TWA DC-2 waiting to depart from Chandler Field. Written on the back is "8-10-38, Fresno Airport."

Two

LET'S HAVE SOME FUN!

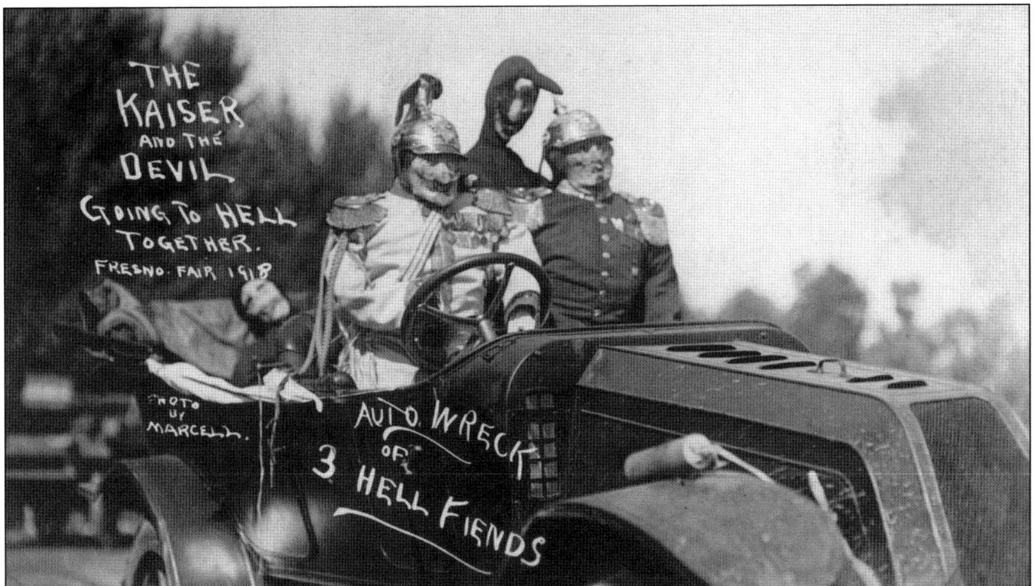

During World War I, a patriotic demonstration was held at the racetrack where an automobile holding effigies of the Kaiser and the Devil was blown up. The caption on this card reads "The Kaiser and the Devil Going to Hell Together—Auto Wreck of 3 Hell Fiends."

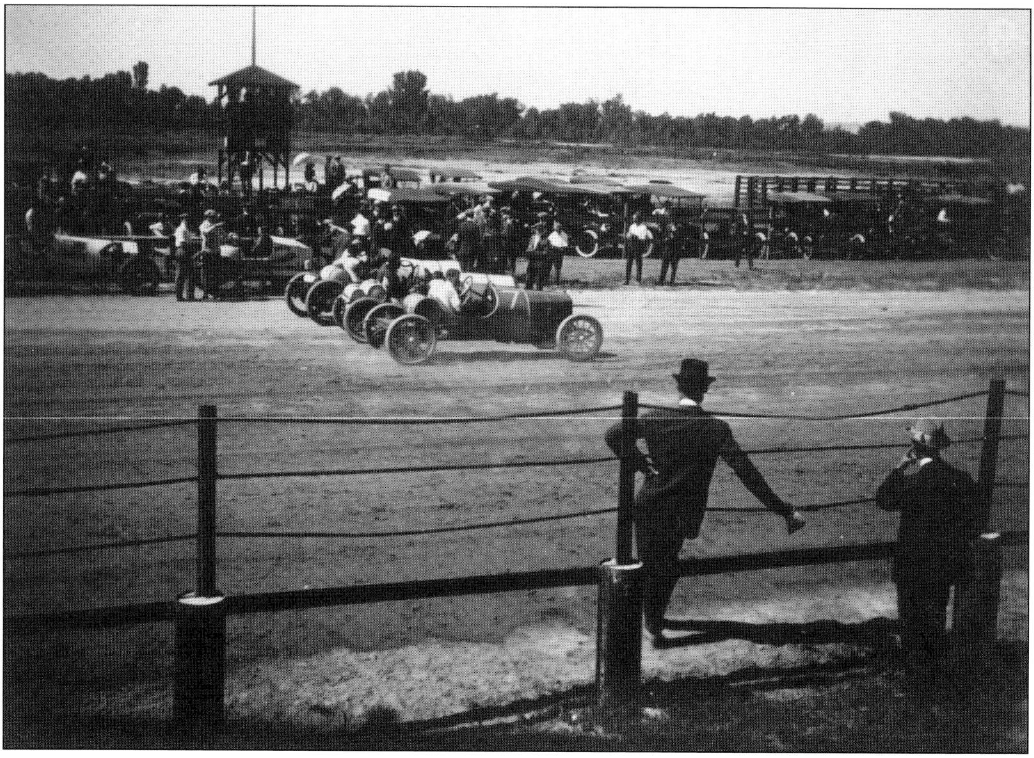

The one-mile dirt racetrack at the Fresno County Fairgrounds was the location of many car races until 1920. In 1904, Barney Oldfield set a world record here with an average speed of 61.64 miles per hour for a 50-mile race. By 1916, two major auto races were held each year. In April, the Raisin Day Classic was held, and in October, it was the Fresno Fair Auto Races.

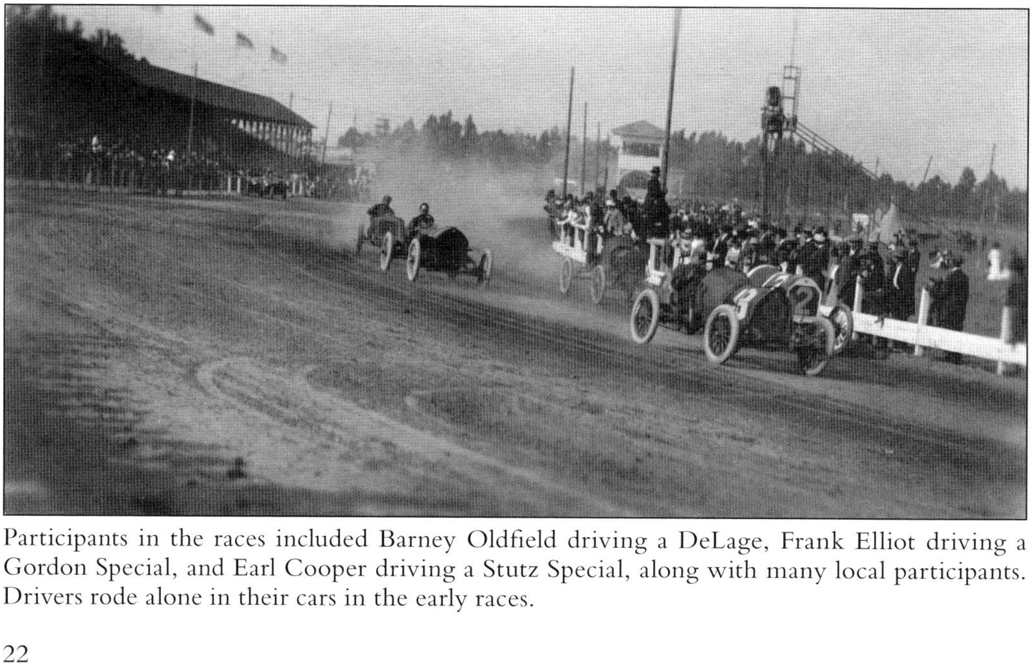

Participants in the races included Barney Oldfield driving a DeLage, Frank Elliot driving a Gordon Special, and Earl Cooper driving a Stutz Special, along with many local participants. Drivers rode alone in their cars in the early races.

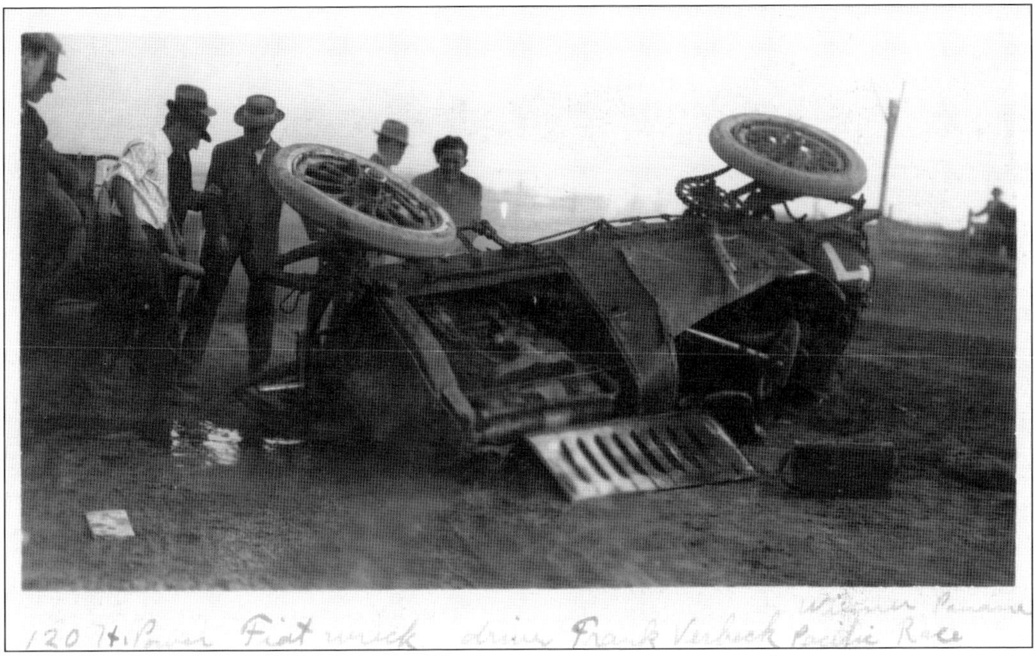

Frank Verbeck wrecked his 120-horsepower Fiat in a Fresno race. He later went on to win the Pan Pacific Expo Auto Race in 1915. Shown here is the aftermath of his wreck.

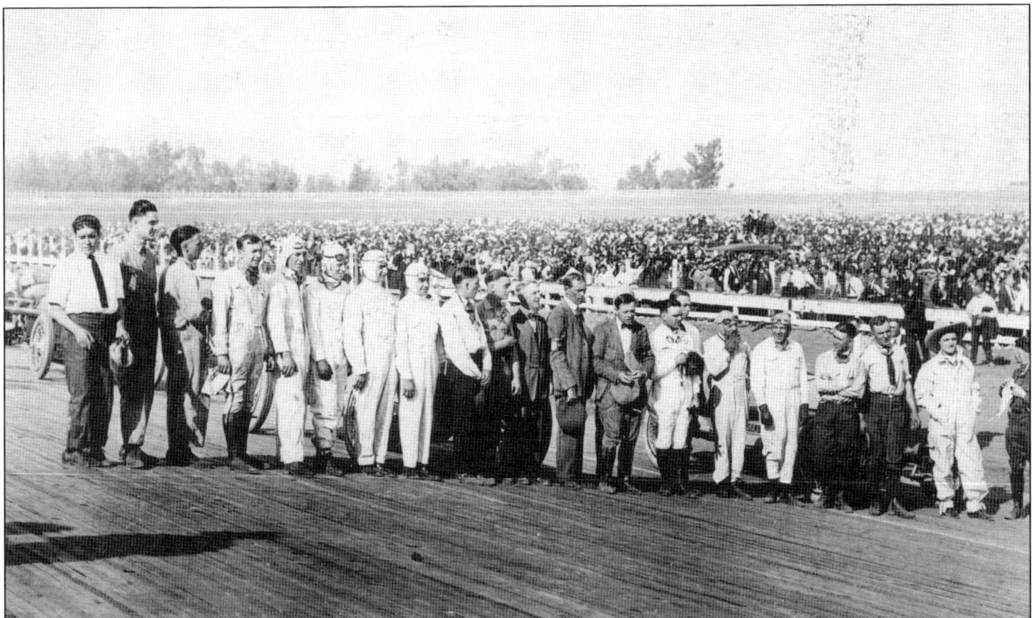

These drivers lined up before a race. They were required to wear heavy coveralls, helmets, and goggles to protect themselves from the flying splinters thrown up by the race cars' tires from the all-wood track.

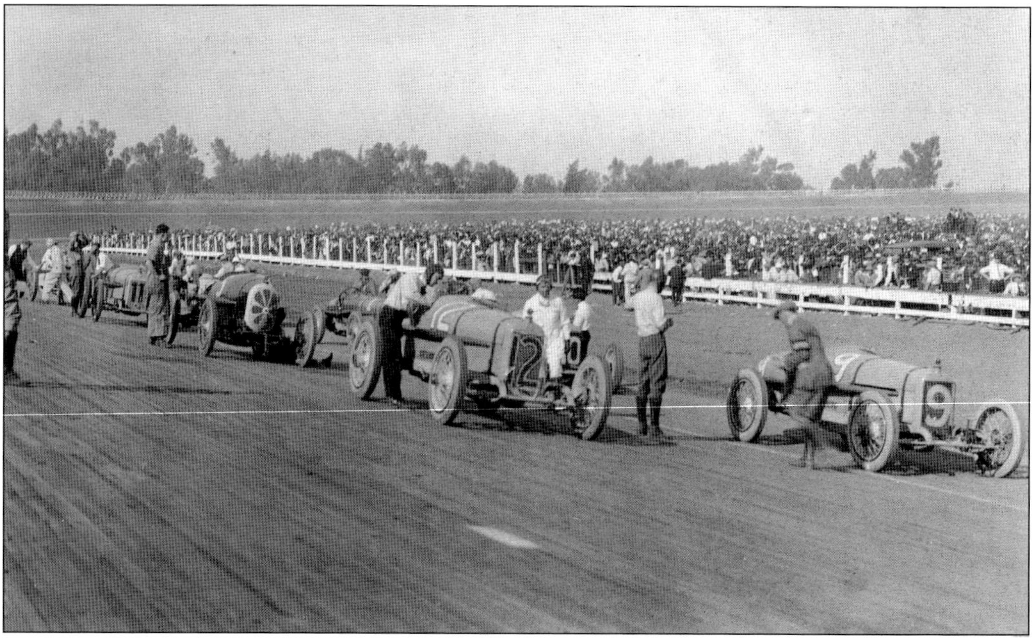

Fresno joined a national circuit and became a red-hot racing city. In 1920, the chamber of commerce and the Fresno District Fair supported the construction of a one-mile, wooden racetrack. The track cost $250,000 and its construction required the use of over 40 tons of nails. October 2, 1920, was the date of the first race, and Jim Murphy won it with an average speed of 96 miles per hour.

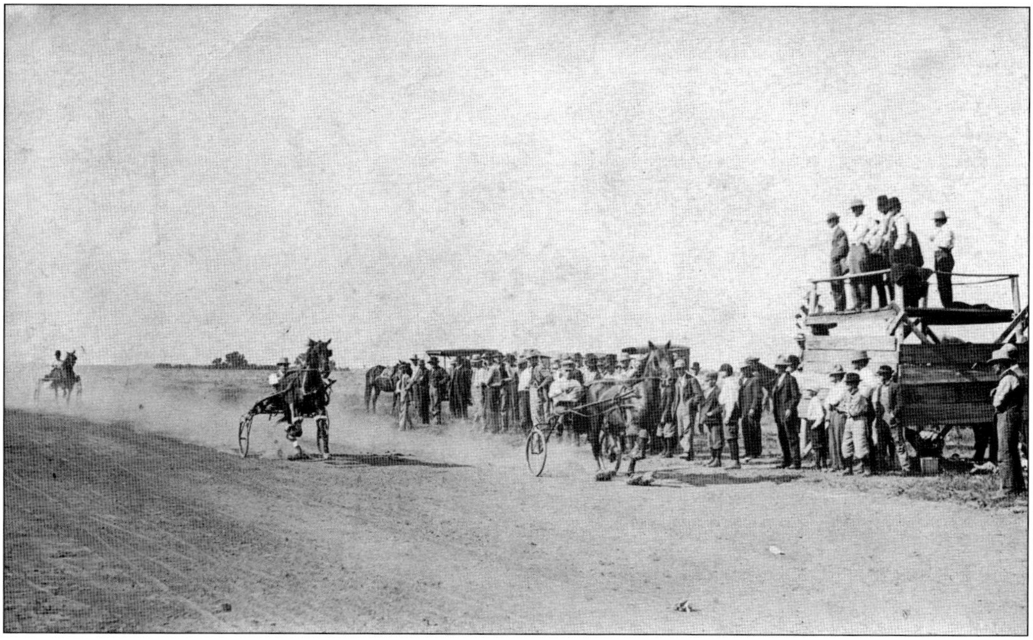

By 1927, interest in auto racing waned, and the wooden track was torn down. The Fresno District Fair Board even banned auto racing. In its place was a dirt track where horses, motorcycles, and bicycles raced again.

Pictured in this image is a postcard of the 8th Annual West Coast Relays, which were held each year in Fresno. The West Coast Relays were organized to replace the car races that were held during the Raisin Day celebration. The event was held in Ratcliffe Stadium from 1927 to 1982. During that time, over 36 track and field world records were broken at the annual event.

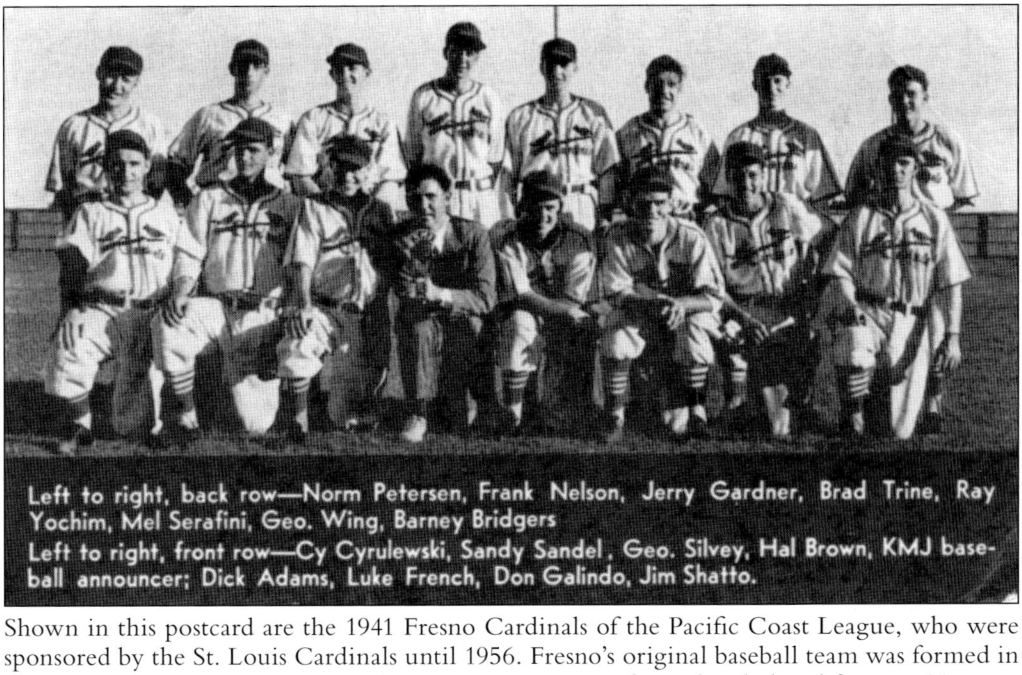

Shown in this postcard are the 1941 Fresno Cardinals of the Pacific Coast League, who were sponsored by the St. Louis Cardinals until 1956. Fresno's original baseball team was formed in 1887 as the Fresno Stars. In 1897, the Fresno Tigers were formed and played for over 20 years. Another team was the Fresno Acorns, a semipro team that played local ball in the 1920s.

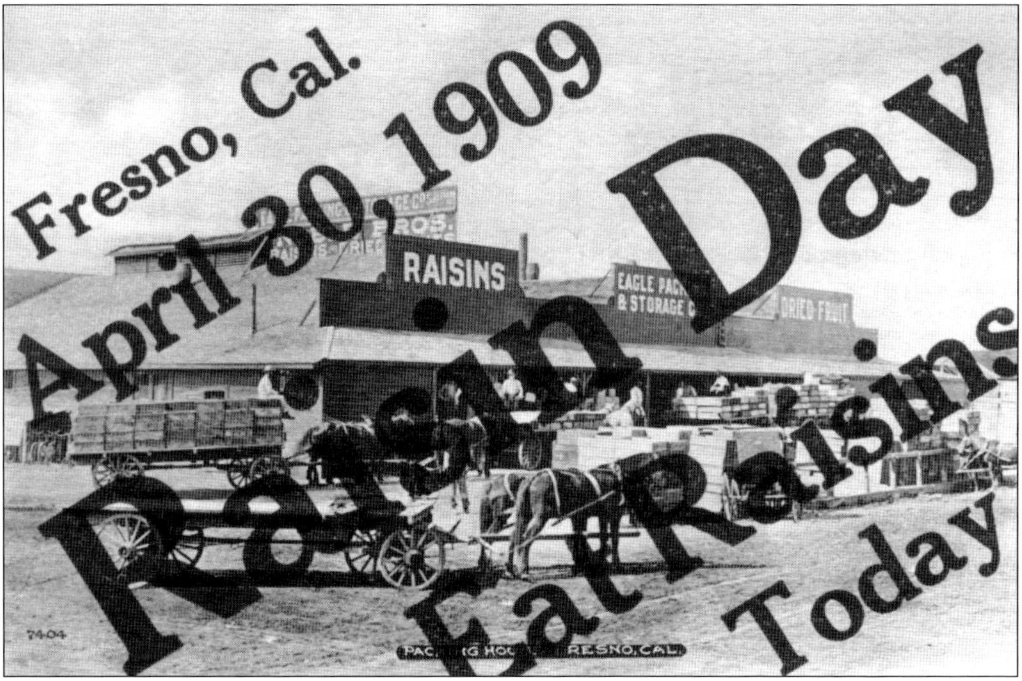

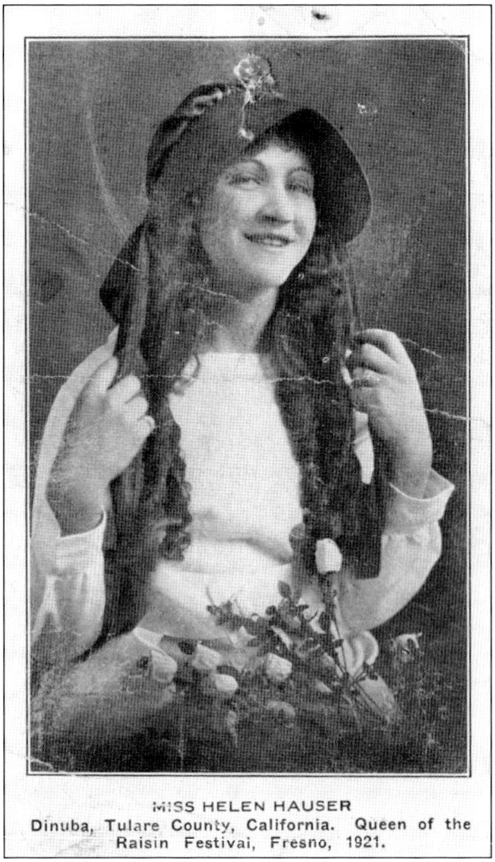

The Raisin Day Festival and Parade was a major event for the entire San Joaquin Valley. Many towns sent floats and queen contestants to promote the major crop—raisins. From 1909 to 1932, the festival attracted fans with exciting events such as the air circus, with wing walkers and acrobats, car races, and in 1927, the first West Coast Relays.

The queen of the 1921 Raisin Festival was Helen Hauser of Dinuba, chosen from among the princesses sent, one from each town, to the contest. The Raisin Day Queen dressed in the Sun Maid Girl costume. This postcard was printed for the Dinuba Chamber of Commerce.

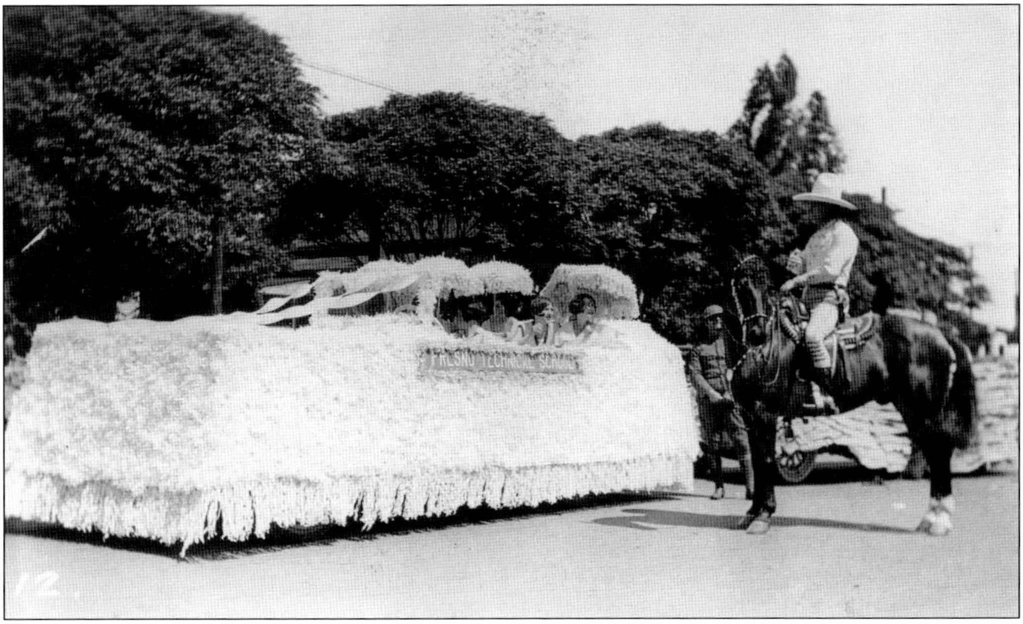

The 1926 king of the Raisin Day Festival was Western movie star Tom Mix. He refused the customary ride on the queen's float and instead rode his horse, Tony, so he could perform his rope tricks. He escorted the decorated car of the princesses, while the queen had her own float.

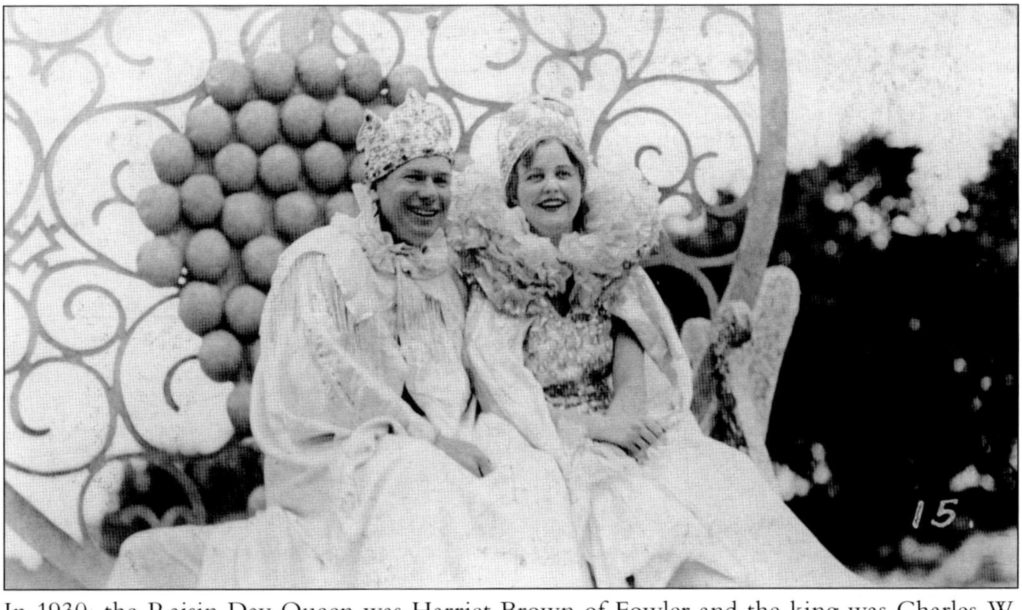

In 1930, the Raisin Day Queen was Harriet Brown of Fowler and the king was Charles W. Paddock, a world-class short-distance runner. He won a total of three gold medals and one silver medal in the 1920 and 1924 Olympics. Behind the royal couple is a representation of a large bunch of grapes.

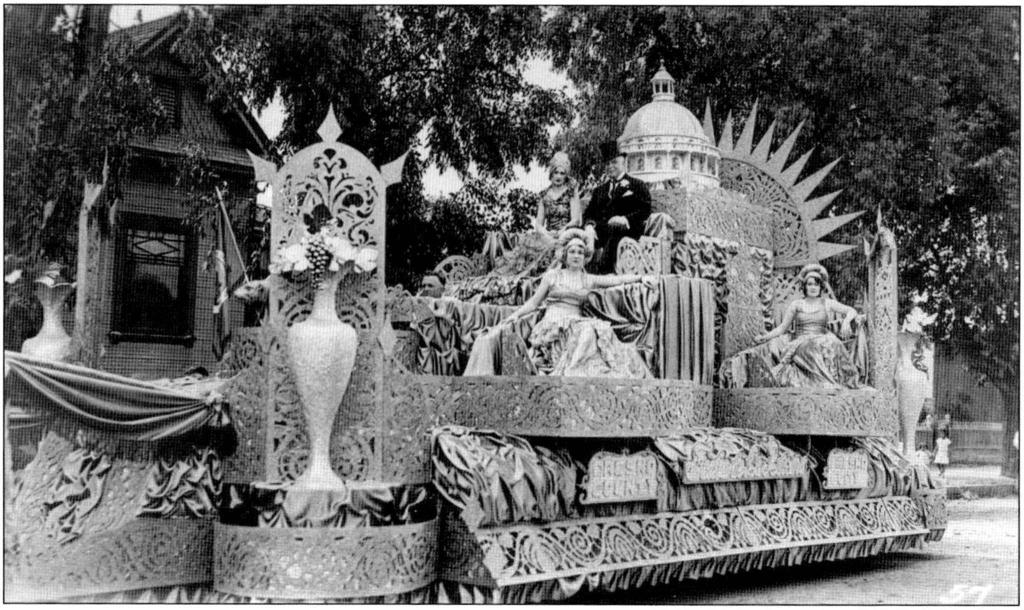

Gov. Ralph Rolph Jr. was Raisin Day King in 1931, riding on a float depicting the state capitol building. The queen was Aileen Higgins of Modesto. Princesses were Enid Ringle of Exeter, Barbara Bringler of Hanford, Marian Copeland of Delano, and Roberta Bergman of Selma.

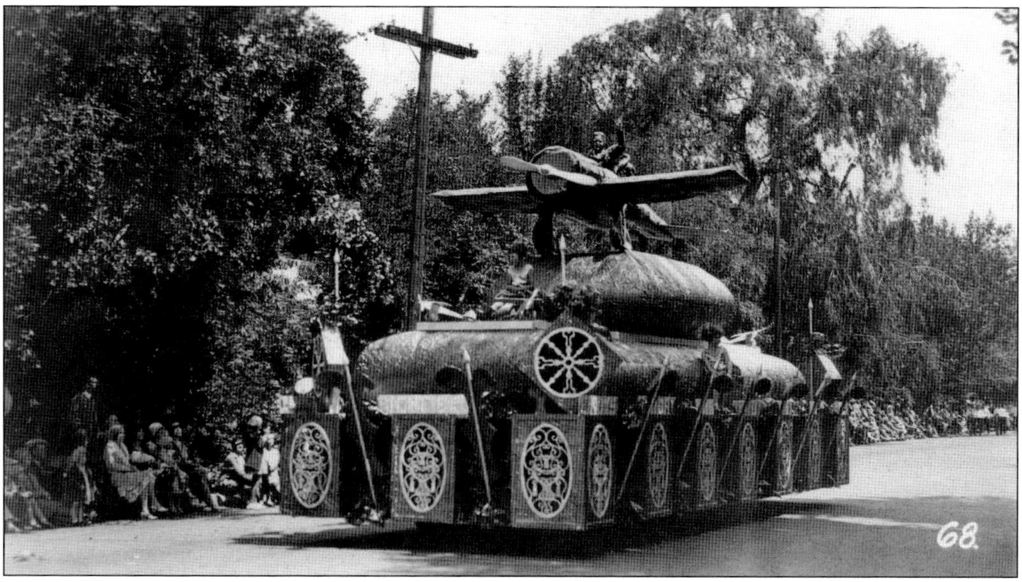

The sweepstakes winner in 1930 was the Richfield Oil Company float, showing an airplane with the pilot waving. Major corporations regularly sent floats to maintain public awareness of their products.

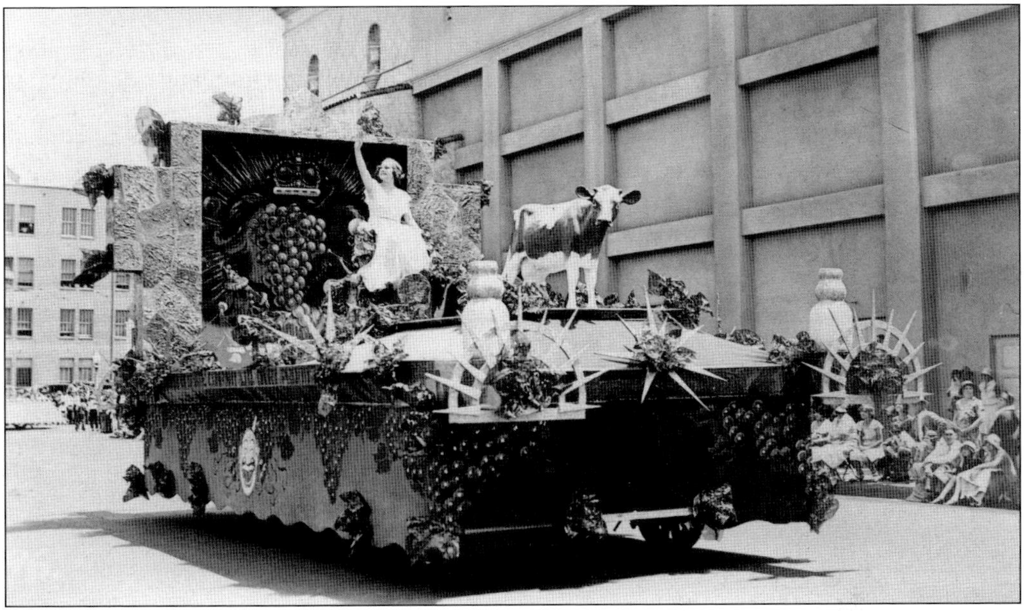

Shown here is the Golden State Company float from the 1931 parade. Golden State was a milk-processing firm in Fresno. The building next to the float is the Sperry Flour Mill at the southeast corner of N and Fresno Streets.

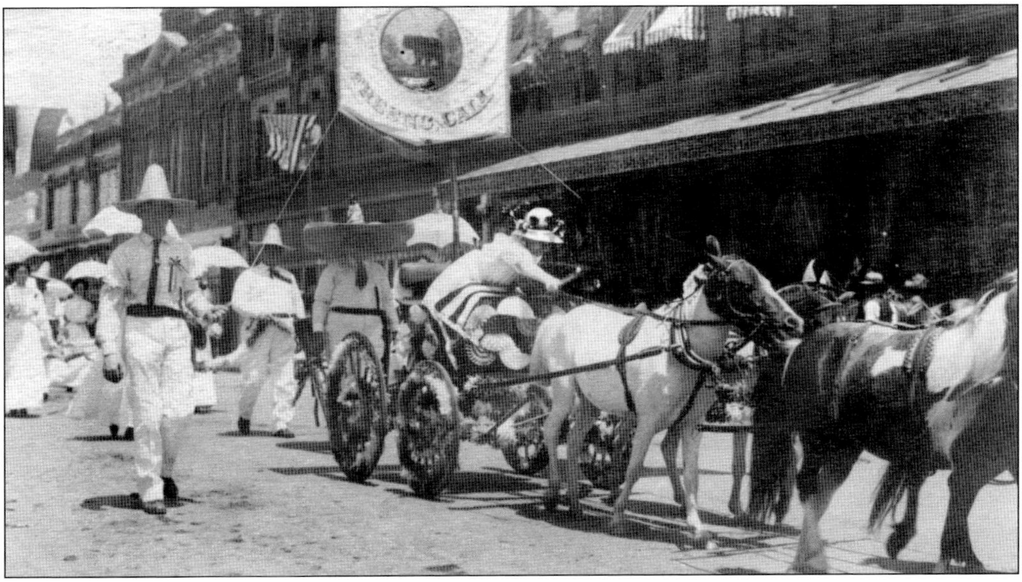

Fresno celebrated many holidays with parades. In the 1911 Fourth of July parade, Leota Burnside Zapp, co-owner of Zapp's Park, drove her four-wheel cart behind three ponies. Leota headed the delegation of The Native Sons and Daughters of the Golden West, whose banner is seen at the top of her carriage.

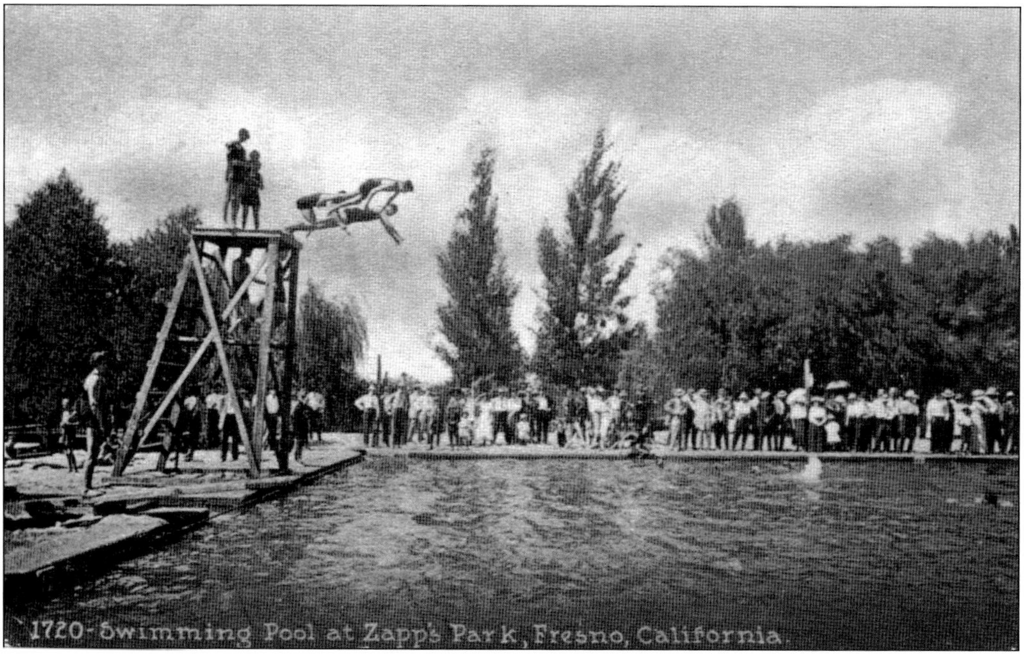

Zapp's Park was developed by John Zapp and his wife, Leota, on part of her family's farm. The park was bounded by Blackstone, Calaveras, Patterson, and Hedges Streets. Sand was removed to form a shallow lake and a swimming hole, which were filled with water from Dry Creek.

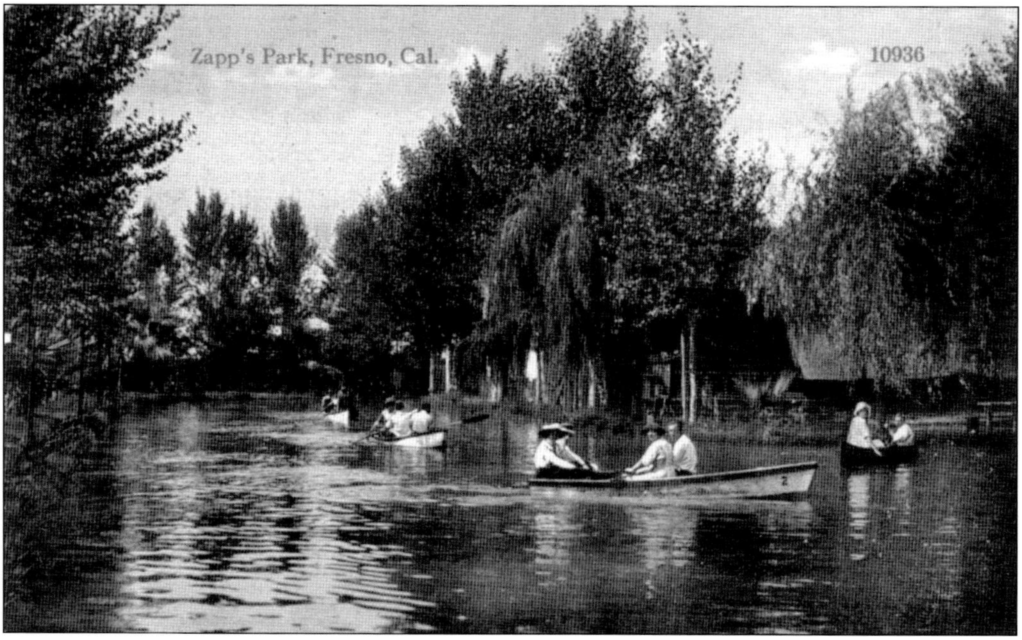

Zapp loved children and animals. Rides such as a Ferris wheel and a roller coaster, along with dancing, bowling, and a picnic area, were located on the south side of Olive Avenue. Located on the north side of Olive Avenue were the baseball field and the zoo. The zoo had elk, a bear, a great tortoise, and kangaroos.

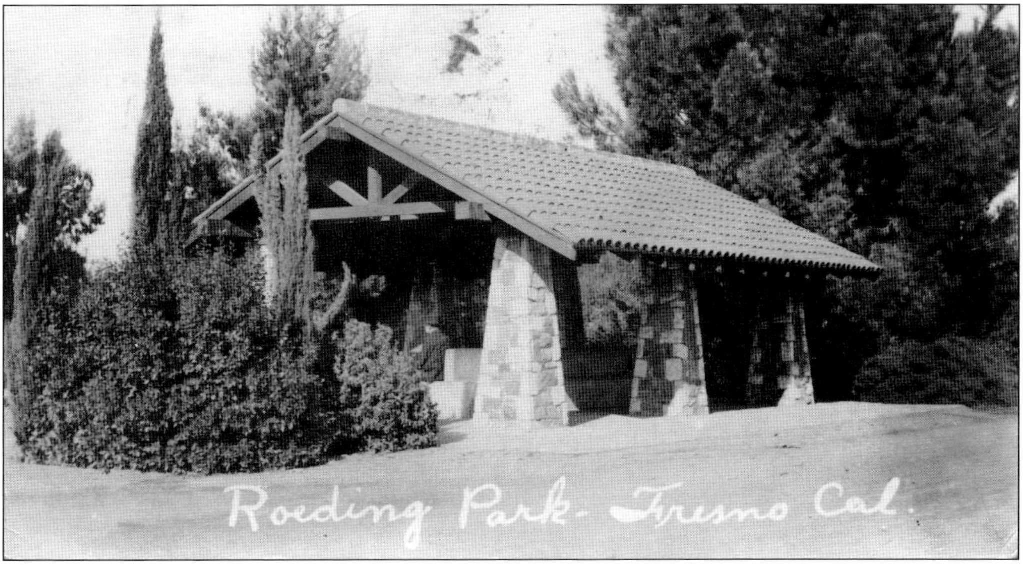

In 1903 and 1908, Frederick Roeding donated two gifts of land, totaling 117 acres, for Fresno's first large public park. Frederick's son George, a nurseryman and a college-trained horticulturist, added trees and shrubs to the park for years. By trading land with the state, Fresno grew the park to 149 acres. In 1912, an electric streetcar line was laid out along Olive Avenue, passing through the park and ending at the Mountain View Cemetery. Shown here is the streetcar depot, which was used until 1939.

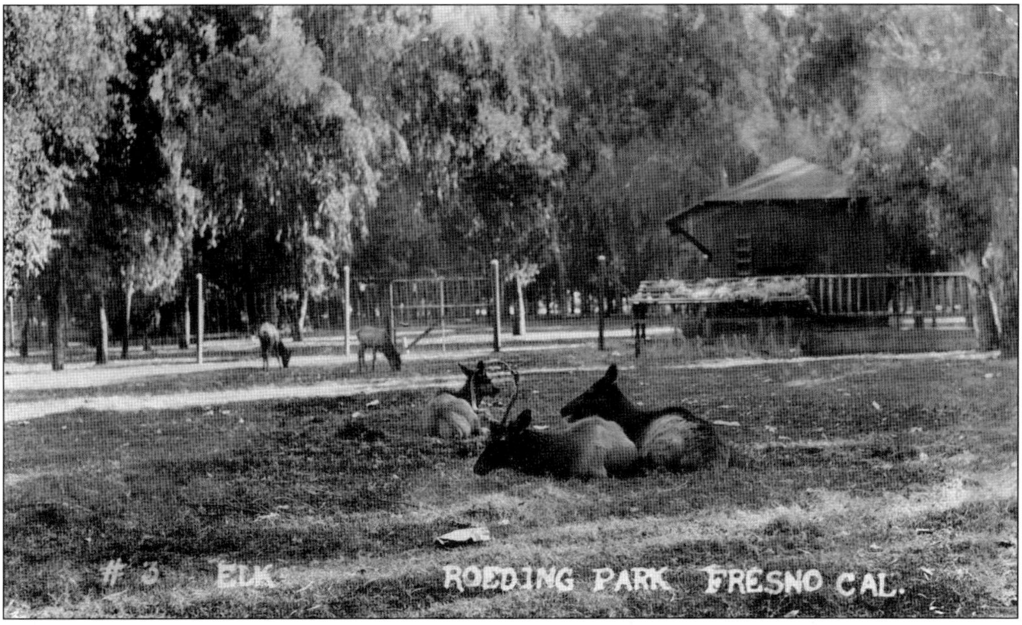

Roeding Park Zoo originally started with donated animals and cages. The City of Placerville donated two mature bears and the *Fresno Bee* raised funds for the bear display. In 1947, the city hired its first zookeeper, E.M. "Curly" Blocker, from the San Diego Zoo. He immediately started a fundraiser to buy a baby elephant. In 1949, the pachyderm was purchased. A contest to name the elephant was won by a 13-year-old girl from Orosi. "Nosey the Elephant" was a long time resident of the zoo until she died in 1993.

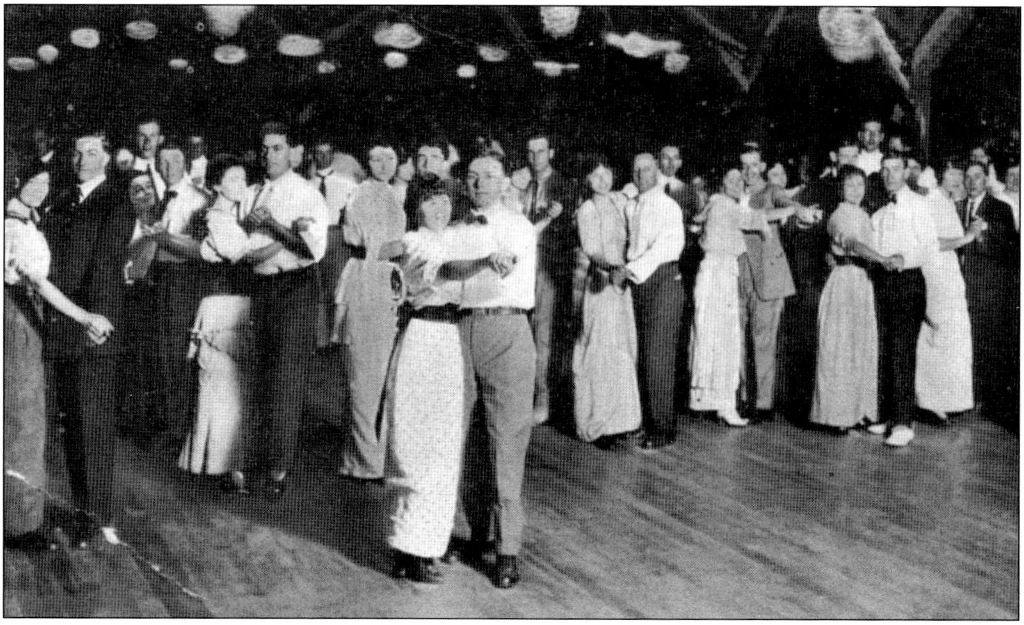

Fresno Beach was located on the south bank of the San Joaquin River and was accessed via the Fresno Beach streetcar from downtown Fresno to River Park. A covered dance pavilion was a popular evening destination for couples and, after dark, for mosquitoes.

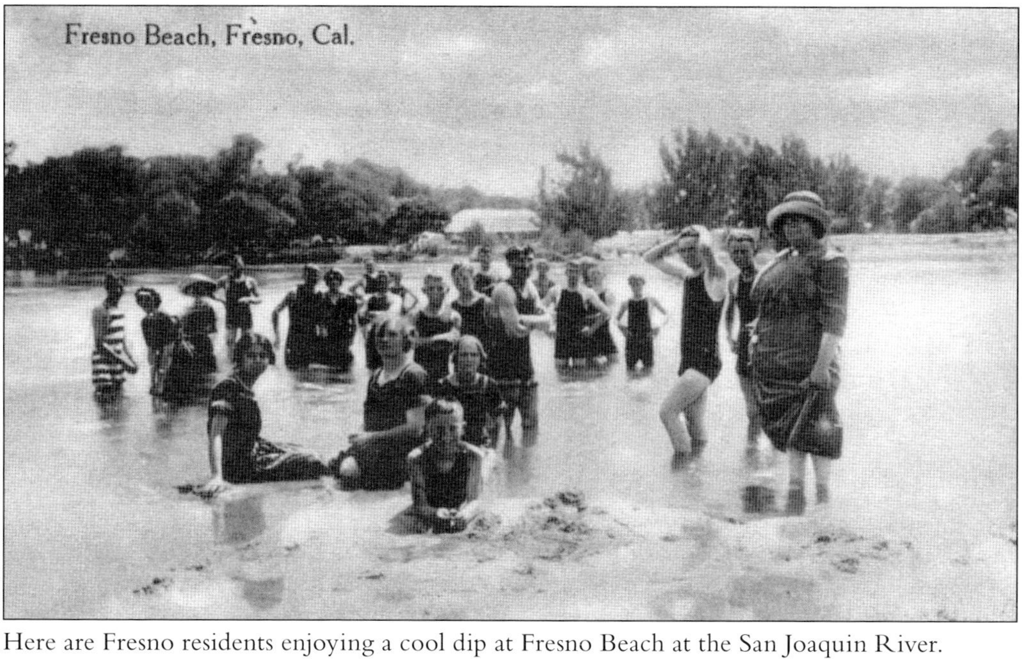

Here are Fresno residents enjoying a cool dip at Fresno Beach at the San Joaquin River.

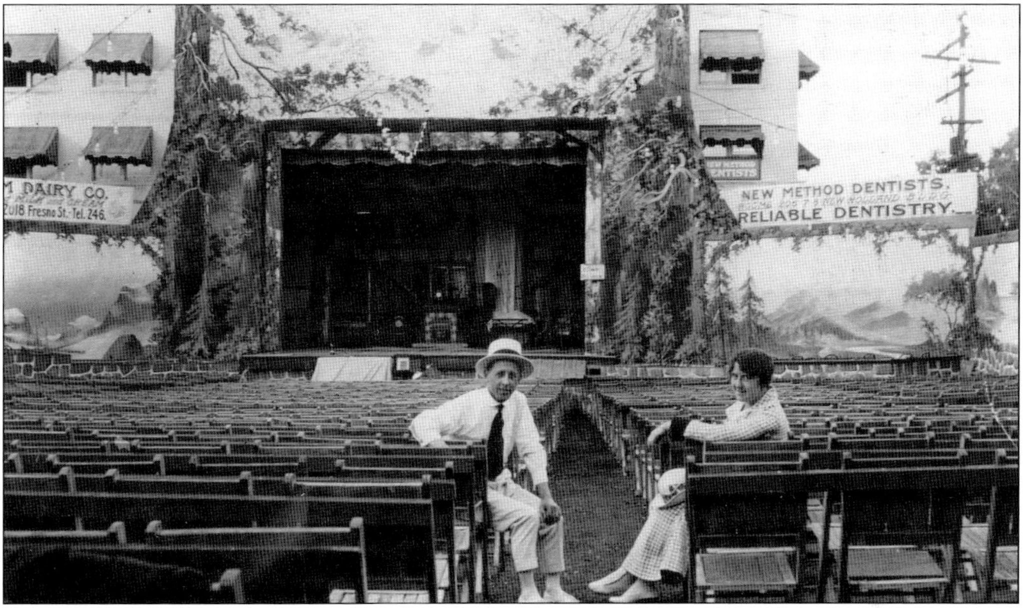

The Plaza Theatre was a summer theater in the 1910s, near the corner of Fresno and K (Van Ness) Streets. Evenings featured comedy drama, singing comedy, roller-skating, dancing, and audience sing-alongs. The Holland Building (with the awnings.) is on the north side of Fresno Street, between K and L Streets.

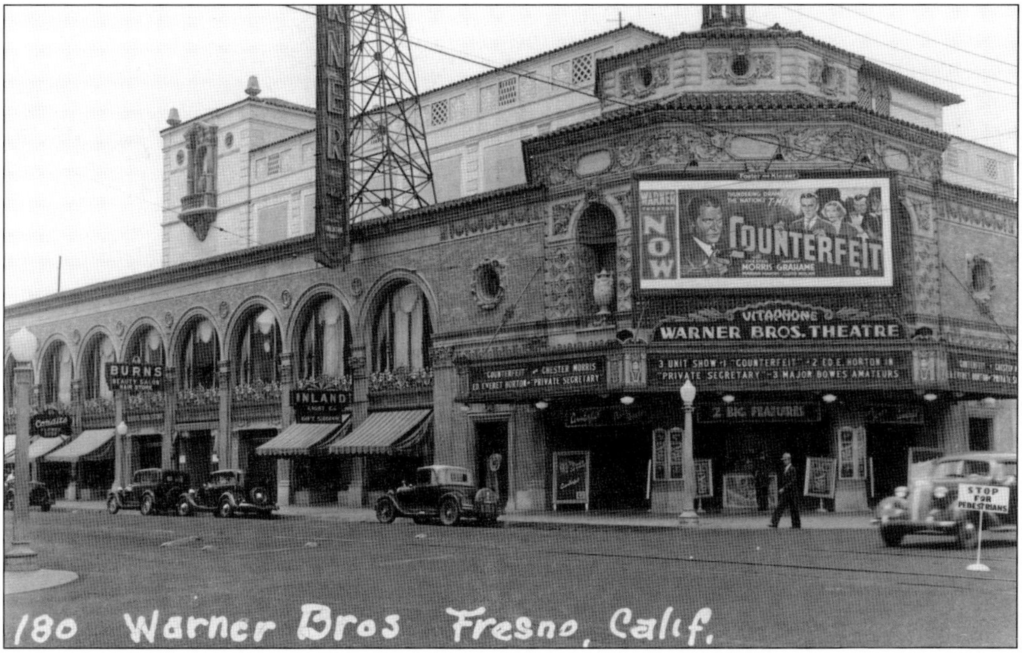

Warner Brothers Theatre at 1400 Fulton Street, a plush and lavish movie palace, was built in the late 1920s as the Pantages Theater. The movie bill advertises two features and Major Bowes Amateur Hour. Warner's was changed to Warnor's after it was sold to private owners. The movie advertised here, *Counterfeit*, debuted in 1936.

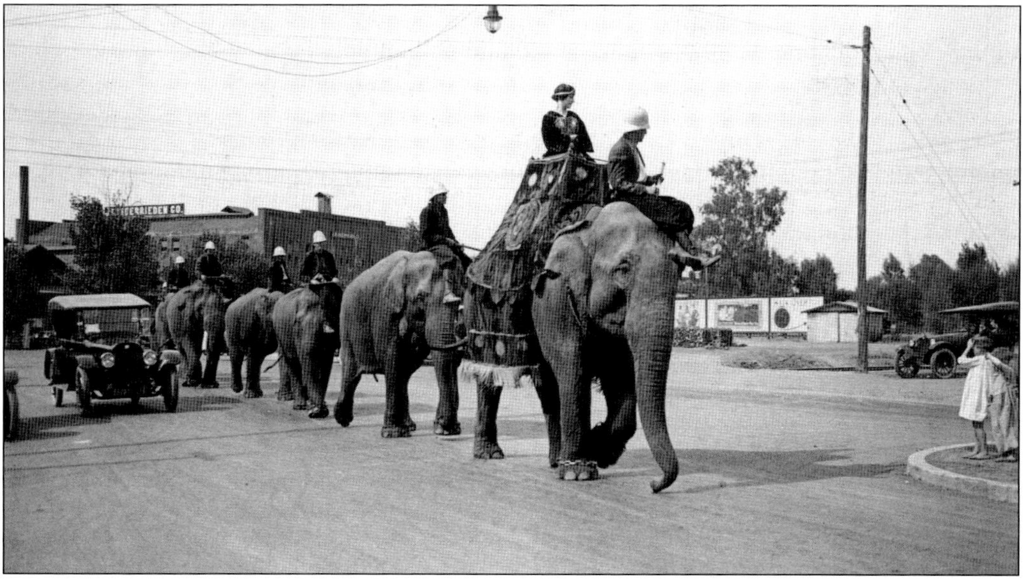

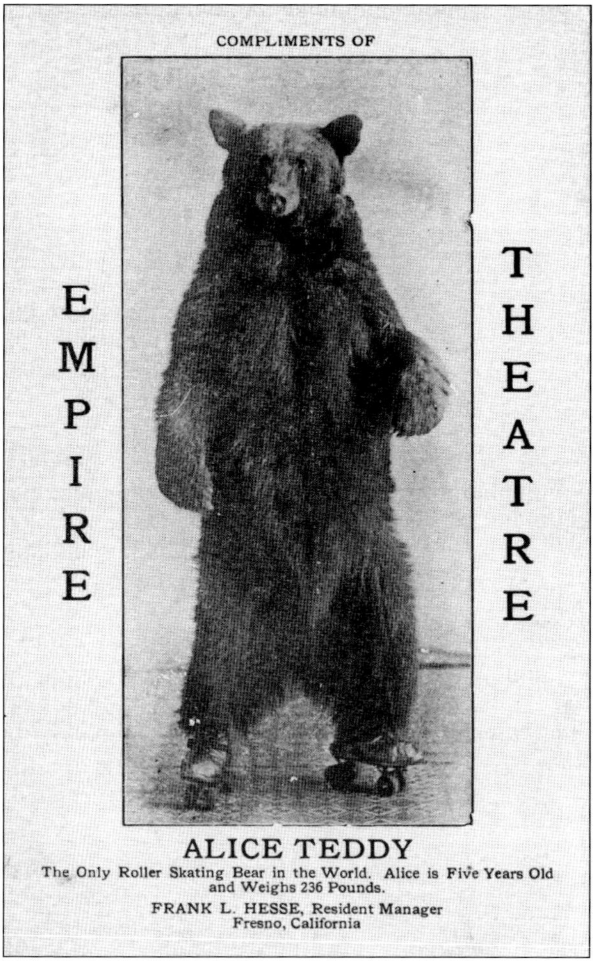

Fresno has seen many traveling circuses since the Conklin's Great US Circus erected a tent north of town near the Southern Pacific tracks in 1873. In this picture, the elephants are walking east along Ventura Avenue. In the background is the Inderrieden Fruit Packing Plant. The plant was built in 1925 on the northwest corner of Ventura and R Streets. Later owners of the building included the Old Spaghetti Factory Restaurant.

Appearing at the Empire Theatre on Fulton between Tulare and Kern Streets was "Alice Teddy—The Only Roller Skating Bear in the World." This card was sent out for promotional purposes and shows Alice on wheels.

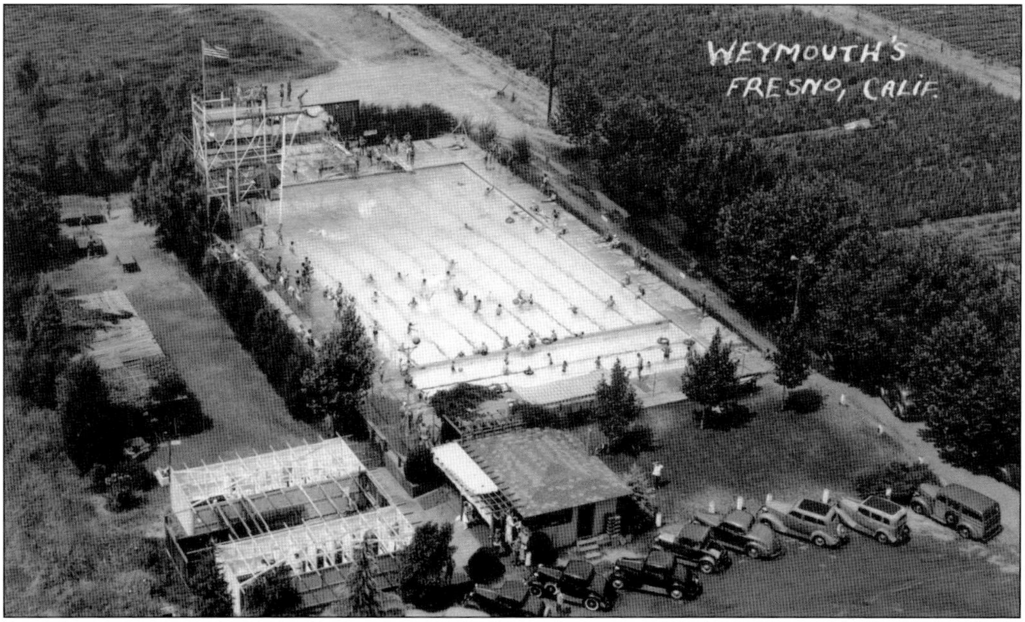

In 1934, Weymouth Swimming Pool opened on West Whitesbridge Road. It had a high diving platform and later had water slides. This is an aerial view of the facility.

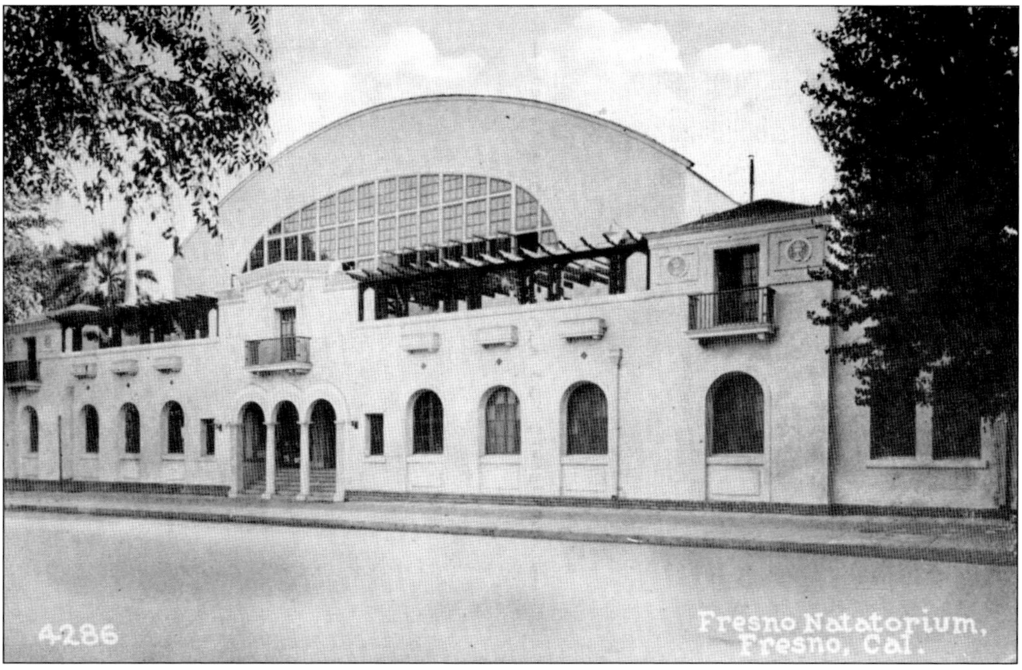

The Fresno Natatorium was Fresno's first indoor swimming pool, built in 1918 for $50,000, and located at 1725 Broadway.

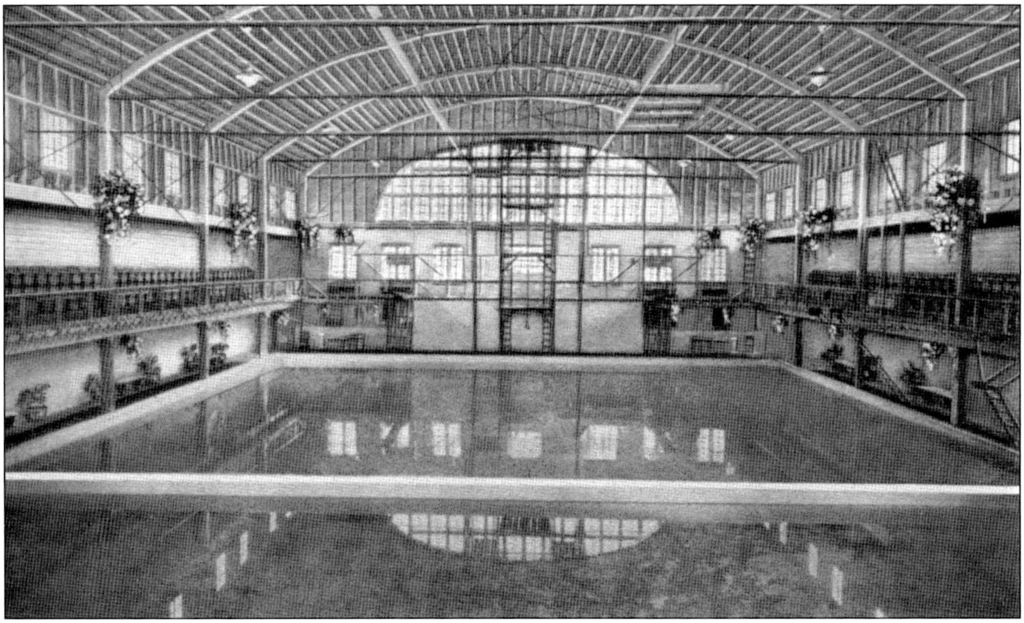

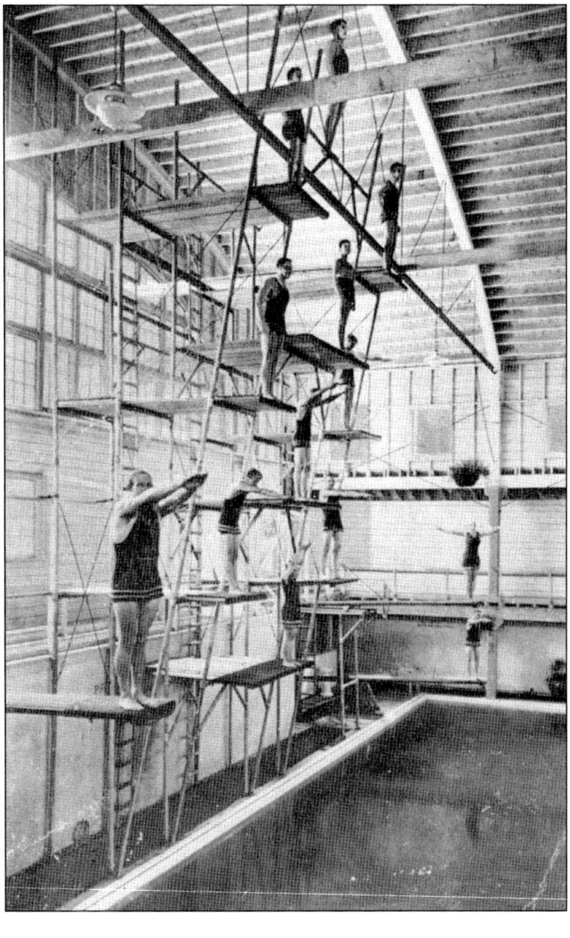

The high roof and many windows gave the 125-foot-by-150-foot pool in the Natatorium lots of light. It had both high and springboard platforms and 165 dressing rooms.

The pool closed around 1930 and was converted to a dance hall. A dance floor was built over the existing pool. Today, the dance hall is known as the Rainbow Ballroom.

Three

The Heart of Downtown

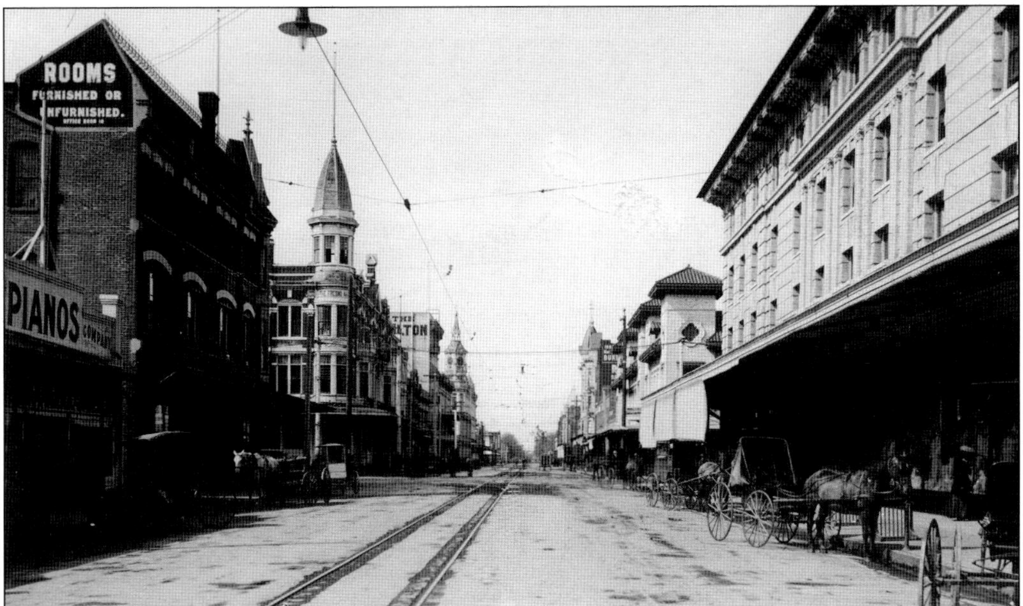

This 1906–1907 postcard view is looking north on Fulton Street at the intersection of Tulare Street. On the left side was the Edgerly Building. The building with the sharp cupola was the Fresno National Bank Building. The building on the middle right was the Patterson Block, with its turrets and dark covers. The structure on the right was the Forsyth Building. Down the middle of the street are streetcar tracks.

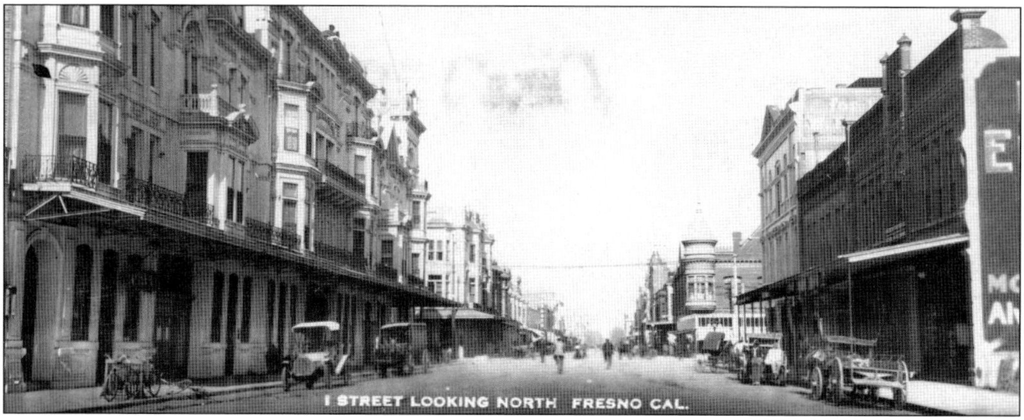

This 1906–1910 image, looking north on I Street (Broadway) at Tulare Street, shows mainly horse-drawn wagons, bicycles, and an early automobile. The Hughes Block is on the left side of the street, and the building with the round cupola was the First National Bank.

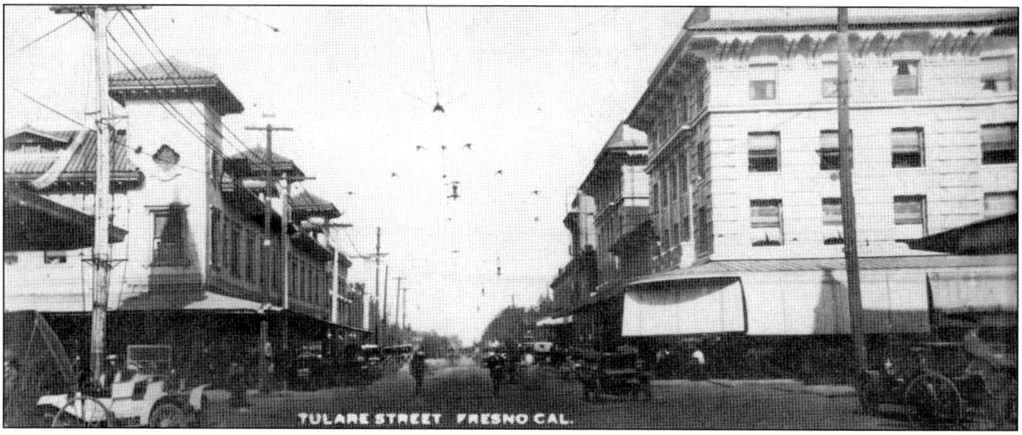

Looking east on Tulare Street from Fulton shows the Patterson Block on the left side of the street and the Forsyth Building on the right. The wires suspended over the street ran power for the electric streetcars.

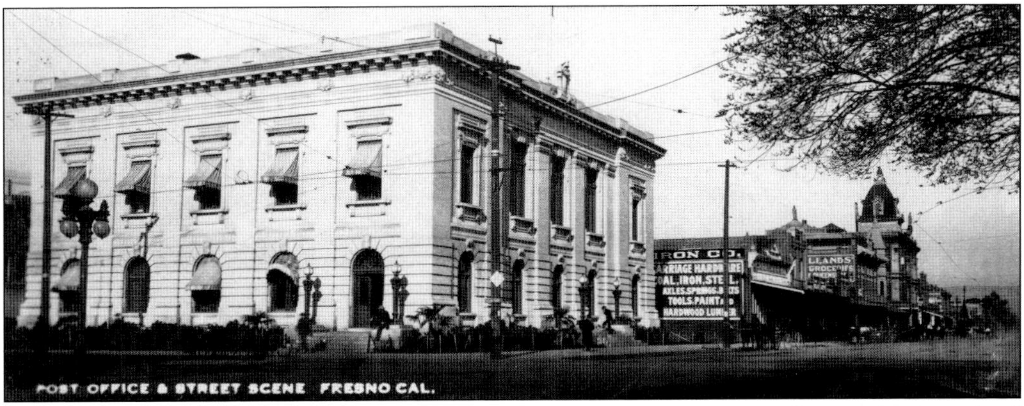

Shown in this image is the building that housed the Fresno Post Office and US Federal Courthouse. The building occupied the northwest corner of Tulare and Van Ness Streets. The building with the dark, pointy tower was the Temple Bar Building. The ground floor was occupied by the Webster Brothers Drugstore, and the upper floors were occupied by lawyers.

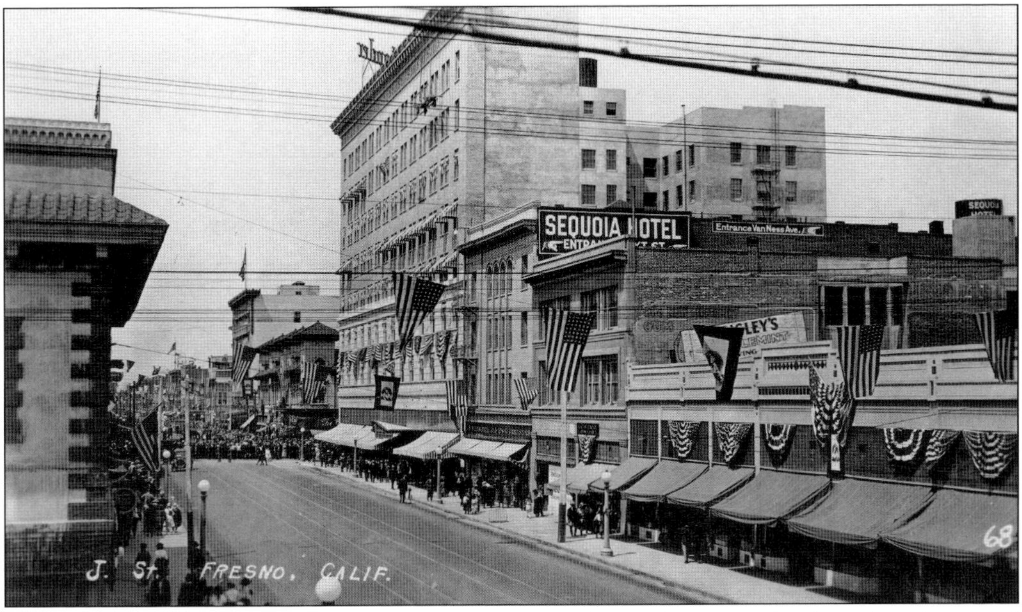

This image is looking north on J (Fulton) Street in the mid-1920s. The flags, buntings, and crowds of people on the street suggest that either the Raisin Day or Fourth of July parade was in progress.

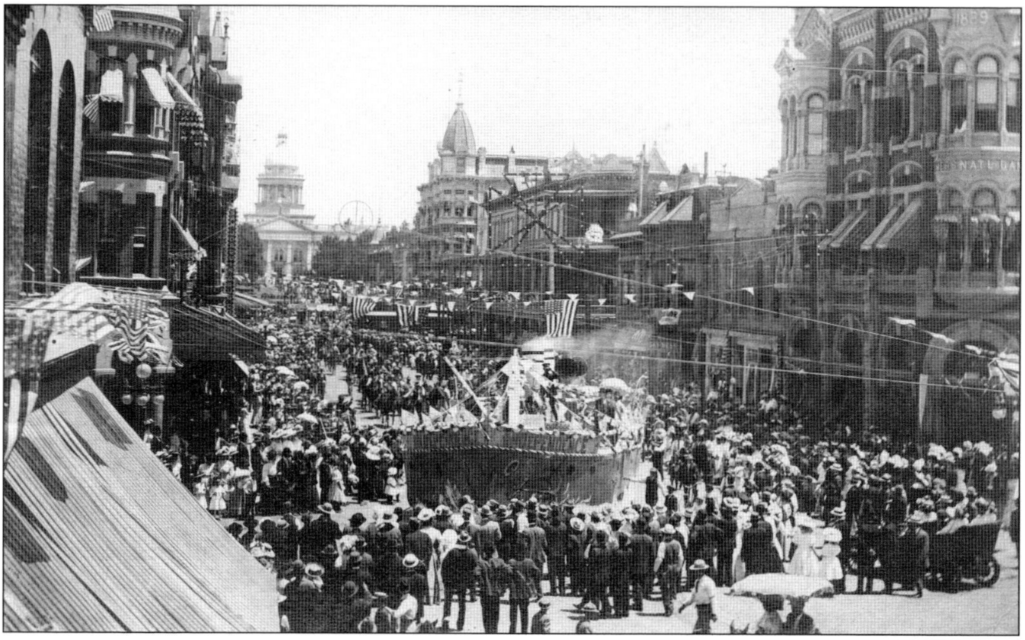

Flags and buntings waved in the air at the Fourth of July parade in Fresno about 1910. The float in the foreground is of a large ship named "Independence." The parade route came down Van Ness Street to the front of the courthouse, turned west on Mariposa, and then north onto Broadway.

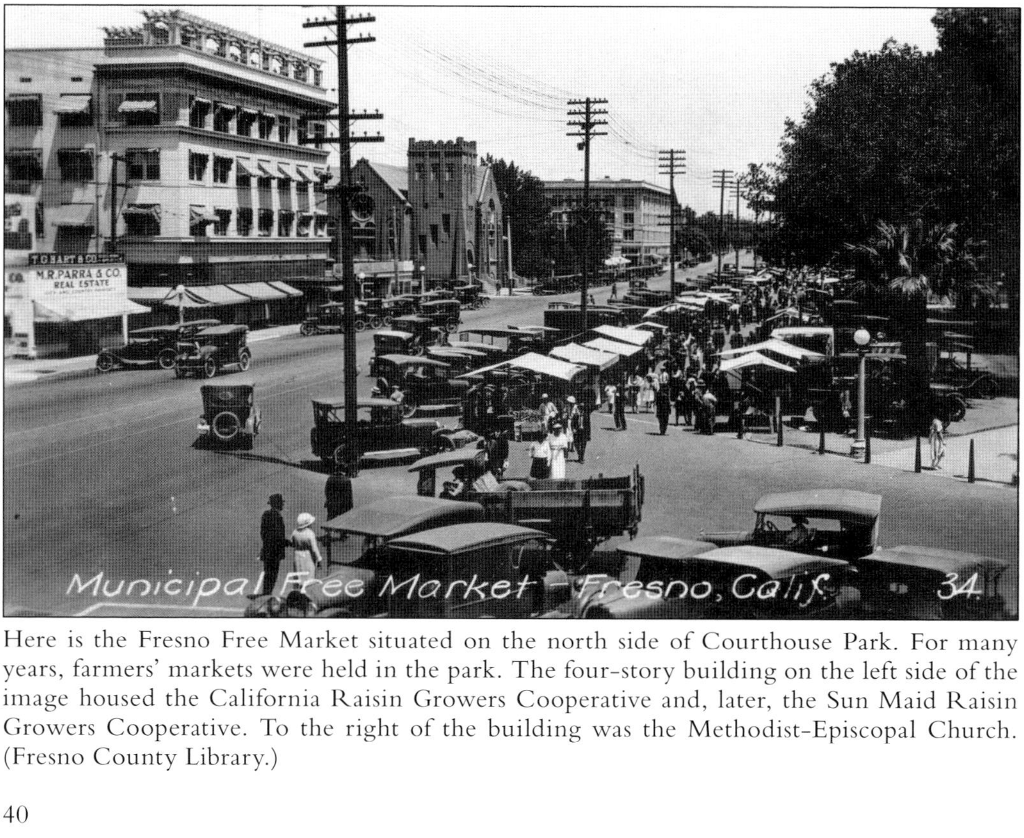

Here is the Fresno Free Market situated on the north side of Courthouse Park. For many years, farmers' markets were held in the park. The four-story building on the left side of the image housed the California Raisin Growers Cooperative and, later, the Sun Maid Raisin Growers Cooperative. To the right of the building was the Methodist-Episcopal Church. (Fresno County Library.)

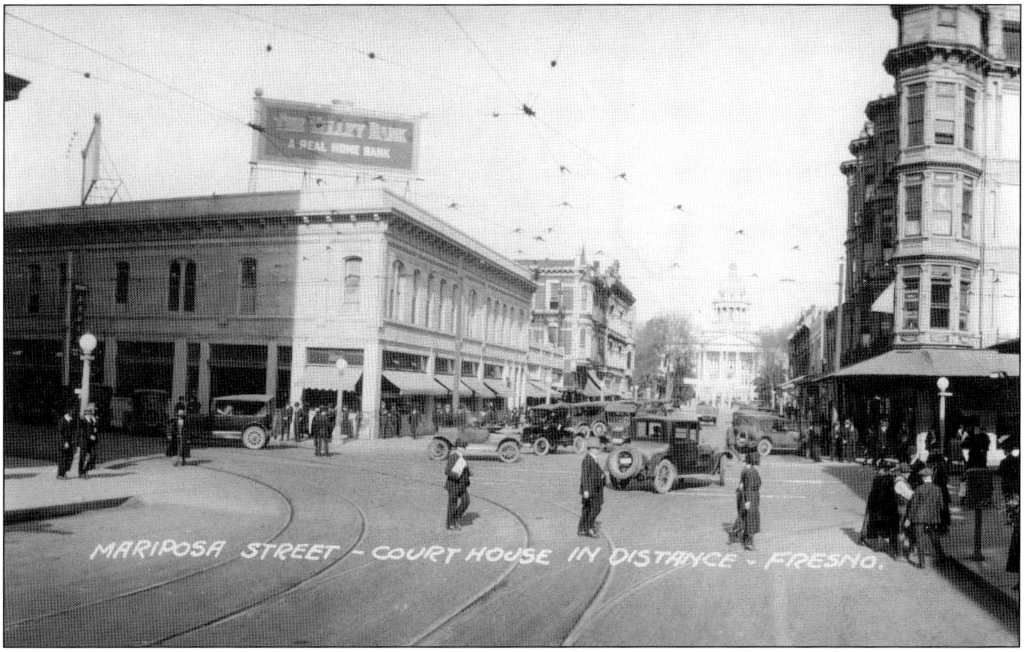

Mariposa Street is seen here looking east from Fulton. This 1921 postcard image shows the county courthouse at the end of Mariposa Street. The building on the left was the location for Valley Bank. The building on the right was the Hutchinson Building, which was built in 1887 and housed the Bank of Central California. The tracks in the street were used by the electric street cars.

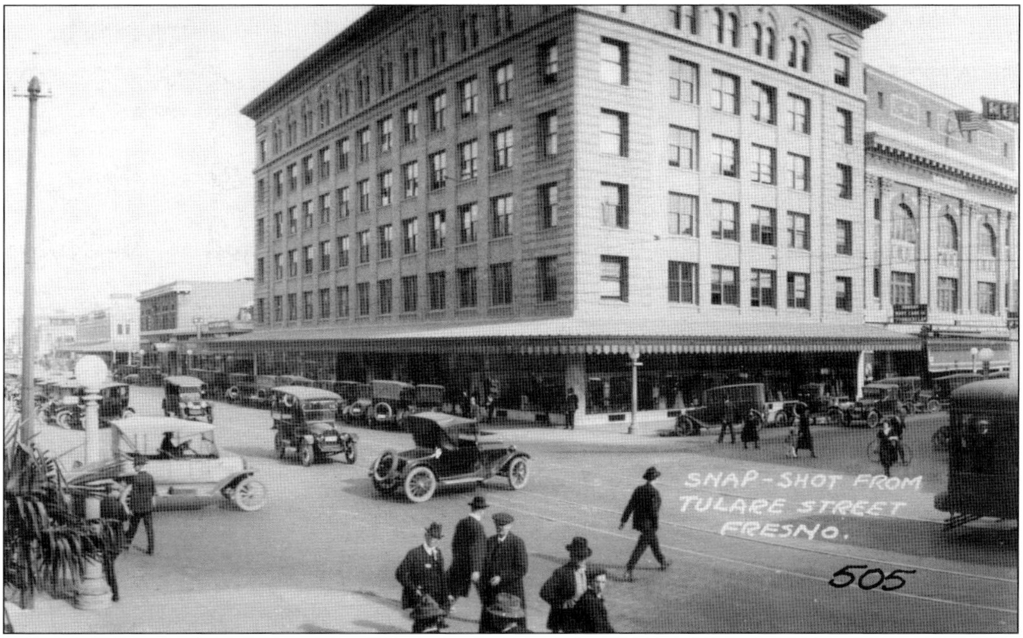

Here is the intersection of Tulare and Van Ness Streets. The six-story building is the 1914 Rowell Building. To the far right is the 1917 Liberty Theater, which had a seating capacity of 1,200. The theater was later renamed Hardy's Theater.

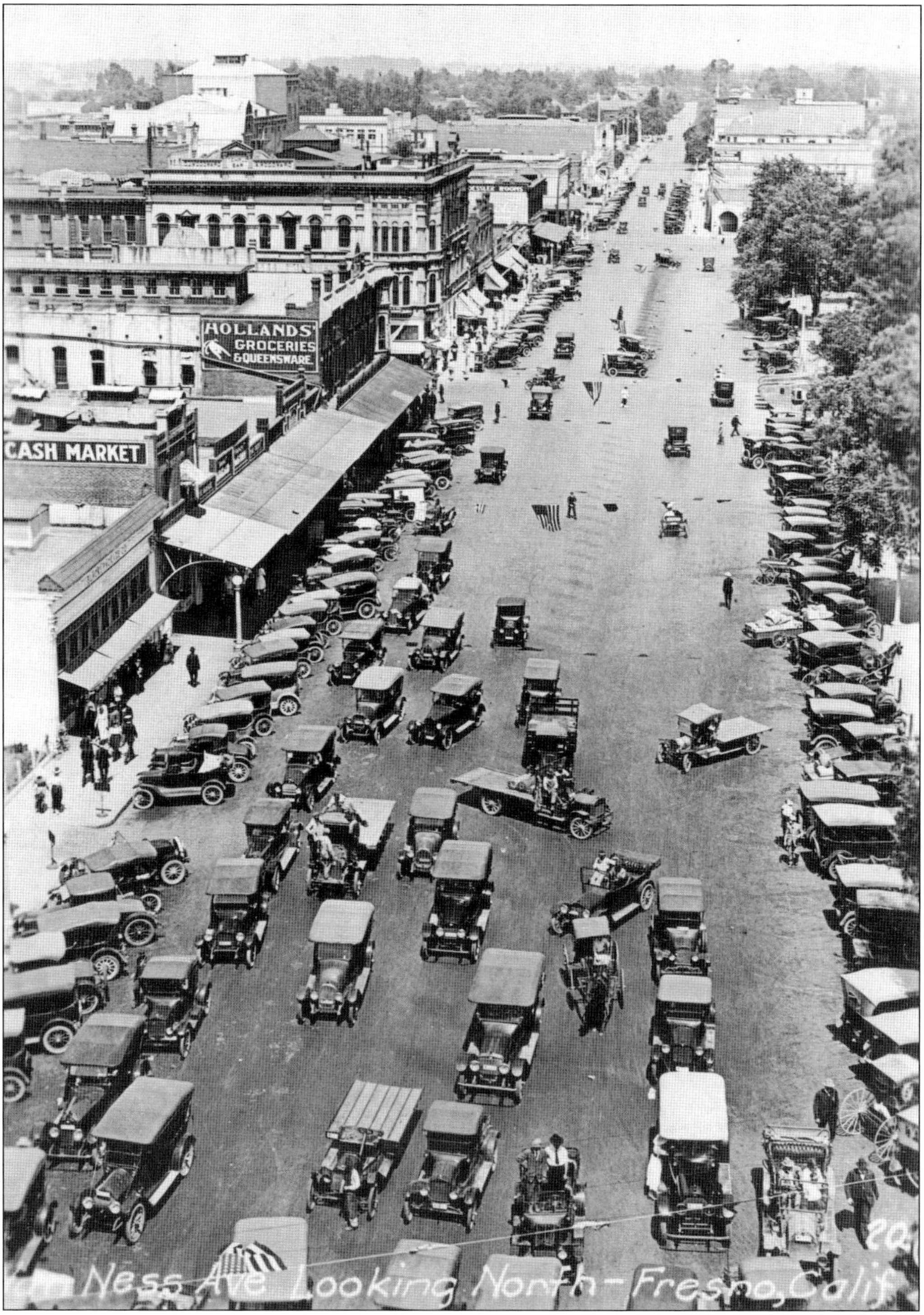

This postcard image shows a busy Van Ness Street, looking north from Tulare Street towards Mariposa and Fresno Streets. The courthouse park is on the right side of the street. Note the markings for diagonal parking spots in the middle of the street.

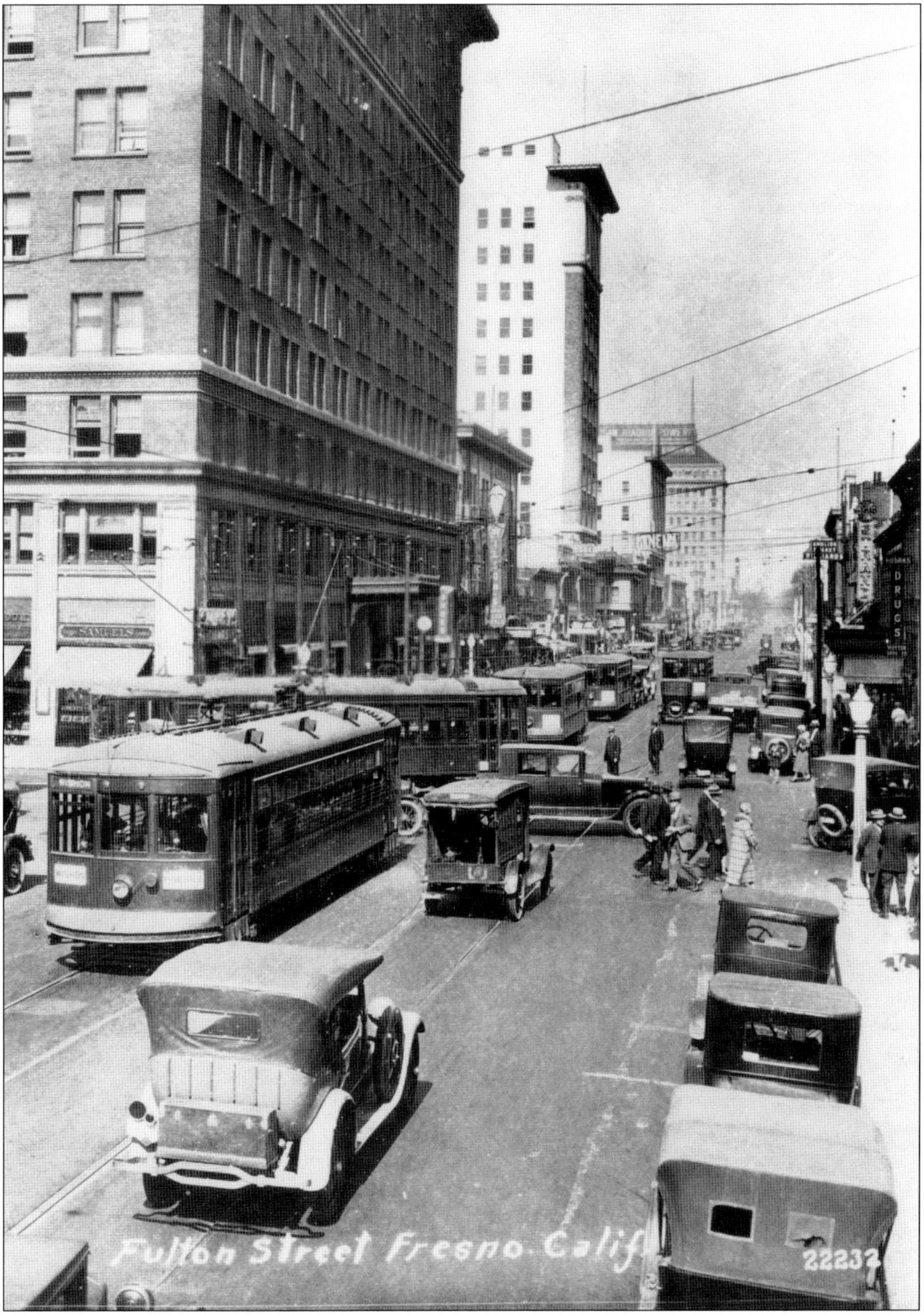

This image shows the extent of public transportation that existed in Fresno over 80 years ago. Fulton Street was the heart of Fresno, and the amount of traffic is a testament to the vibrant business that existed downtown. (Fresno County Library.)

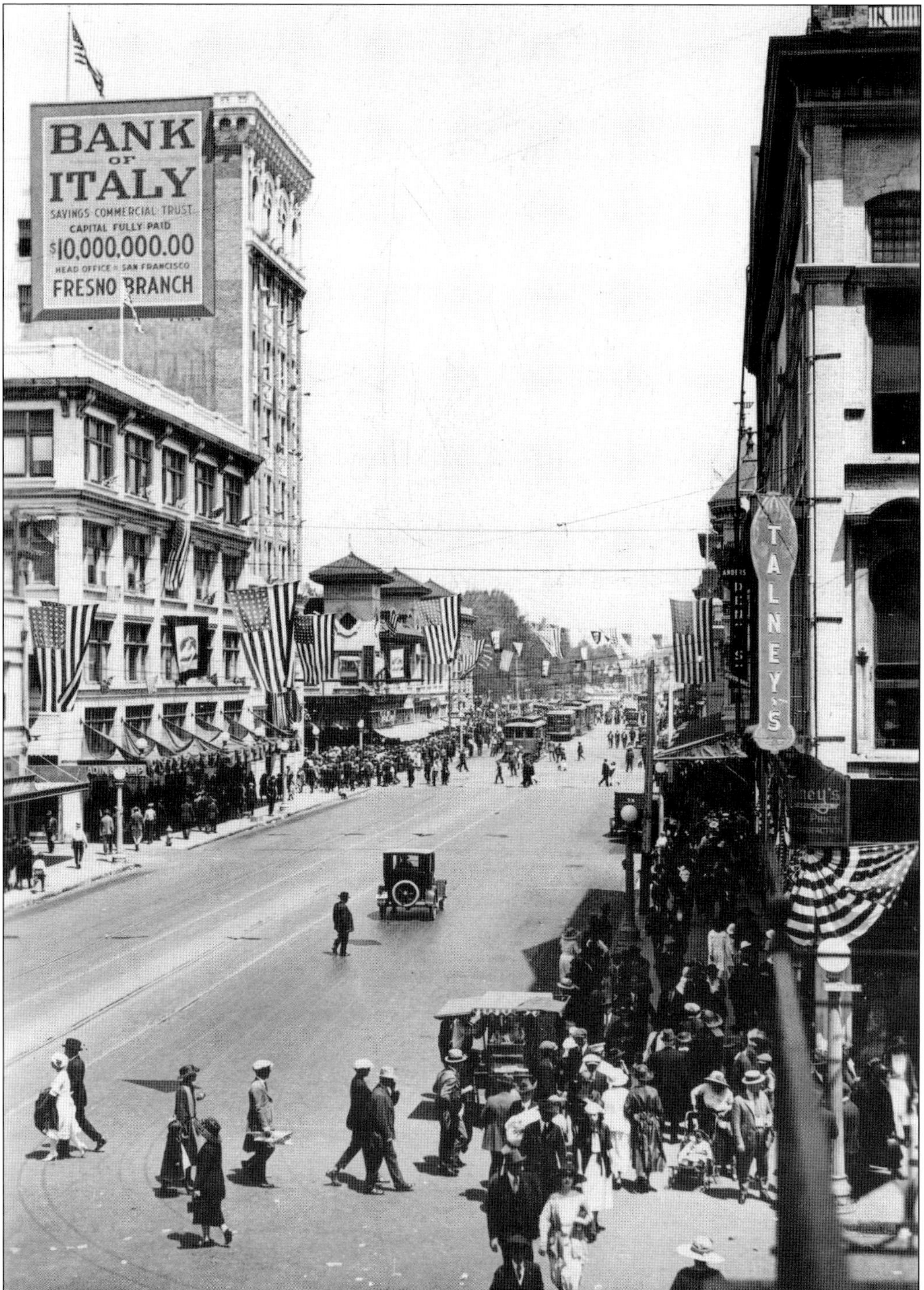

Here is a busy shopping day in Fresno near Tulare and Broadway Streets. The Bank of Italy stands out on the left. The building, completed on August 1, 1918, used 280 tons of steel in its construction. To the left was the Radin and Kamp Department Store.

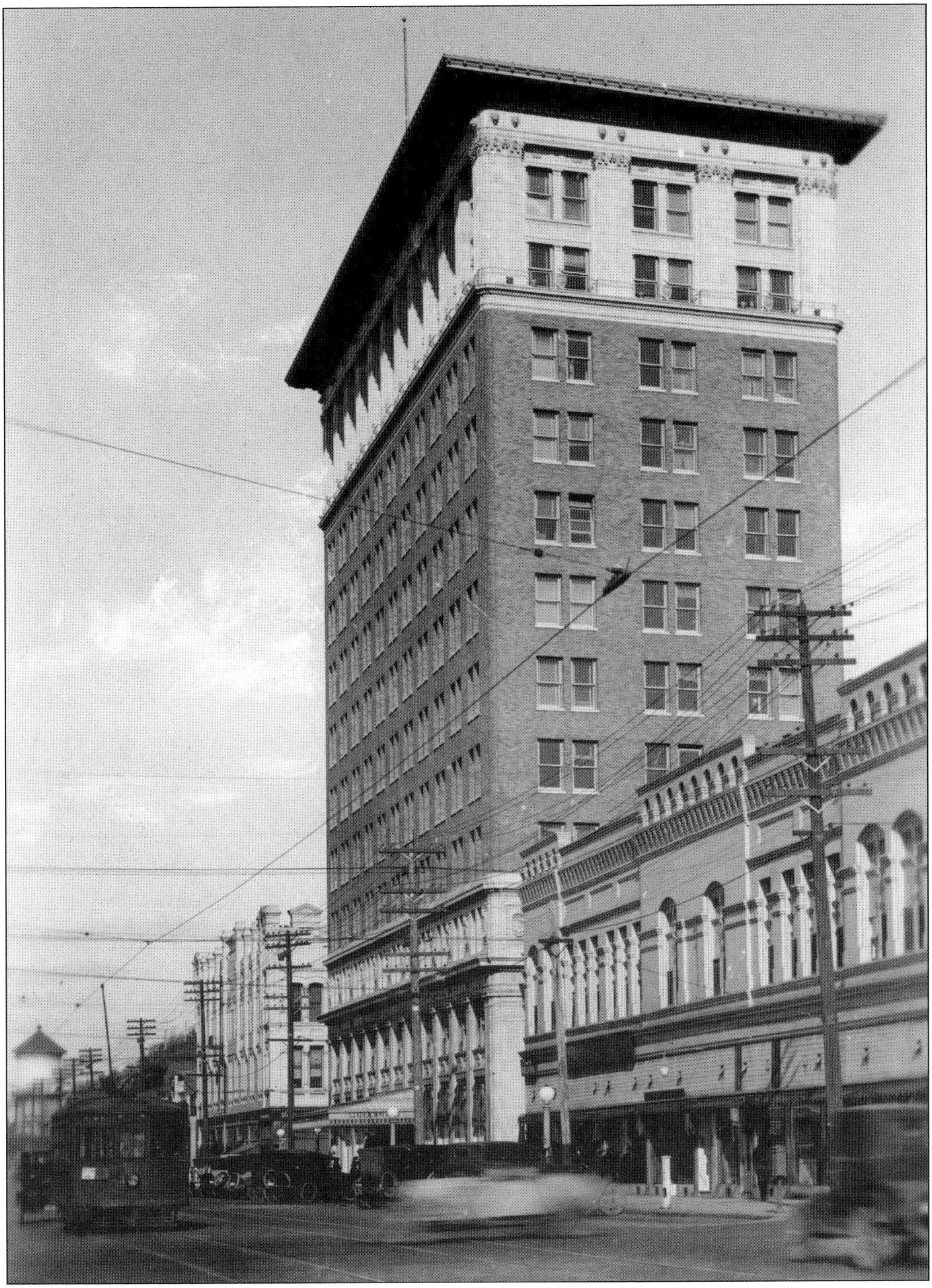

The 12-story Mattei Building was completed in 1920 at a cost of $1.2 million and is located at 1177 Fulton Street. It was designed by Eugene Mathewson in the Classic Revival style. Andrew Mattei was a local farmer who owned 1,200 acres of wine grapes. He lost the building to Bank of America during the Depression. In 1961, it was purchased by Fresno Guarantee Savings and Loan.

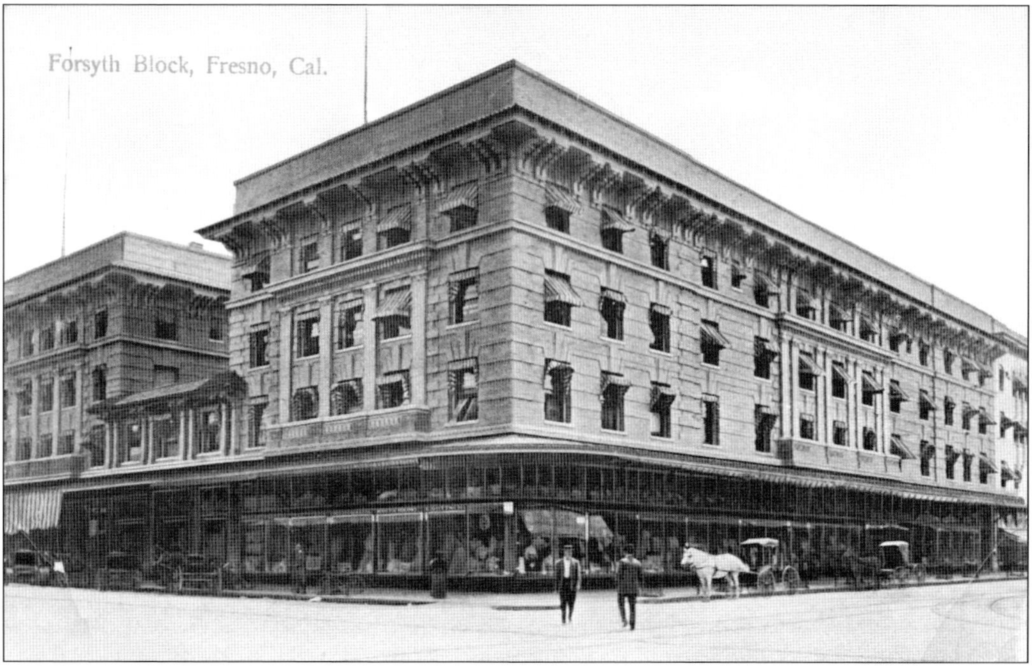

The Forsyth Building was constructed in 1904 by Col. William Forsyth, T.W. Patterson, and W.A. Nevills and occupied the southeast corner of Tulare and Fulton Streets. One of the original tenants was Gottschalks Department Store, which occupied the ground floor from 1904 through 1913, before they built their own building in 1914.

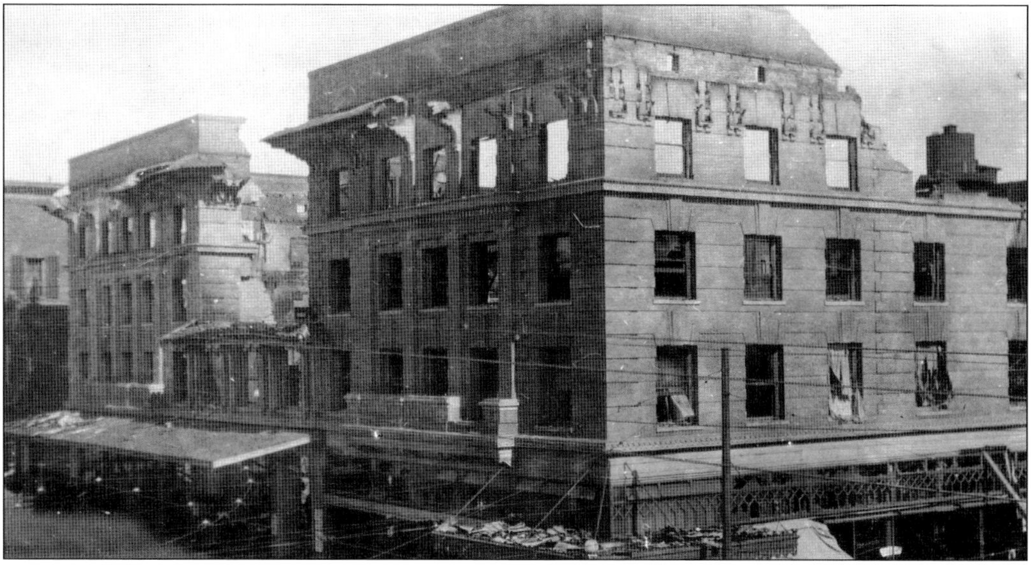

Shown here is the Forsyth Building after it was destroyed by fire. According to the *Fresno Bee*, a fire started at approximately 8:30 p.m. on Saturday, March 19, 1921, in the basement of The Wonder, a women's apparel store located on the ground floor of the building, and quickly spread to all four floors.

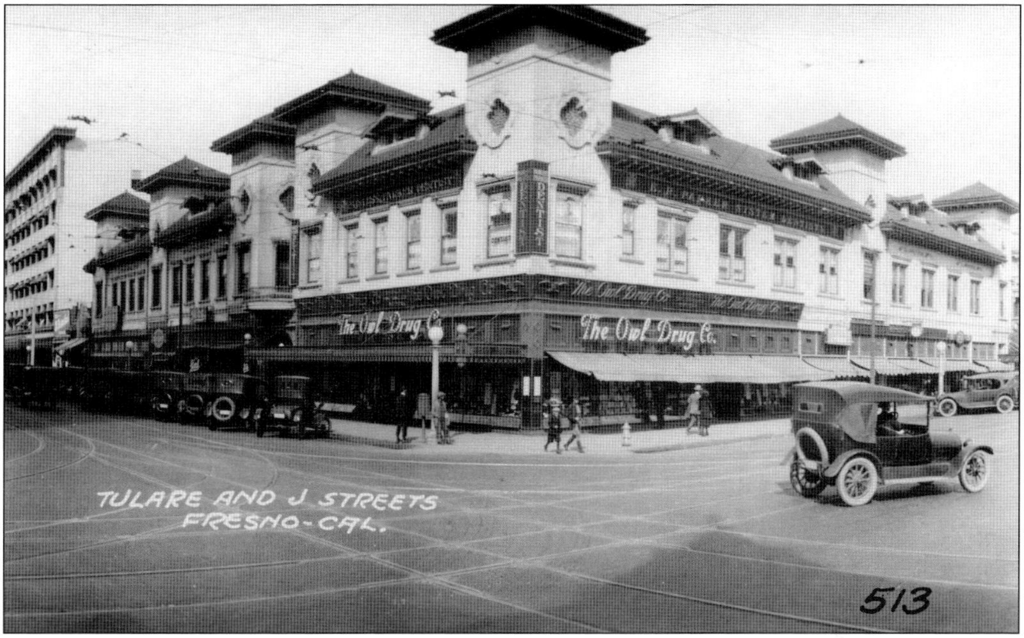

The Patterson Block Building is located on the northeast corner of Tulare and Fulton Streets. The original ground floor tenant of the building was H. Graff and Co., a local grocery store. A more recent occupant was The Owl Drug Company. This photograph was taken in 1921.

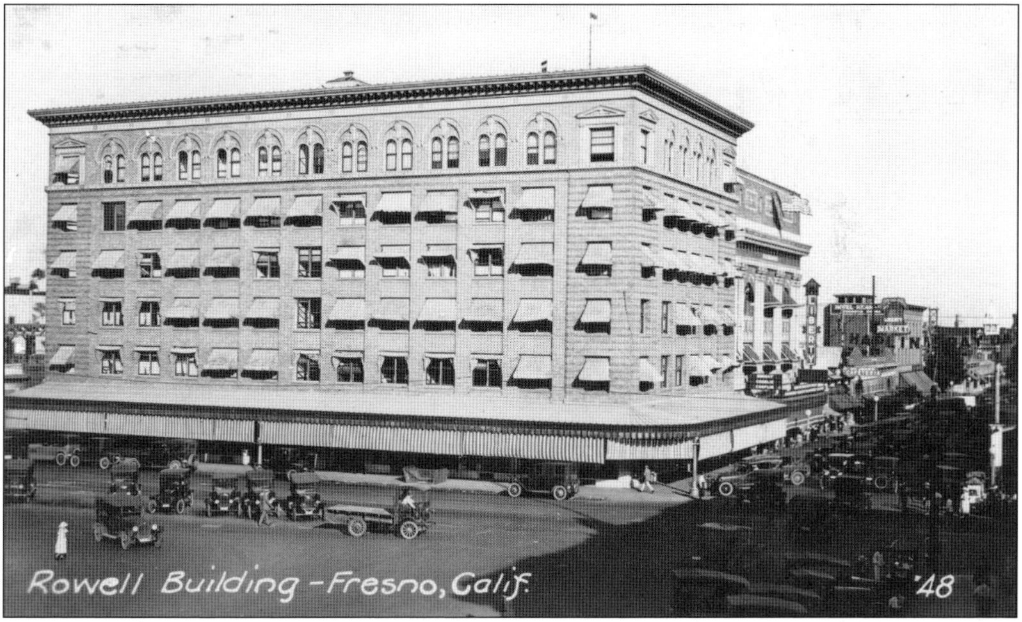

The six-story Rowell Building was completed in 1914 and was Fresno's first all steel framed high rise. It was designed in the Renaissance Revival style by R.F. Felchin & Company. The owners were Dr. Chester Rowell and Wilber Chandler, who later donated land for the airport named after him. Dr. Rowell was a doctor, newspaper owner, city mayor, and California state senator. The Rowell Building is located on the southeast corner of Tulare and Van Ness Streets.

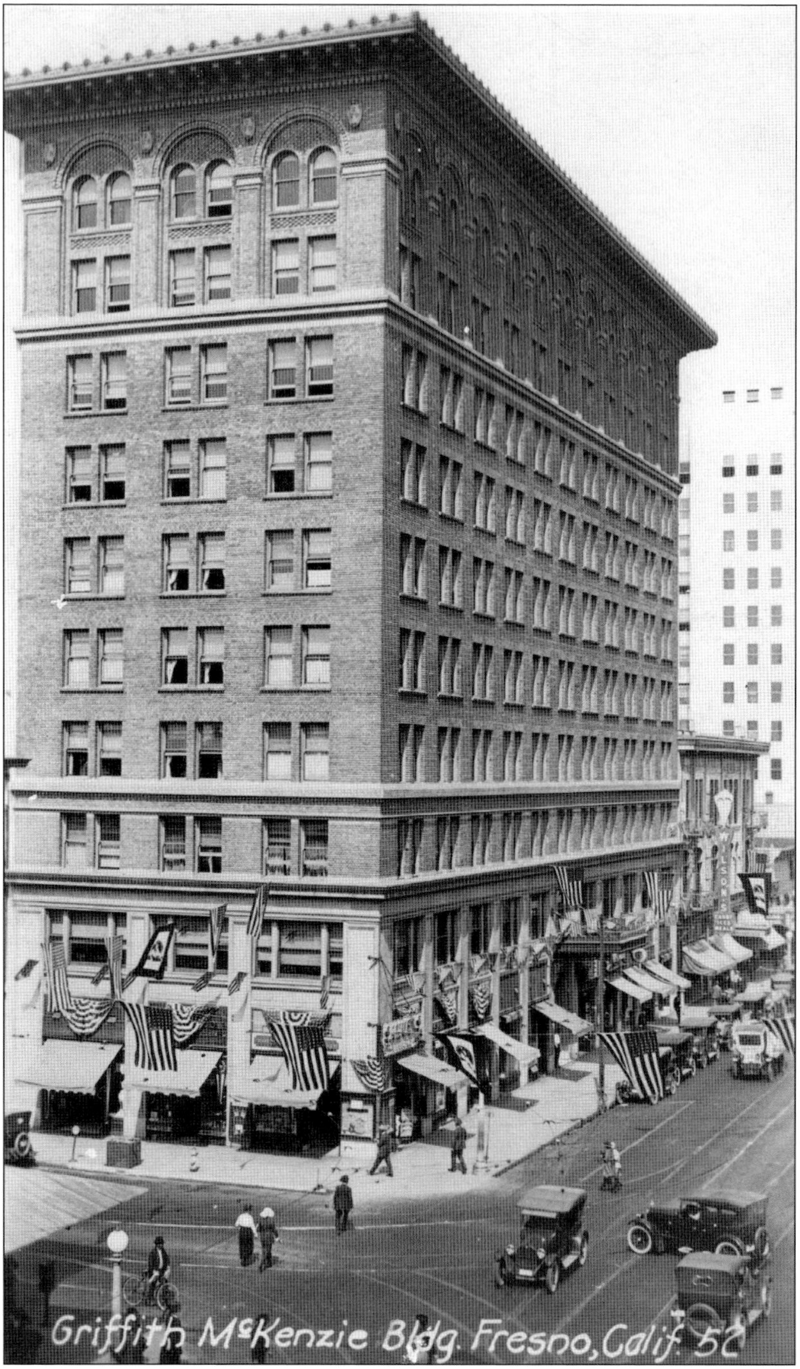

The Griffith McKenzie/Helm Building is located on the northwest corner of Fulton and Mariposa Streets. It was designed by George Kelhan in the Renaissance Revival style. Construction began in 1913 and was completed the following year. Floors two to ten housed mainly offices, while the ground floor was occupied by Campbell's Ice Cream Parlor and Samuel's Smokehouse and Tobacco Store. Later, the building was purchased by the Helm Family and renamed in honor of Frank Helm.

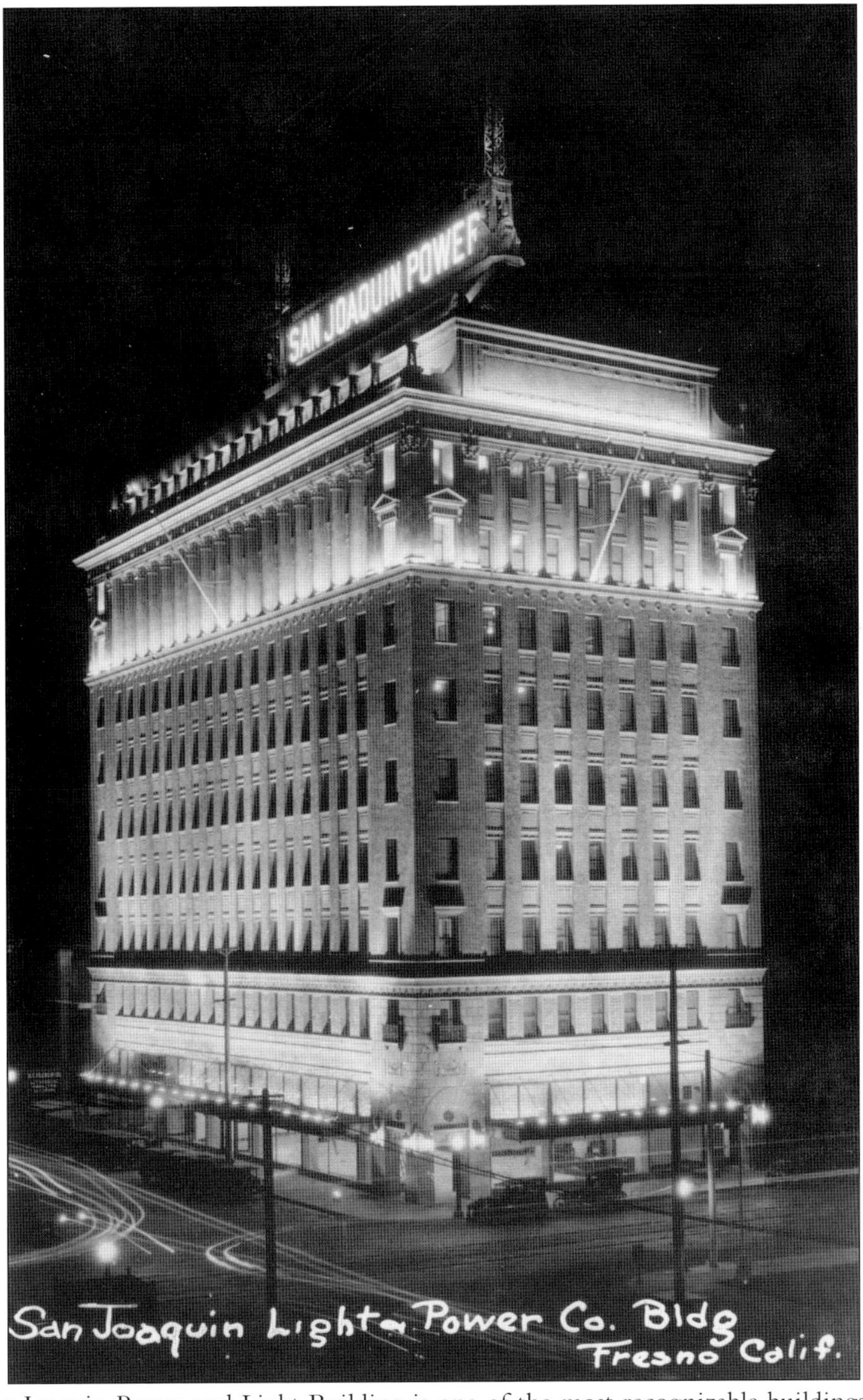

The San Joaquin Power and Light Building is one of the most recognizable buildings of the Fresno downtown area. Completed in 1922, the 10-story building occupies the northwest corner of Fulton and Tuolumne Streets. The architectural firm of Felchin, Shaw, and Franklin designed it in the Italian Renaissance Revival style. The building had a bright neon sign on its roof reading, "San Joaquin Power."

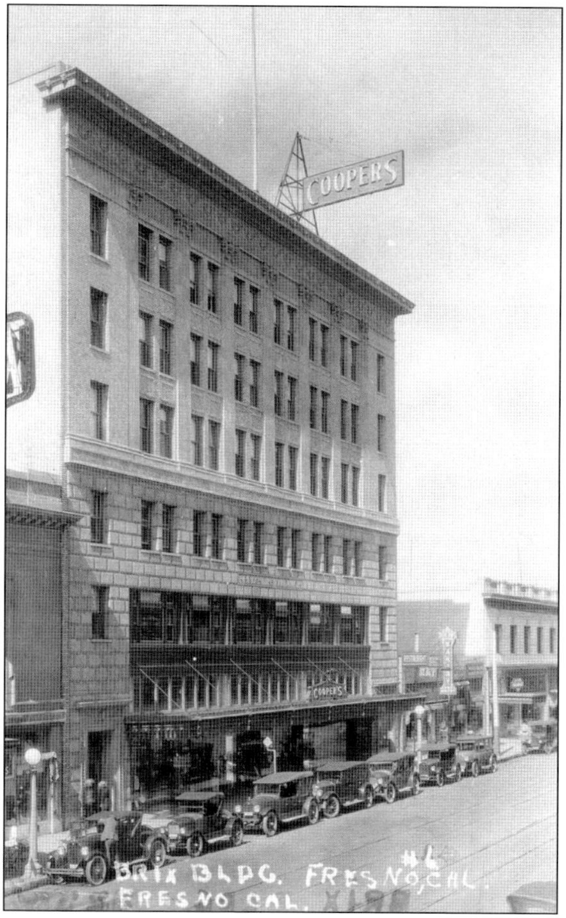

The six-story Brix Building, located at 1221 Fulton Street, was completed in 1922 at a cost of $350,000. The Brix Family, immigrants from Germany, made their fortune in the early oil boom of Fresno County. Designed by Eugene Mathewson, the building reflects the Early Classical style of design. The sign at the top of the building shows that an early tenant was Cooper's Department Store.

The H.H. Brix mansion was built in 1911 for Herman and Helena Brix at 2844 Fresno Street. The building was designed by Edward T. Foulkes in the Italian Renaissance style. It is considered to be one of the finest representations of period Italian Villa in the Central Valley.

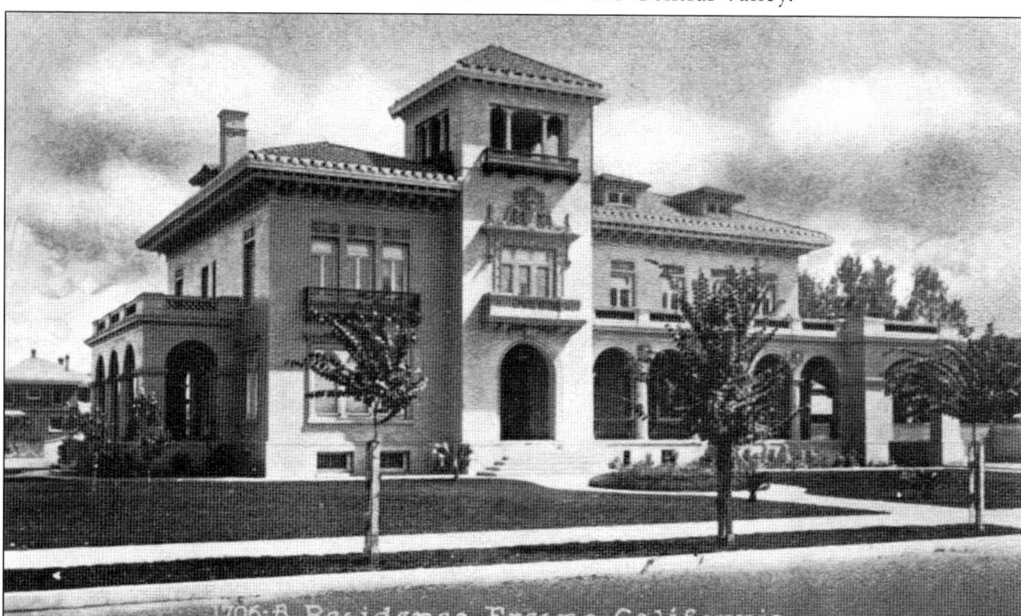

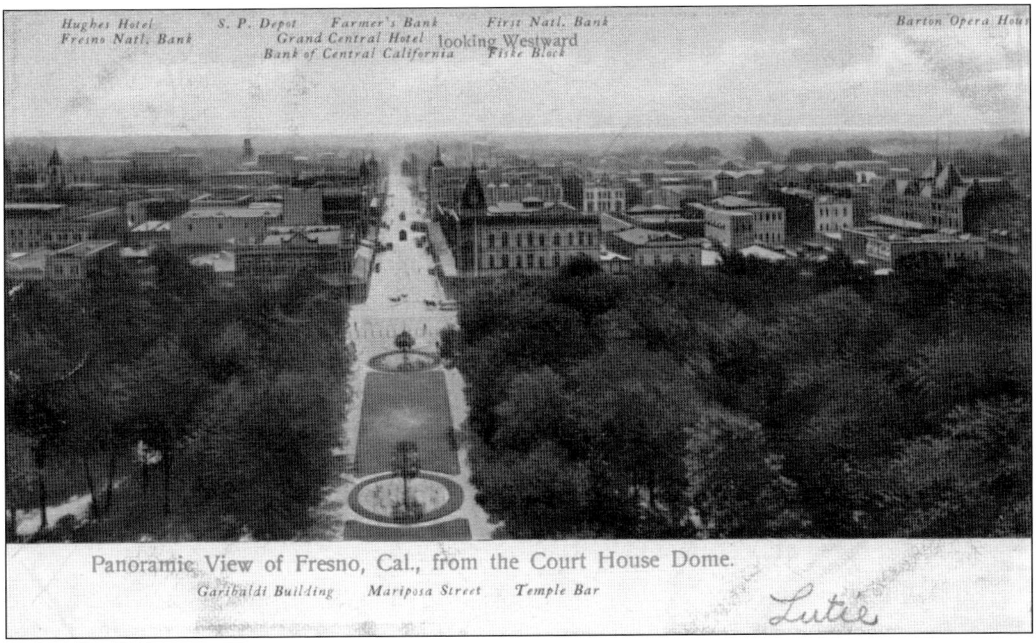

This west-facing view of downtown Fresno is one of four taken from the courthouse dome. Van Ness Street runs left to right between the park and business district. The card identifies many of the major buildings in the downtown area.

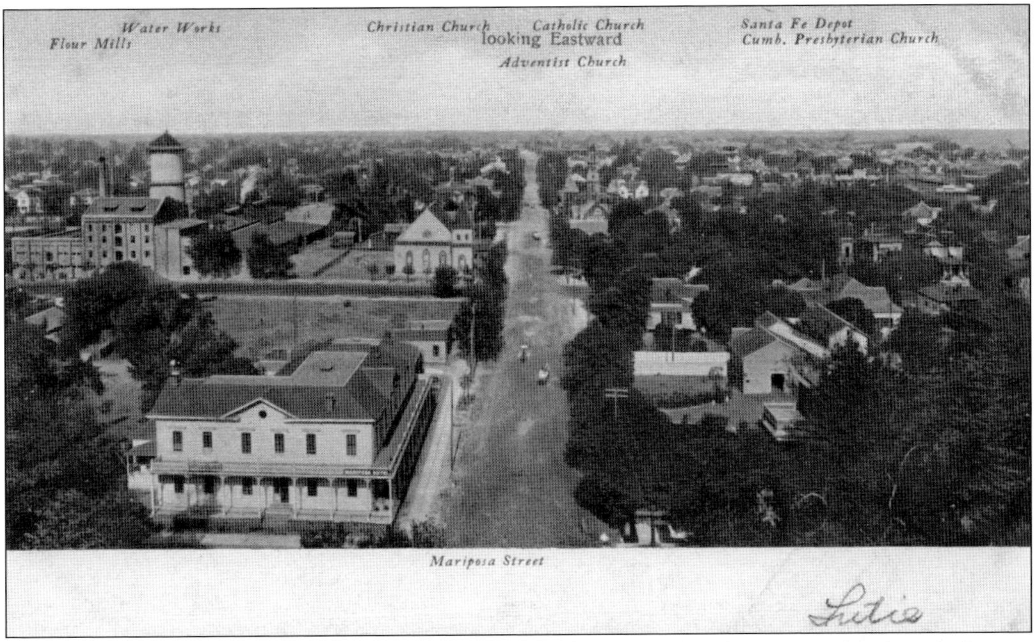

This is the view facing east from the courthouse dome, looking down unpaved Mariposa Street. This part of Fresno was mainly churches and residences. In the foreground is the Mariposa Hotel. Behind it along Mariposa Street is the First Christian Church. To the far left is the Sperry Flour Mill.

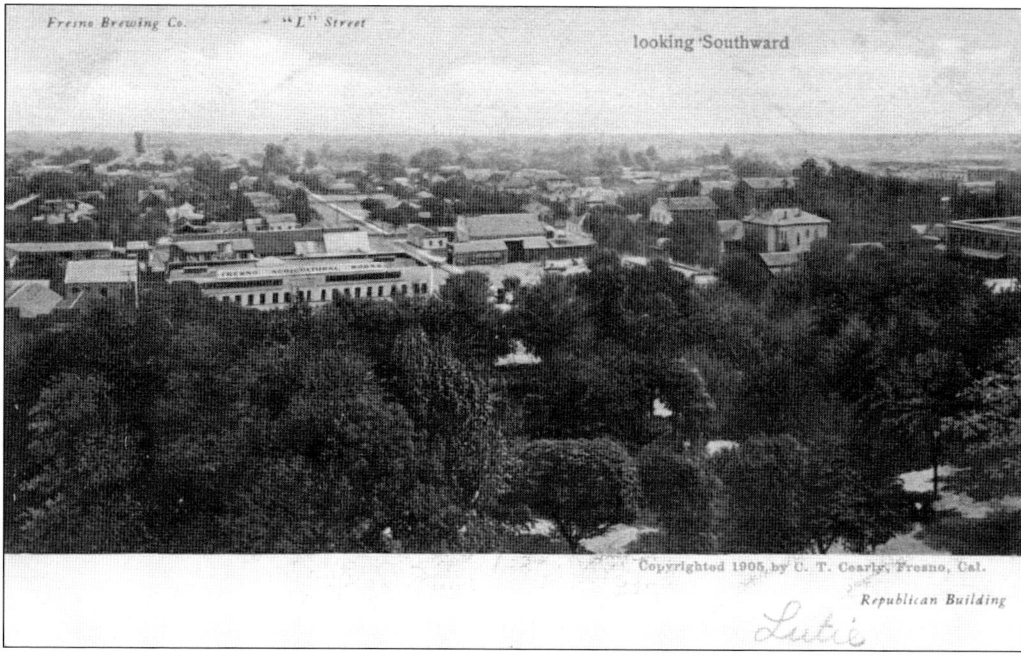

Shown here is the view south from the courthouse. The many-windowed building peeking above the trees is the Fresno Agricultural Works. This company manufactured the Fresno Scraper, a farm implement that allowed for easy leveling of land and helped transform vast tracts of farmland all over the world. The business still operates today under the name of Fresno Ag Hardware.

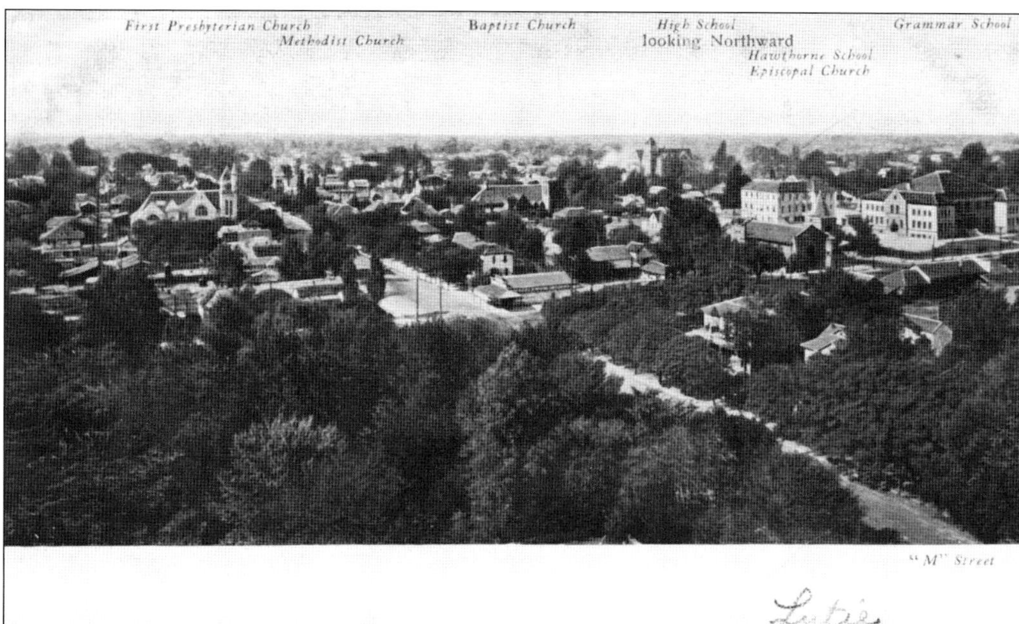

The fourth image from the courthouse dome provides a perspective on how far Fresno extended north from the downtown area. This neighborhood was the location of many churches and was also where the grammar and high schools stood.

Four

City and County Buildings

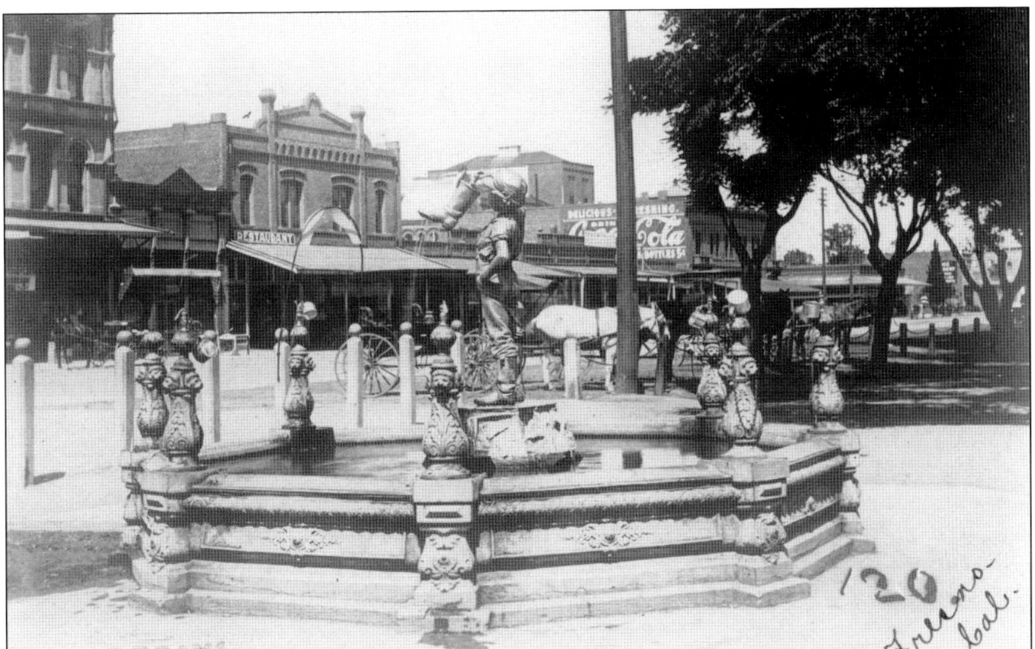

"The Boy with a Leaky Boot" drinking fountain was installed in August 1895 at the edge of Courthouse Park at the intersection of Mariposa and Van Ness Streets. It had six tin cups and several faucets available for the public to use for drinking water. Today, the statue is located in the County Plaza across Tulare Street from the Hall of Records in Courthouse Park.

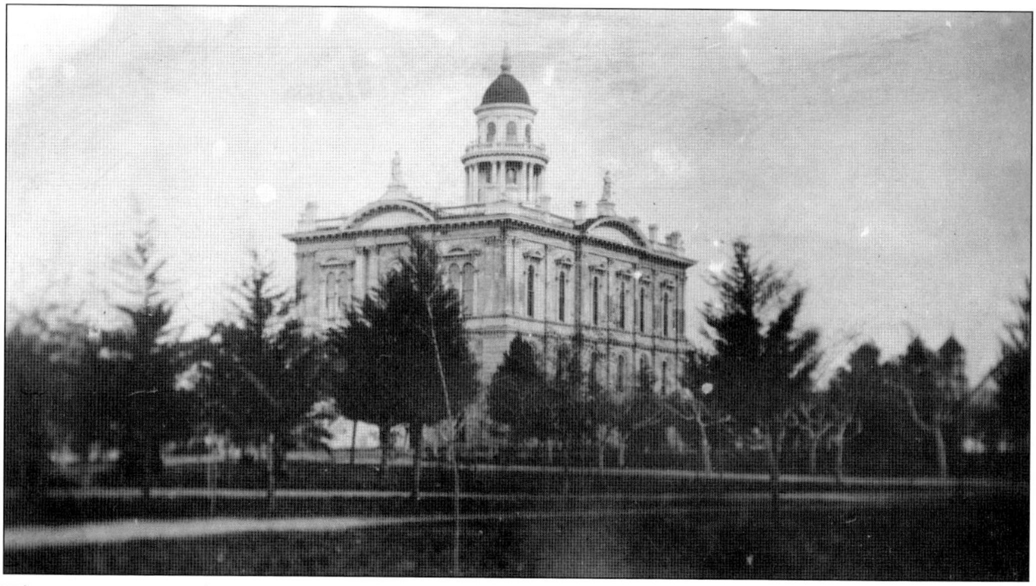

The cornerstone for Fresno County's first courthouse was laid on October 8, 1874. The cornerstone held many objects and documents including gold coins and an 1874 local newspaper. By the time the courthouse was completed in 1876, Fresno's population had grown to 600 people, including 200 Chinese.

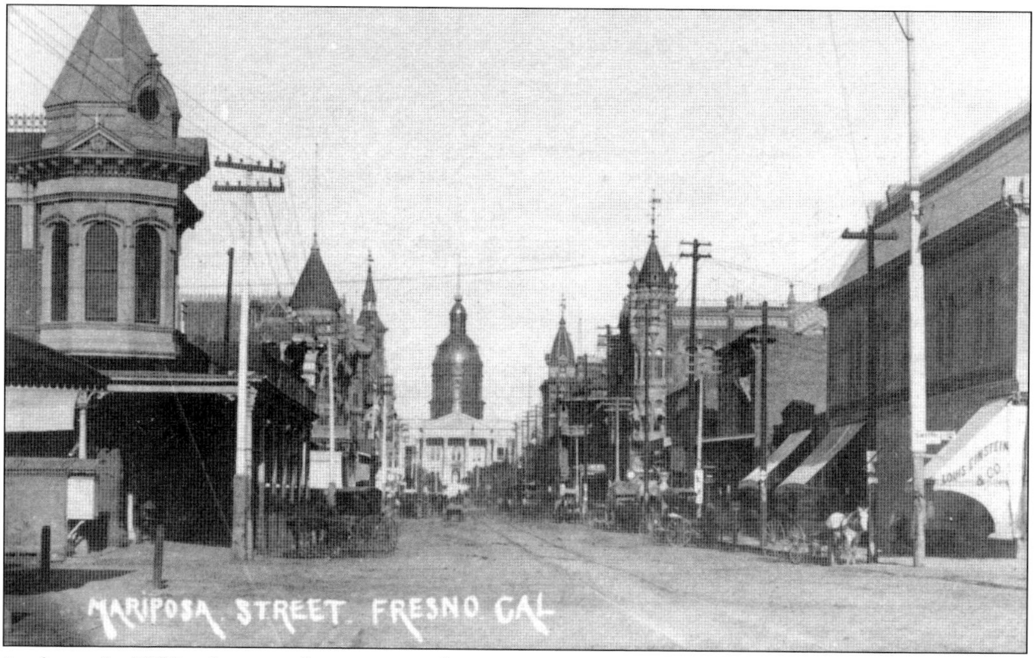

In the early 1890s, the courthouse grew short of office space for all of the departments. Sections were added on to each side of the original building and a copper dome was installed in 1893. On July 29, 1895, a fire caused heavy damage to the courthouse, and the copper dome was destroyed. (Mark Jost Collection.)

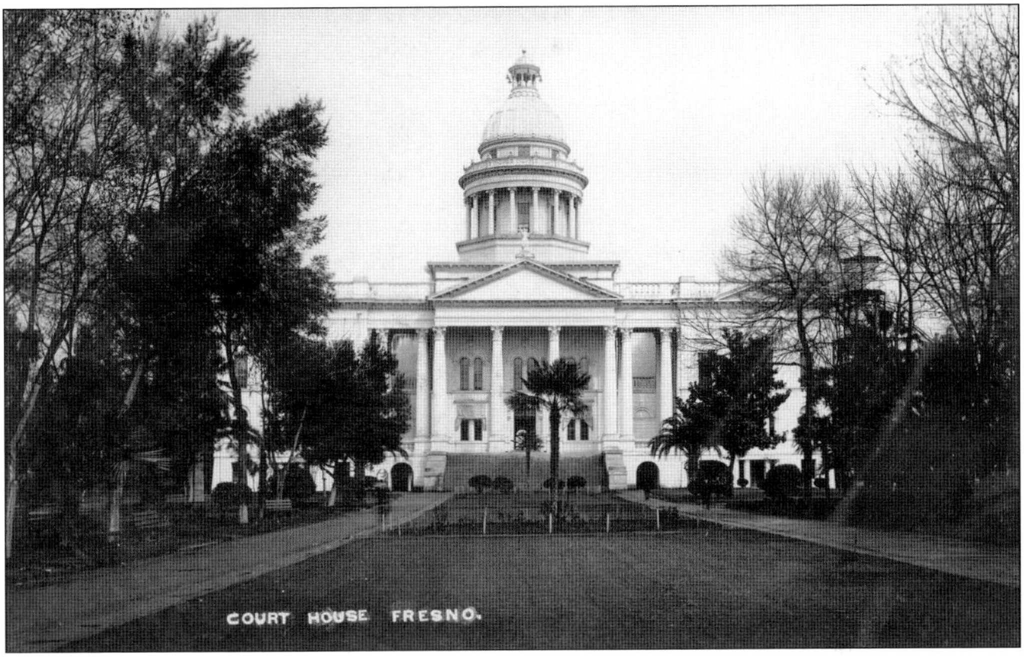

The courthouse was repaired, and a more modest dome was installed. Shown here is the third and final version of the building in 1907.

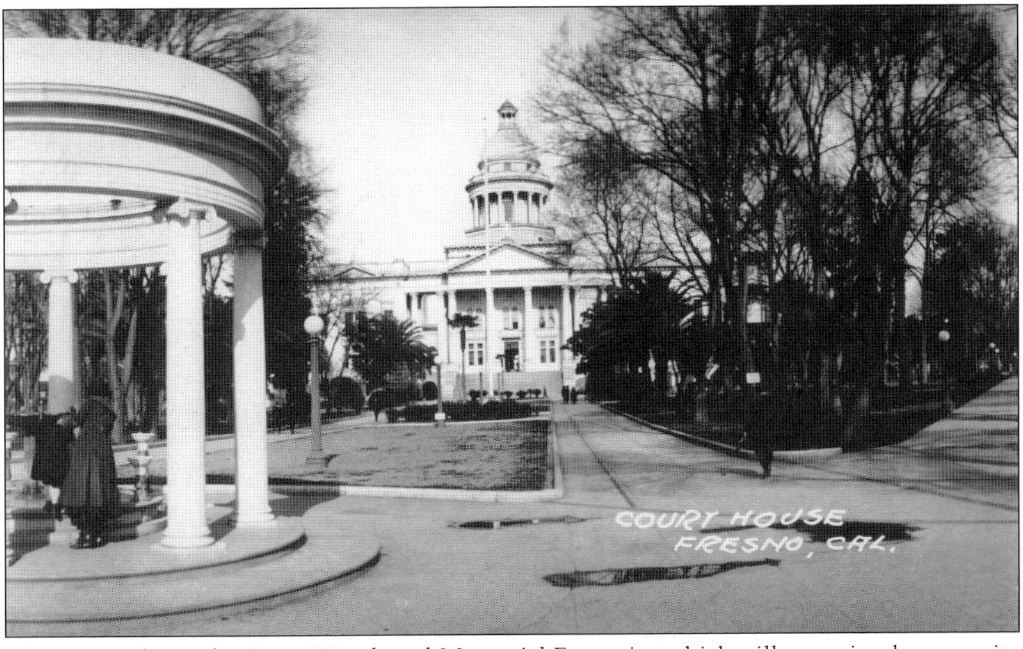

This image shows the Anna Woodward Memorial Fountain, which still occupies the same site in the park.

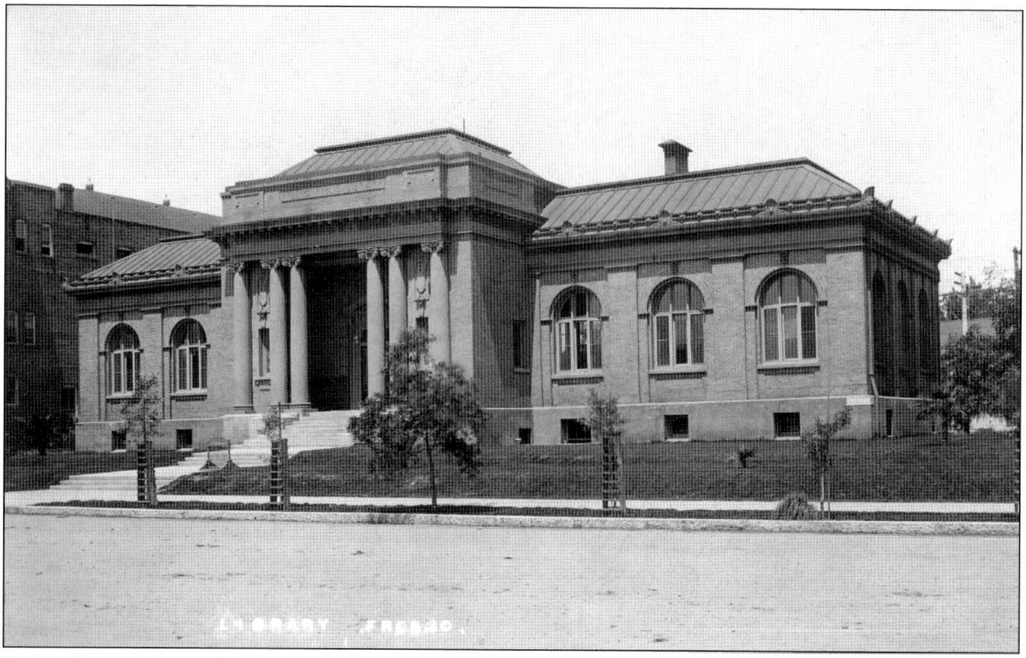

Fresno's Carnegie Library was designed by Copeland and Dole of New York City and was built by Fresno contractors C.P. Pierce and J.Q. Anderson. Andrew Carnegie gave $30,000 to fund the construction, and it was built on a donated site at 1330 Broadway. The cornerstone was laid on December 8, 1902, and construction was completed April 2, 1904.

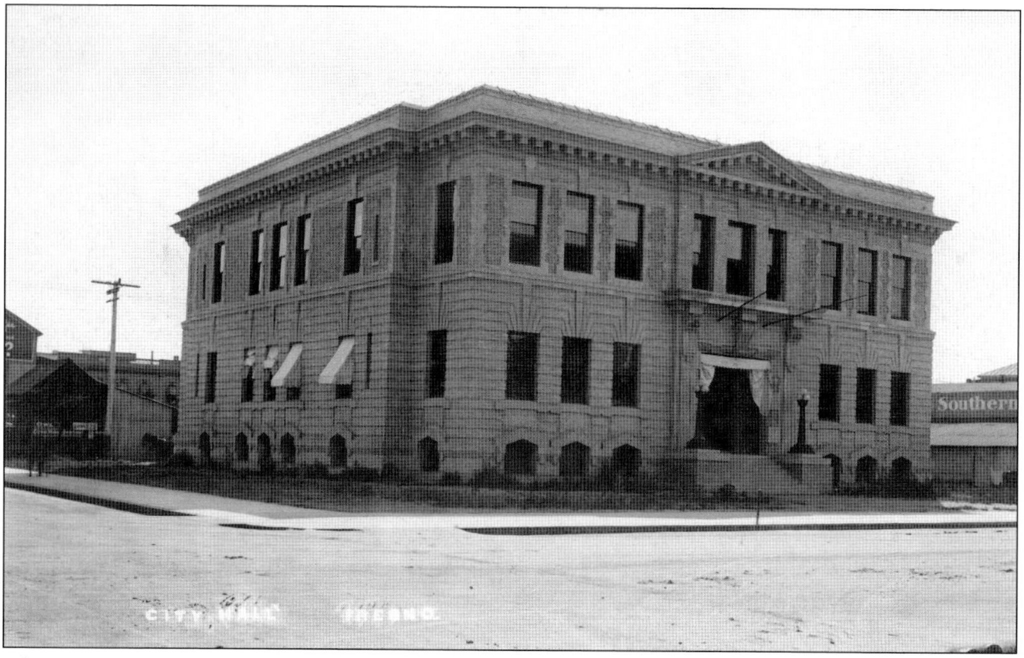

The two-story brick city hall was located on the southeast corner of Broadway and Merced Streets. It was built in 1907 at a cost of $75,000. The Fresno police department and city first aid station were located in the building's basement.

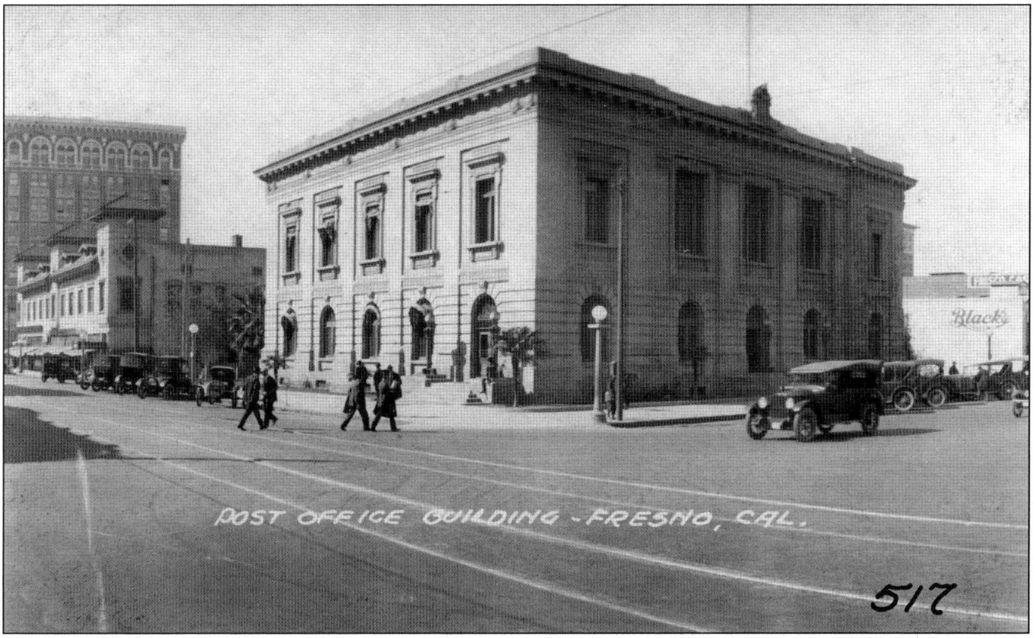

Fresno's first US Post Office and US Courthouse were located at the northwest corner of Tulare and Van Ness Streets. Built in 1906–1907 at a cost of $100,000, the building was vacated in 1940 and demolished in 1951. Prior to this location, the post office was in various rented locations throughout the downtown area.

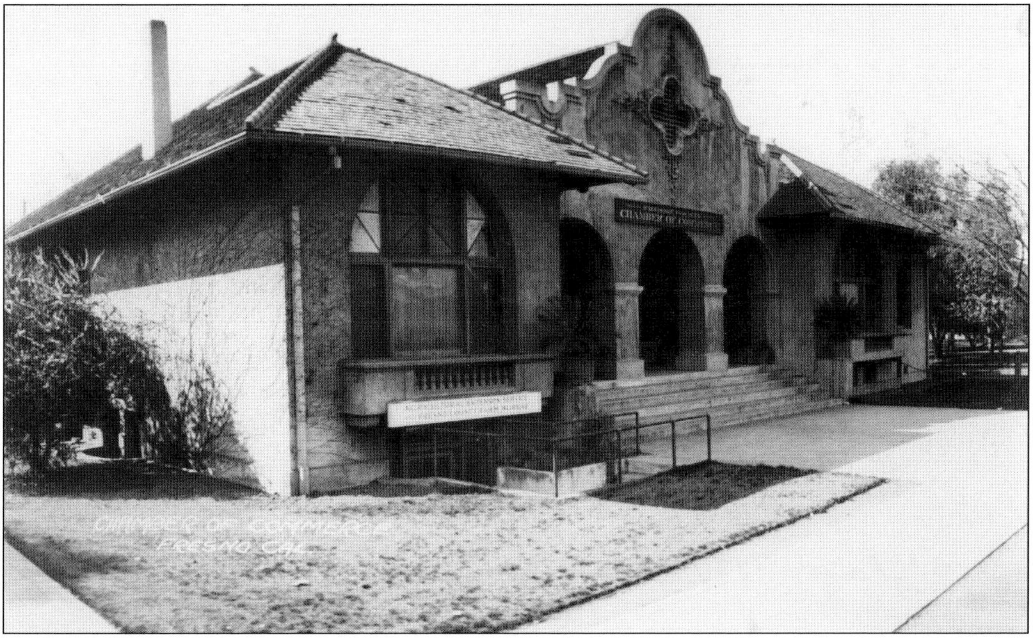
The chamber of commerce building for Fresno City and County was built in 1903 in a small park in front of the Southern Pacific Depot at Tulare and H Streets. At that time, the chamber boasted of a membership roster of over 800 individuals and businesses.

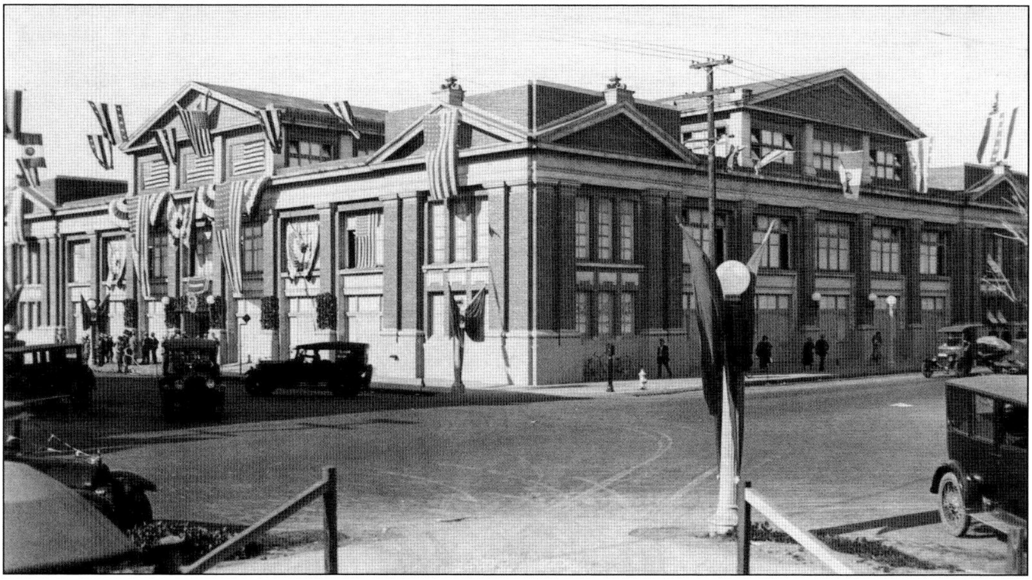

Fresno's first public auditorium was located at the northeast corner of L and Kern Streets. Promoted by Mayor Chester Rowell and designed by C.K. Kirby Jr., construction on the structure began in October 1911 and was completed at a cost of $105,000, three times the projected cost of $35,000. The building was dedicated on March 2, 1914. The Del Webb Building occupies the site today.

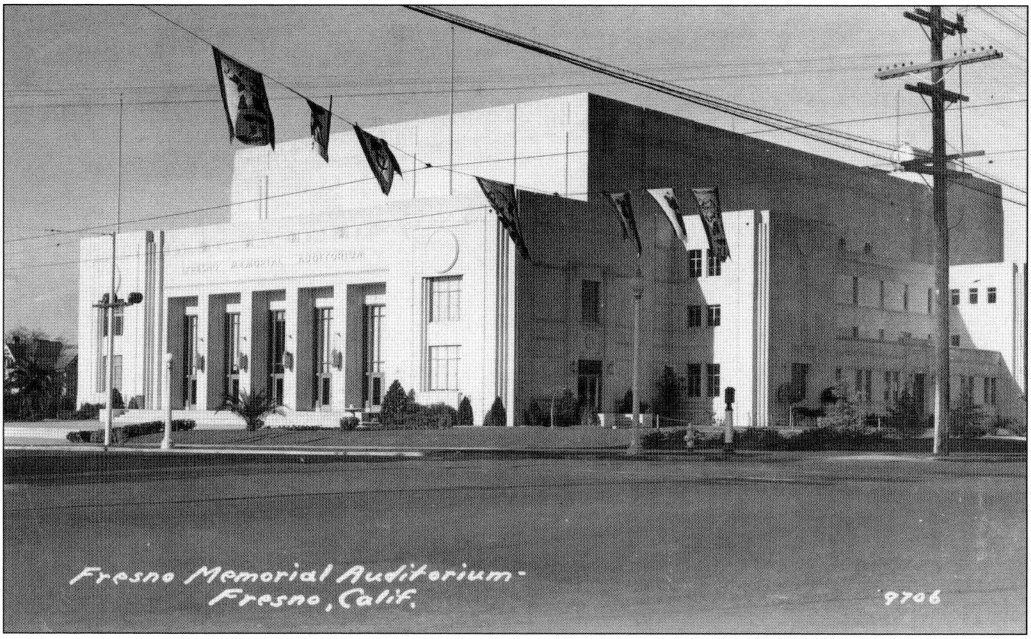

Across from the Fresno Water Tower stands the Fresno Memorial Auditorium. Designed by Allied Architects of Fresno, it was constructed in 1936 at a cost of $400,000. It was designed in the Monumental Modern style and seated 3,500 people. Today, it is home to the Legion of Valor Museum, the first veterans' museum on the West Coast. (Fresno County Library.)

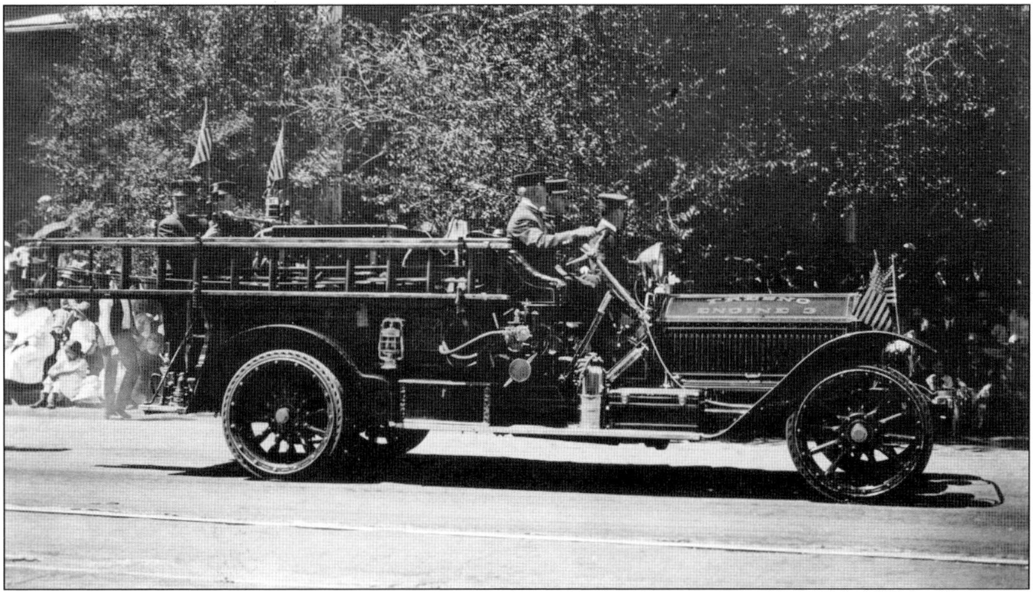

The Fresno Fire Department had a truck in most parades including Raisin Day, The Fourth of July, and Armistice Day. Shown here is Fire Engine no. 4 in front of Courthouse Park in the 1920s. Its home was station no. 4, which was located at Kern and U Streets.

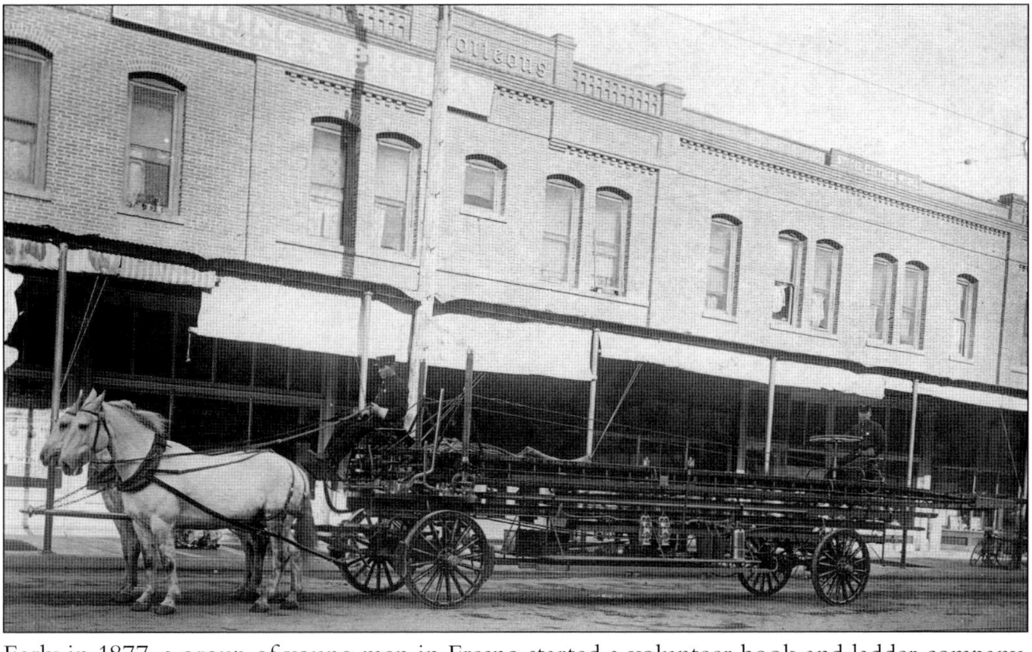

Early in 1877, a group of young men in Fresno started a volunteer hook and ladder company. Leopold Gundlefinger was its first foreman. The pictured horse-drawn hook and ladder unit was purchased in 1895 for the volunteer company. The first motorized hook and ladder was purchased in August 1916. By 1917, all horse-drawn units were retired.

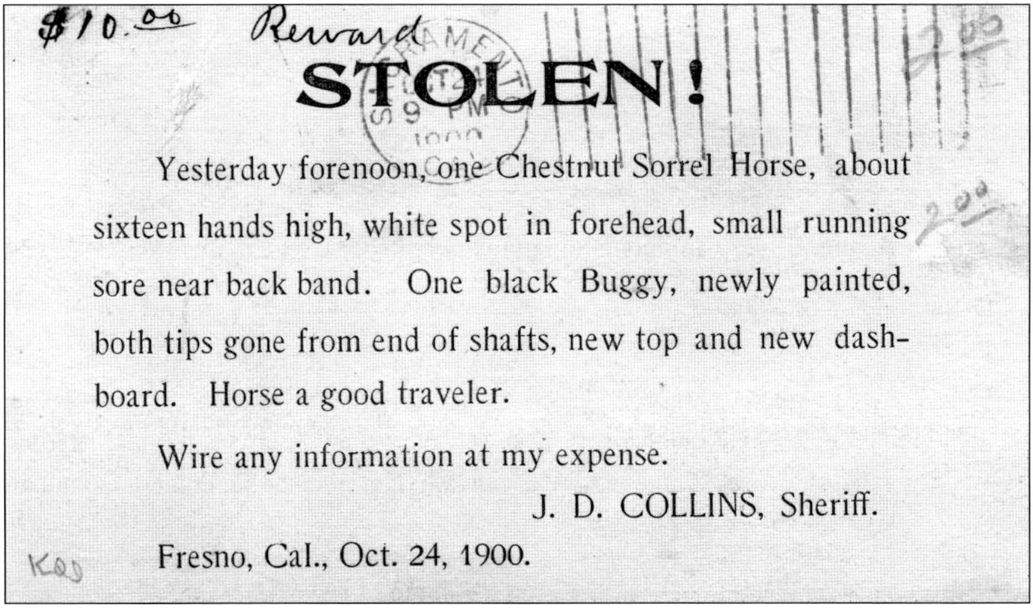

$10.00 Reward

STOLEN!

Yesterday forenoon, one Chestnut Sorrel Horse, about sixteen hands high, white spot in forehead, small running sore near back band. One black Buggy, newly painted, both tips gone from end of shafts, new top and new dash-board. Horse a good traveler.

Wire any information at my expense.

J. D. COLLINS, Sheriff.

Fresno, Cal., Oct. 24, 1900.

Postcards were widely used by city and county police departments to notify other law enforcement agencies in the state of their wanted criminals. These cards were placed into albums for officers to review. Shown here are several examples of local cards.

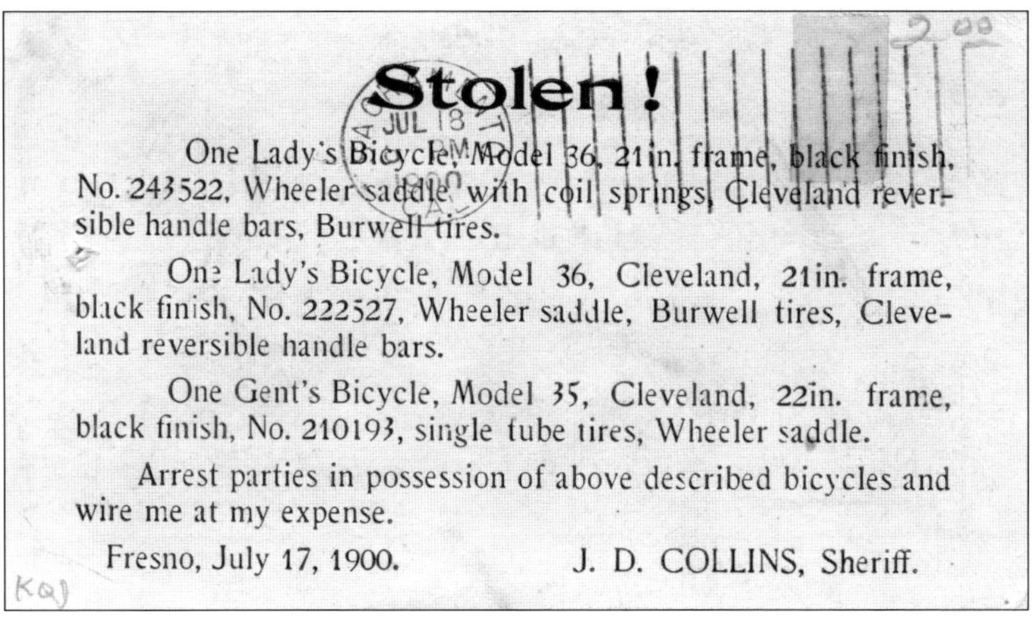

Stolen!

One Lady's Bicycle, Model 36, 21in. frame, black finish, No. 243522, Wheeler saddle with coil springs, Cleveland reversible handle bars, Burwell tires.

One Lady's Bicycle, Model 36, Cleveland, 21in. frame, black finish, No. 222527, Wheeler saddle, Burwell tires, Cleveland reversible handle bars.

One Gent's Bicycle, Model 35, Cleveland, 22in. frame, black finish, No. 210193, single tube tires, Wheeler saddle.

Arrest parties in possession of above described bicycles and wire me at my expense.

Fresno, July 17, 1900. J. D. COLLINS, Sheriff.

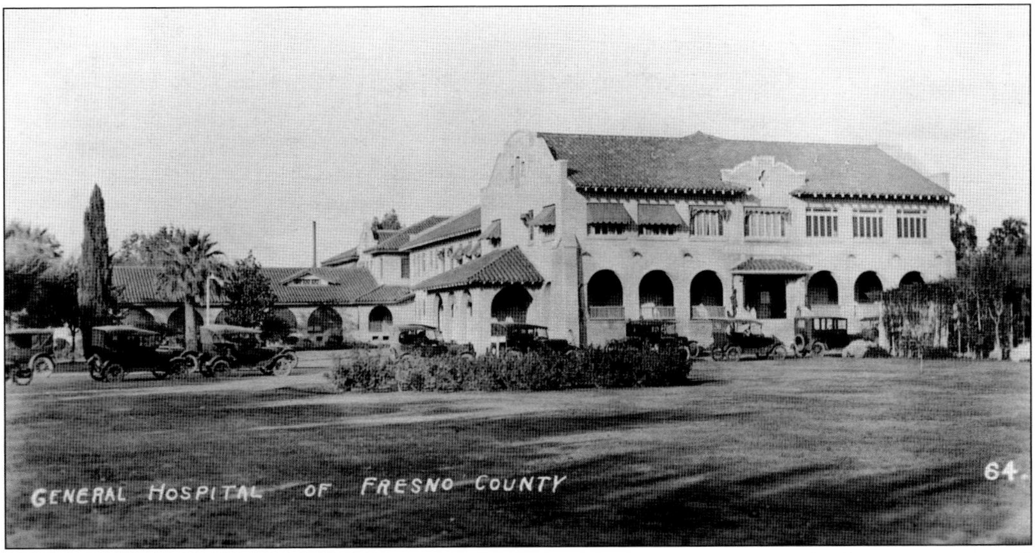

In June 1921, the Fresno County Hospital was renamed "General Hospital of Fresno County." The hospital building was located on an 80-acre site bordered by Cedar Avenue, Barton Street, Huntington Boulevard, and Ventura Boulevard. The site was purchased in 1887 for $96,000.

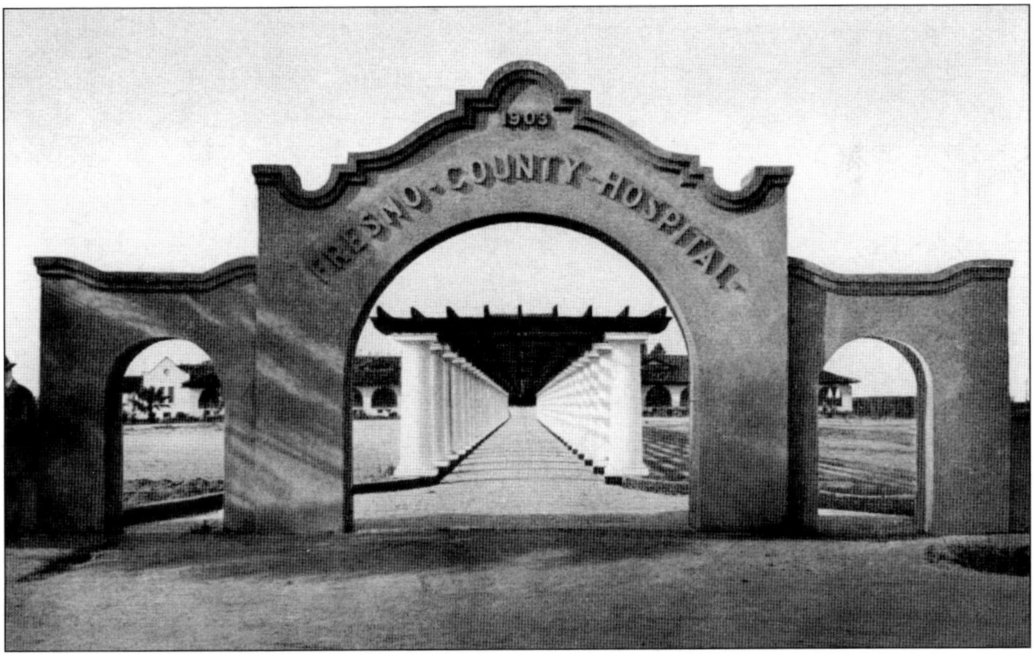

Shown in this image is the Mission-style archway of the Fresno County Hospital. The hospital was built in 1903 after the original structure burned down. This walkway faced Ventura Boulevard between Cedar and Barton Streets.

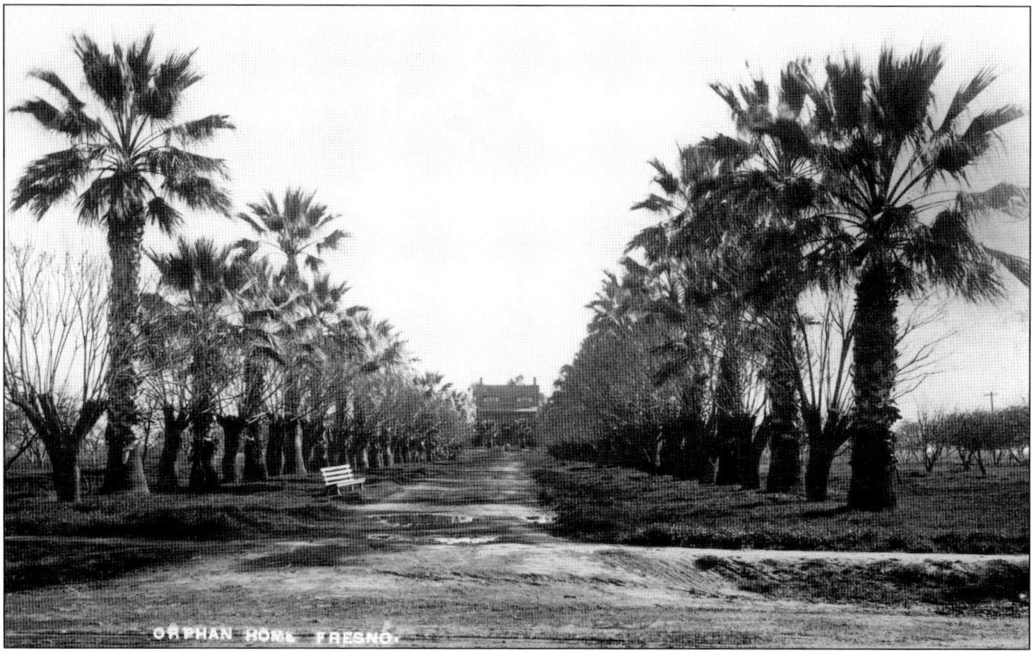

In the early 1890s, the county needed to expand the orphanage, so it purchased a 10-acre site located at Ventura Boulevard and Tenth Street. Included with the purchase was a large, two-story house along with other structures. Shown here is the long driveway that led to the home. The county juvenile hall is located at the site today.

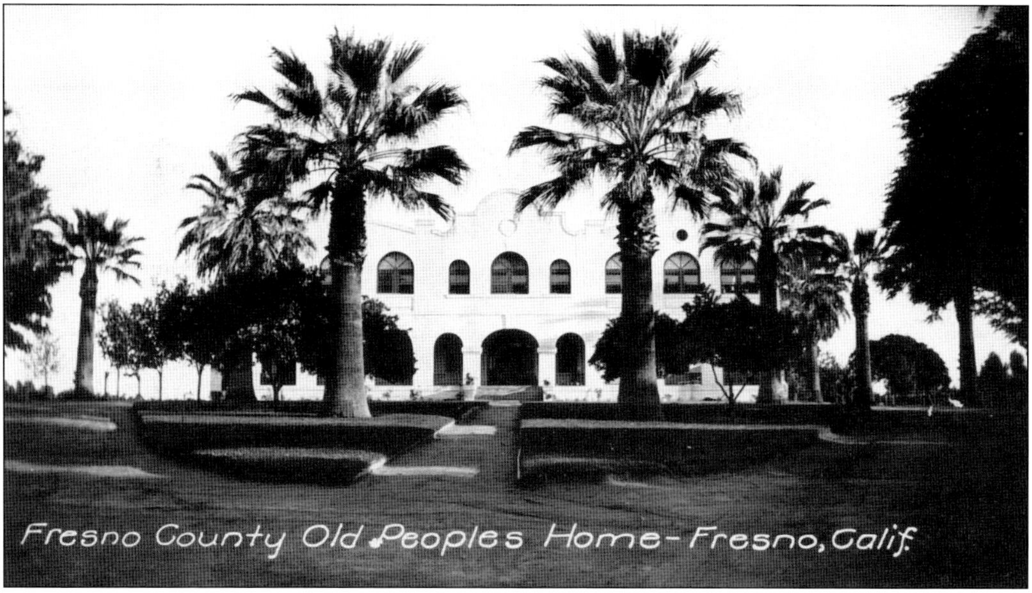

In 1918, the county orphanage closed, and the building remained vacant until 1922. In that year, it was remodeled and reopened as the Fresno County Old Peoples Home.

Five

Fresno Businesses

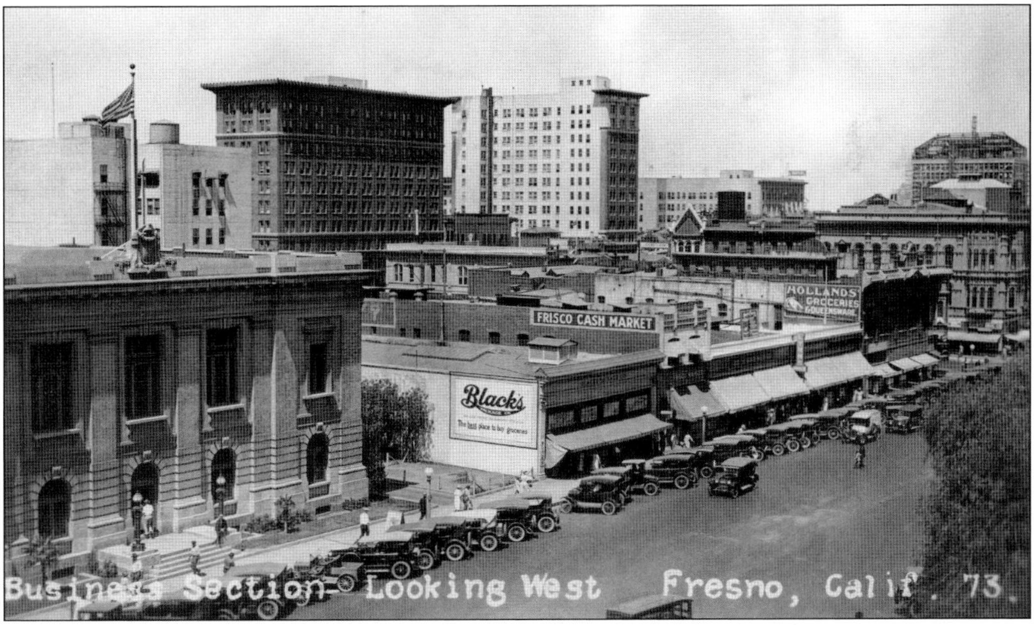

This card looks north on Van Ness Street, between Tulare and Fresno Streets, and is dated to the mid-1920s. Shown together on the same block are three competing grocery stores: Blacks, Frisco Cash Market, and Holland Grocery.

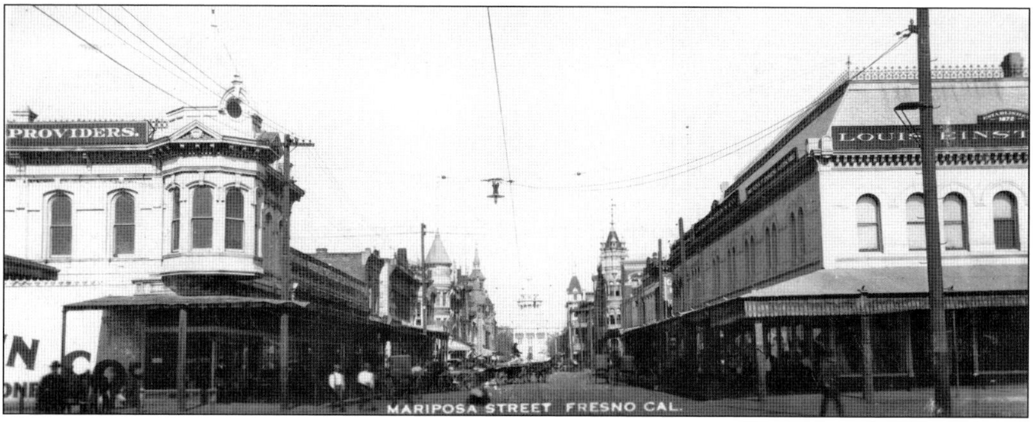

The intersection of Broadway and Mariposa Streets shows the Fresno County Courthouse at the east end of Mariposa. At this intersection were two major general merchandise stores of early Fresno. On the northeast corner was the Kutner-Goldstein store, known as "The Universal Provider." Occupying the southeast corner was The Louis Einstein & Company store, known as the "Pioneer Store" due to its early roots in Fresno. (Mark Jost Collection.)

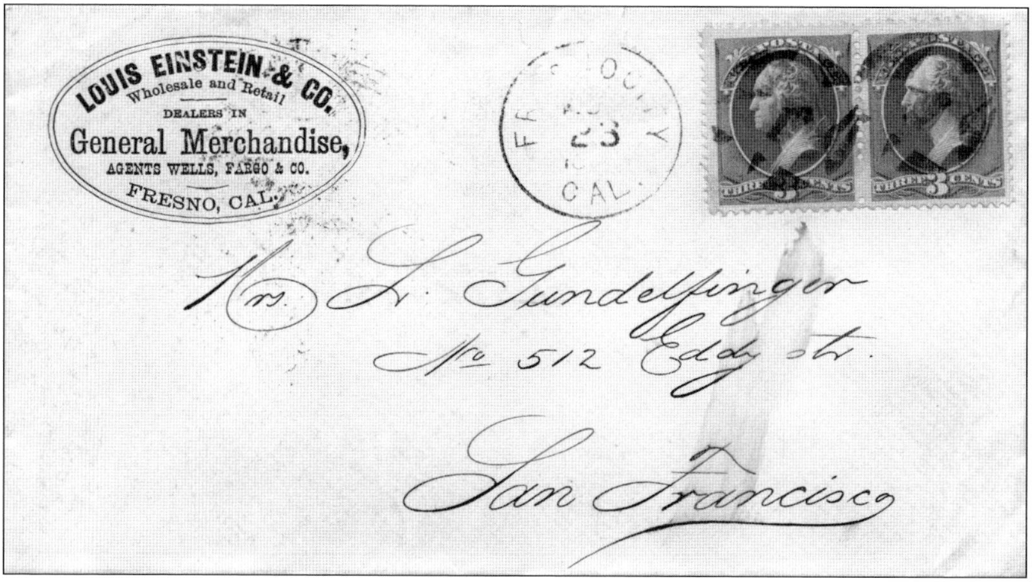

This early business envelope for Louis Einstein & Co. announces its ability to provide any goods at wholesale and retail. Being a Wells, Fargo & Co. agent required them to have a stage and mail service.

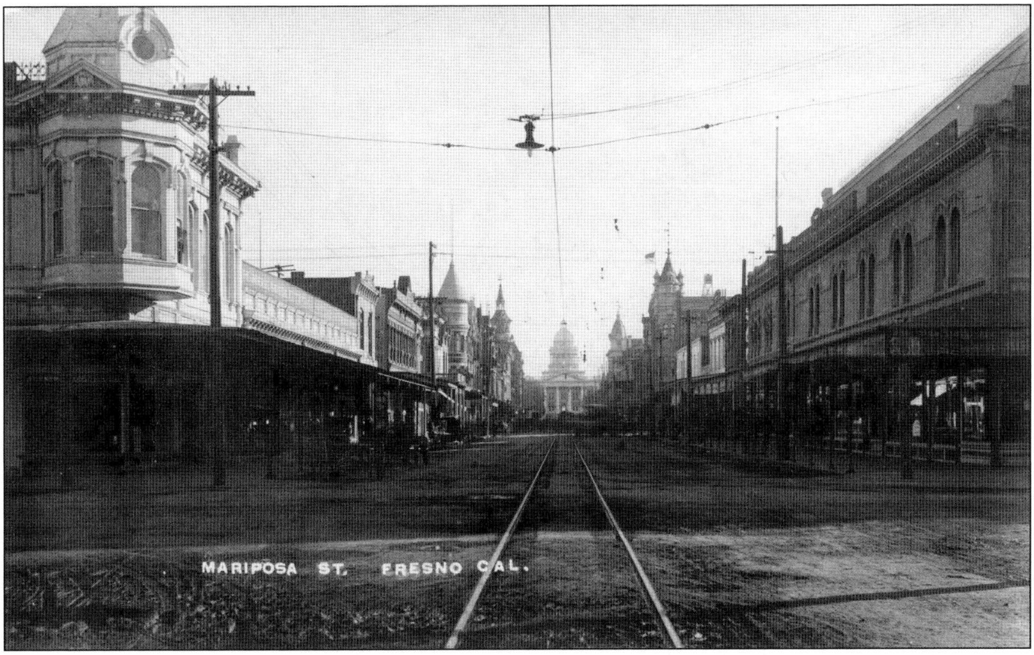

This 1907 street view is looking east on Mariposa Street across Broadway Street toward the county courthouse. On the left is the location of the Kutner-Goldstein Universal Provider Store.

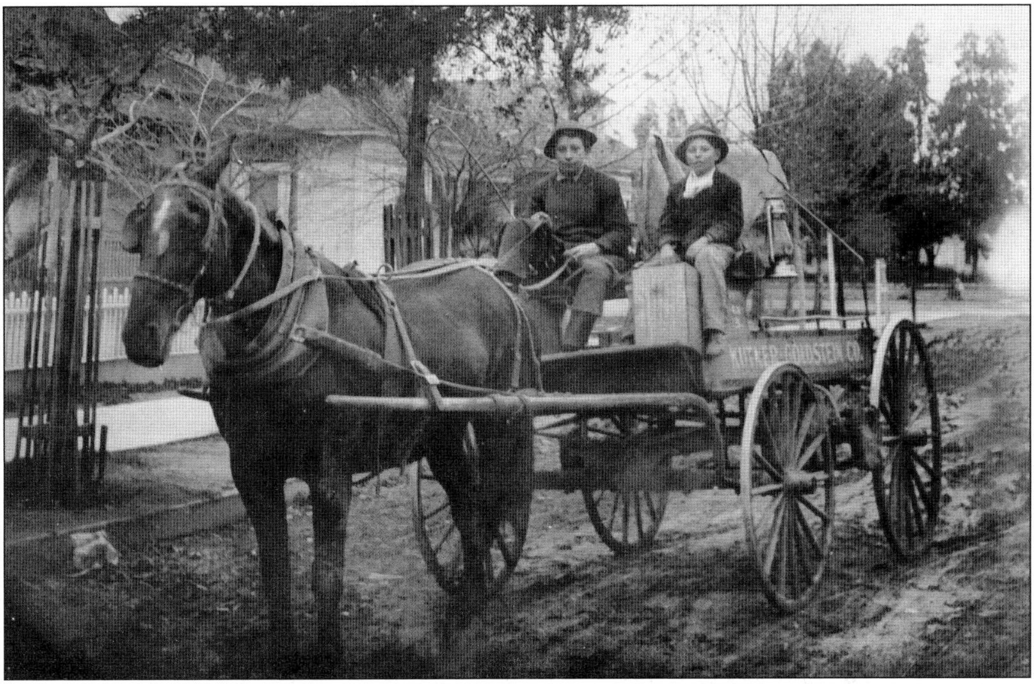

Depicted in this image is an early Kutner-Goldstein delivery wagon. The passenger on the right has a large metal container probably holding kerosene. Painted on the side of the wagon are the words "Kutner-Goldstein Co. Phone Ext 3." Orders received in the morning were delivered to the customer by the end of the day. Delivery was a common practice with early merchants. (Fresno County Library.)

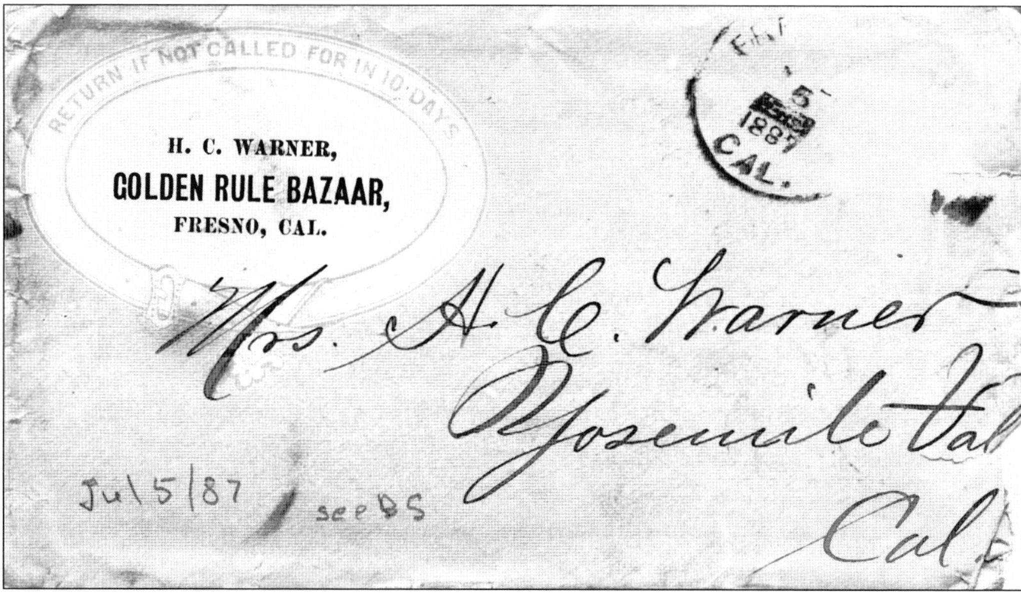

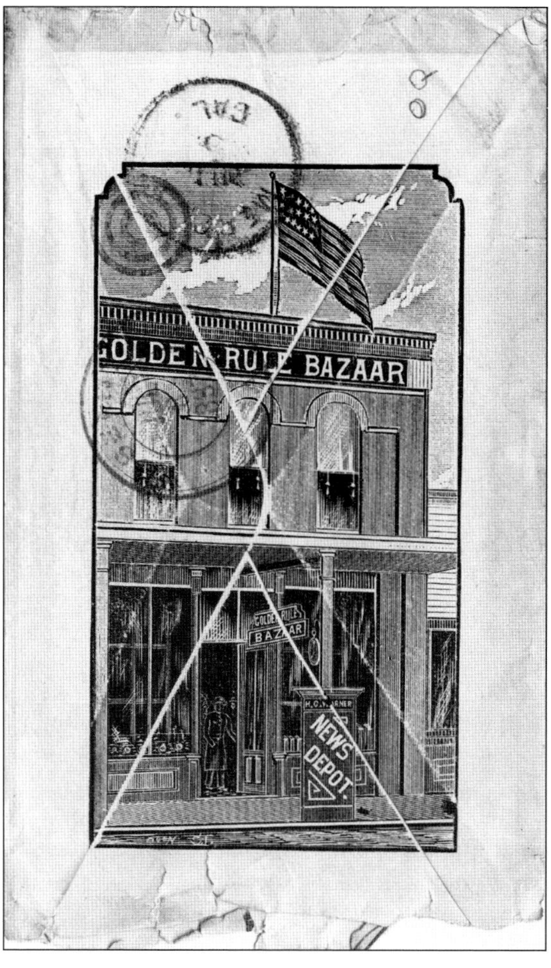

One of Fresno's earliest businesses was a jewelry store operated by Henry Conrad Warner. It was known as "H.C. Warner—dealer in—Watches and Jewelry." Shown here is an early envelope postmarked September 8, 1880, and addressed to Warner's wife, who was still living in Gilroy at the time. Warner was also a dealer in Galvanic Belts, a quack medical device that claimed it could cure headaches, rheumatism, paralysis, and deformities.

The Golden Rule Bazaar was the early name of H.C. Warner's jewelry business in Fresno. This 1885-postmarked envelope shows a printed image of the store on Mariposa Street, between Broadway and Fulton Streets. Five generations of the family operated the store from 1880 until it was sold in 1993.

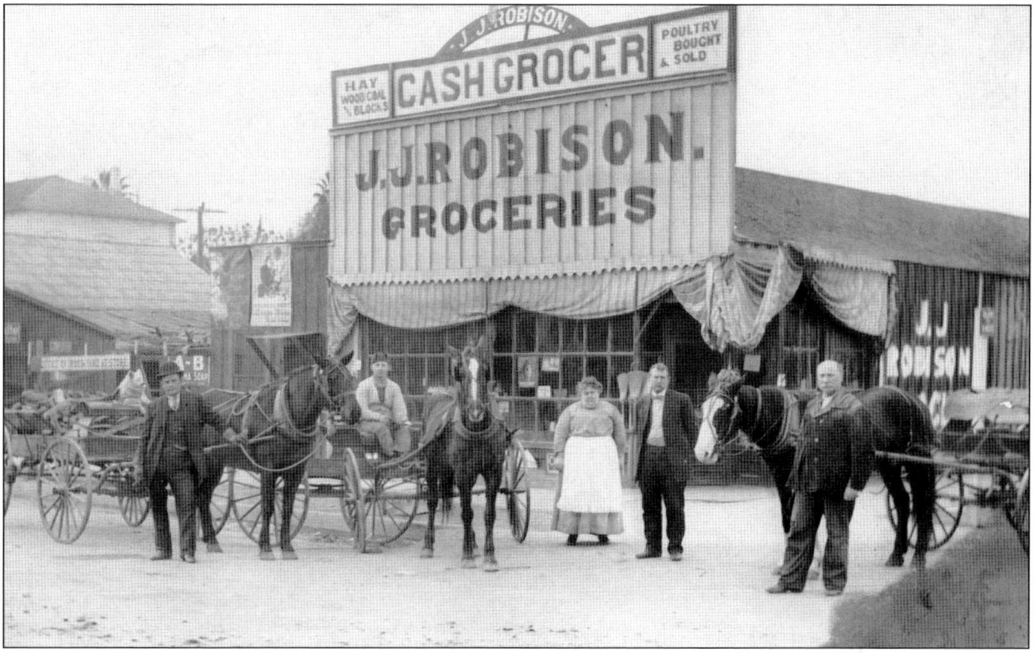

John J. Robison operated a cash grocery store at 2148 Tulare Street (according to the Fresno City Directory, 1905–1909) and at 2147 Kern Street (Fresno City Directory 1910–1913). Standing between the two horse buggies are Robison and his wife. (Fresno County Library.)

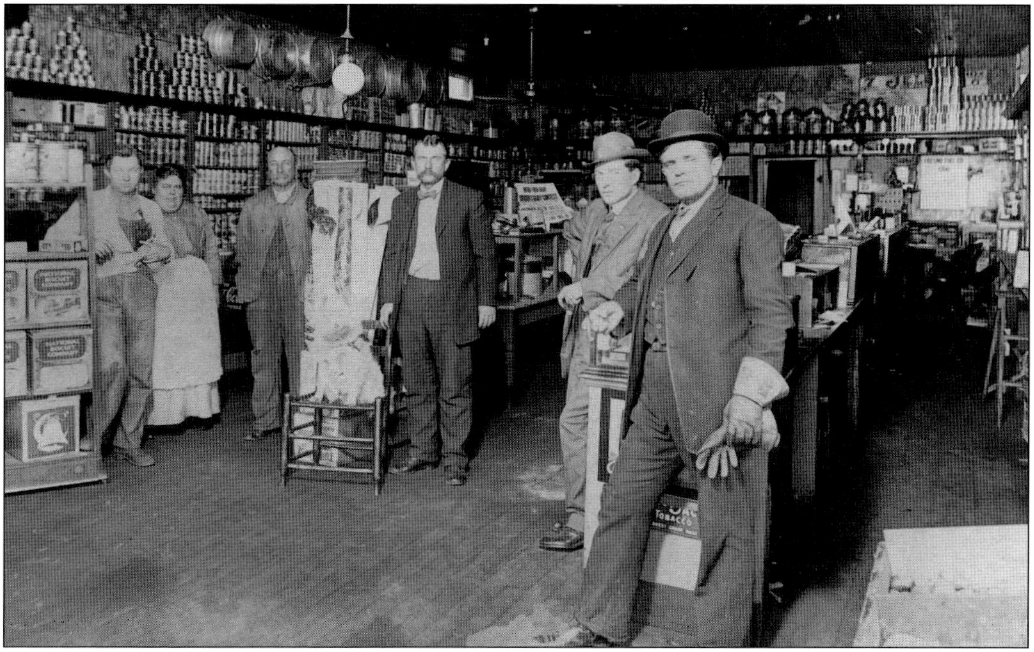

The interior of the John J. Robison store shows the extent of merchandise offered, from canned goods and tobacco to washtubs and lunch buckets. (Fresno County Library.)

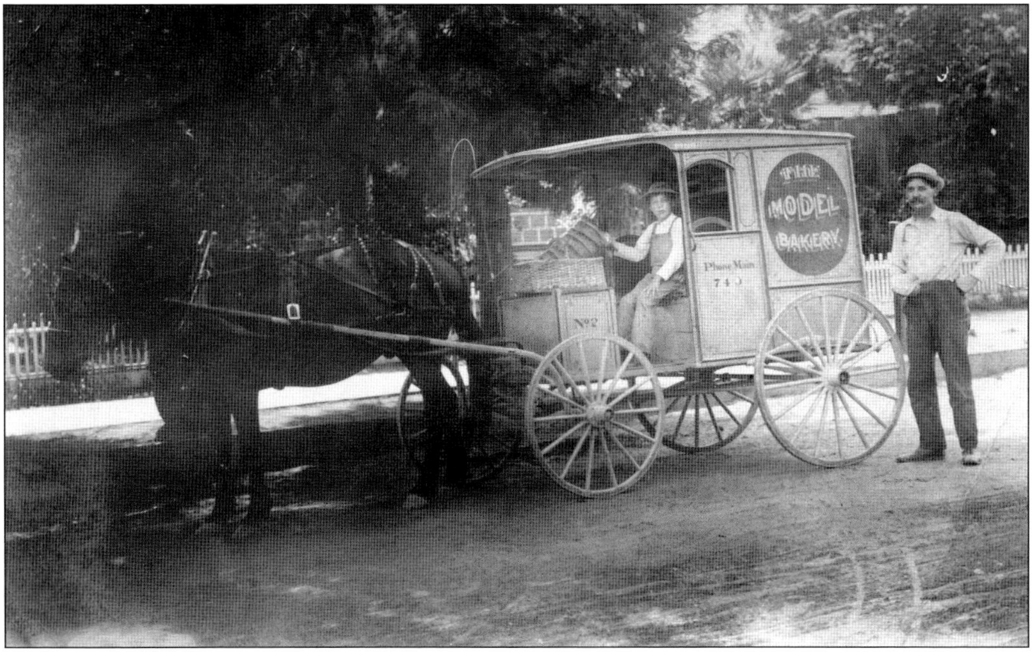

This image shows a delivery wagon from the Fresno business The Model Bakery, phone no. 749. Horse-drawn wagons delivered groceries, ice, bakery goods, fresh vegetables, milk products, and even petroleum products such as kerosene to customers in town. (Fresno County Library.)

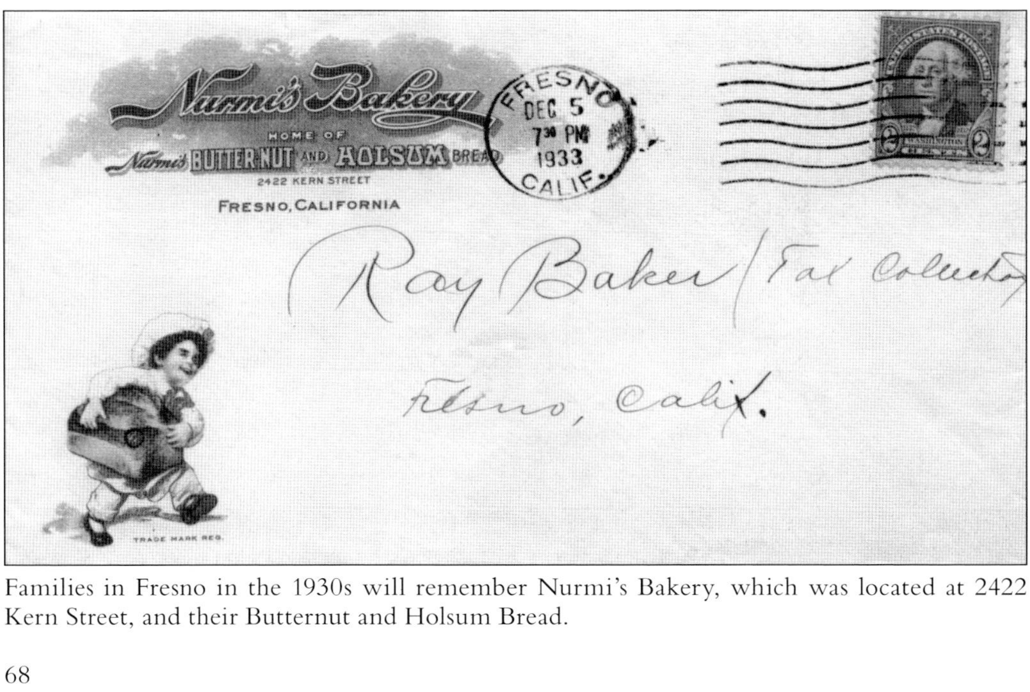

Families in Fresno in the 1930s will remember Nurmi's Bakery, which was located at 2422 Kern Street, and their Butternut and Holsum Bread.

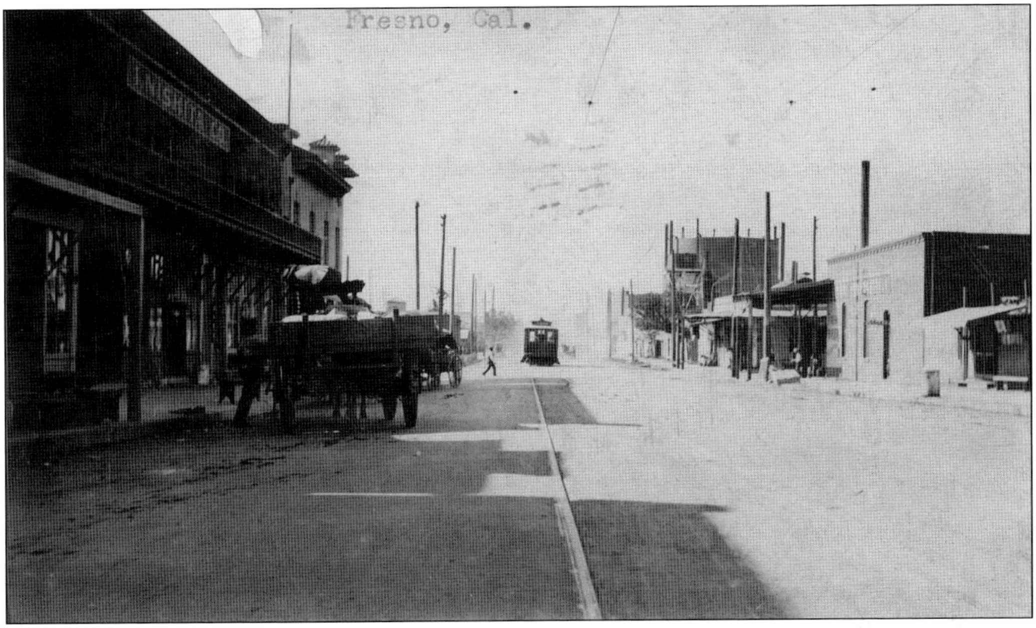

The I. Nishita Company general merchandise store was located at 943 F Street in Chinatown. The store is shown here on the left. Streetcars provided transportation all over the city.

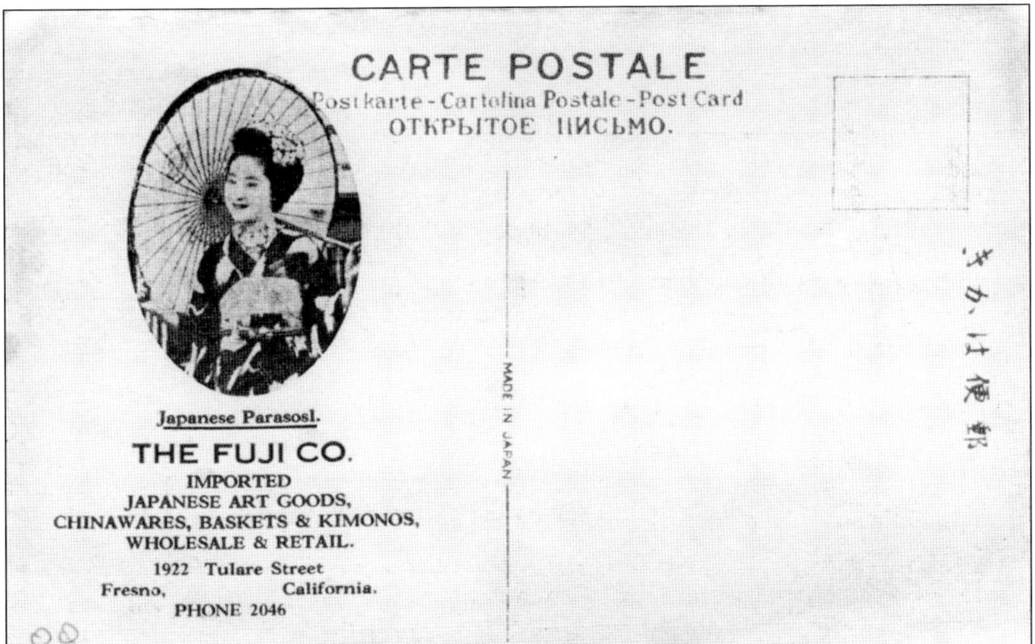

The Fuji Company was located at 1922 Tulare Street and sold imported Japanese art goods, chinawares, baskets, kimonos, and Japanese parasols. The store was west of the Southern Pacific railroad tracks in Chinatown.

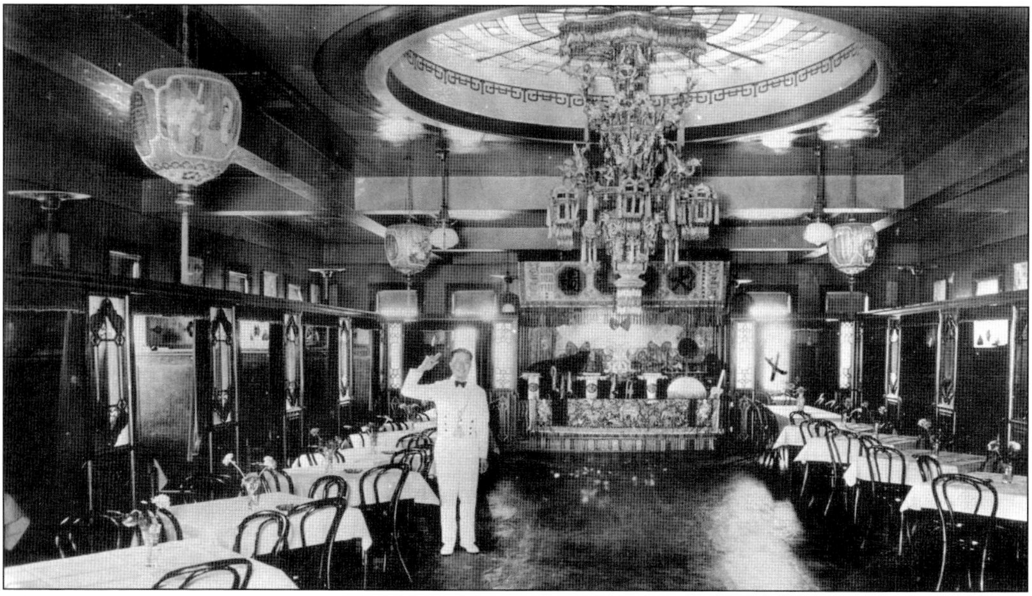

The New Shanghai Café was located at 1538 Tulare Street. The small bandstand provided live music. The handwritten message on the face of the card states, "Have dinner here tonite—X marks our nook." (Fresno County Library.)

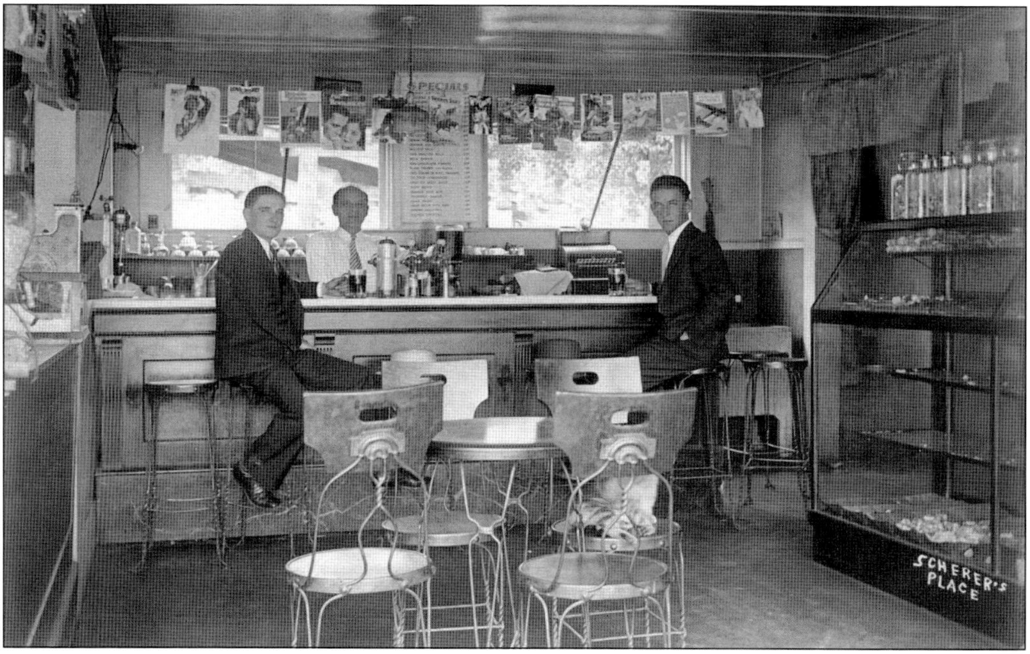

Scherer's Place was located at 1417 San Benito Street and sold candy, magazines, and comic books. There was a soda fountain, booths to enjoy the treats, and a small dance floor for everyone to gather.

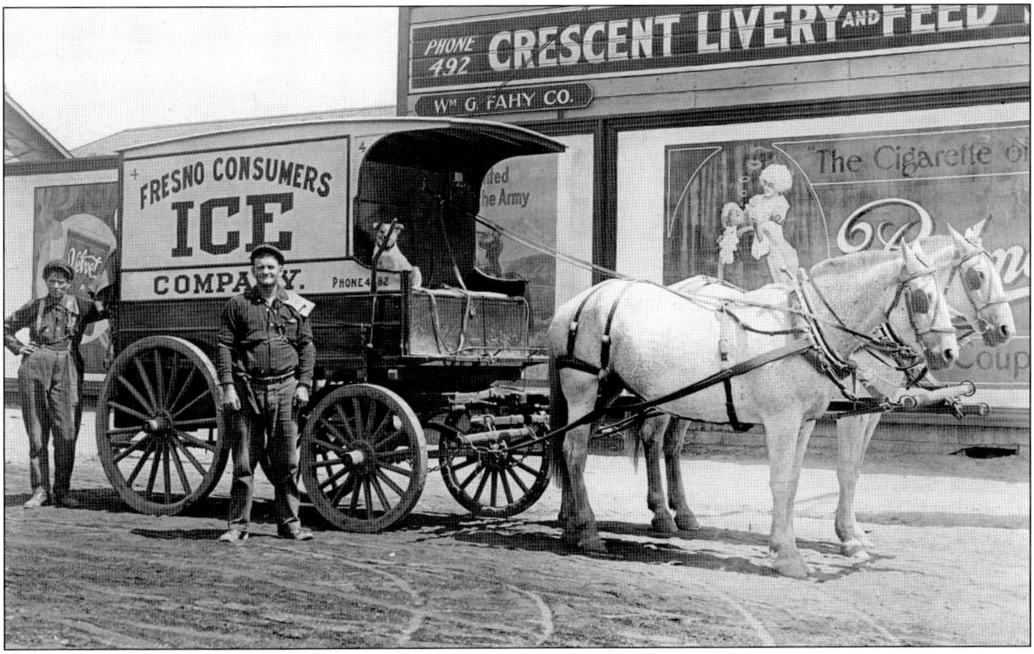

Until 1924, Fresno Consumers Ice employed horse-drawn wagons to deliver ice to individual homes and businesses. Shown here is a typical delivery wagon with its operators and dog mascot. When ice was delivered, it was cut to order in front of the home or business. Children would follow the wagon and pick up the small pieces of ice that were left by the cutting.

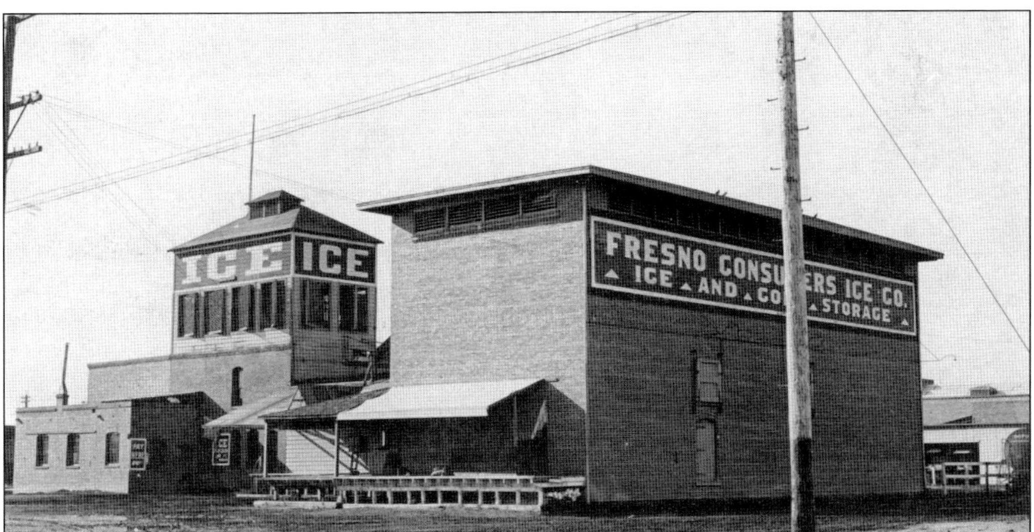

This postcard shows the Fresno Consumers Ice Company at 702 P Street. The company started in 1903 and was at the time the largest ice-making facility on the Pacific Coast. The building was designed by Eugene Mathewson and built of industrial brick.

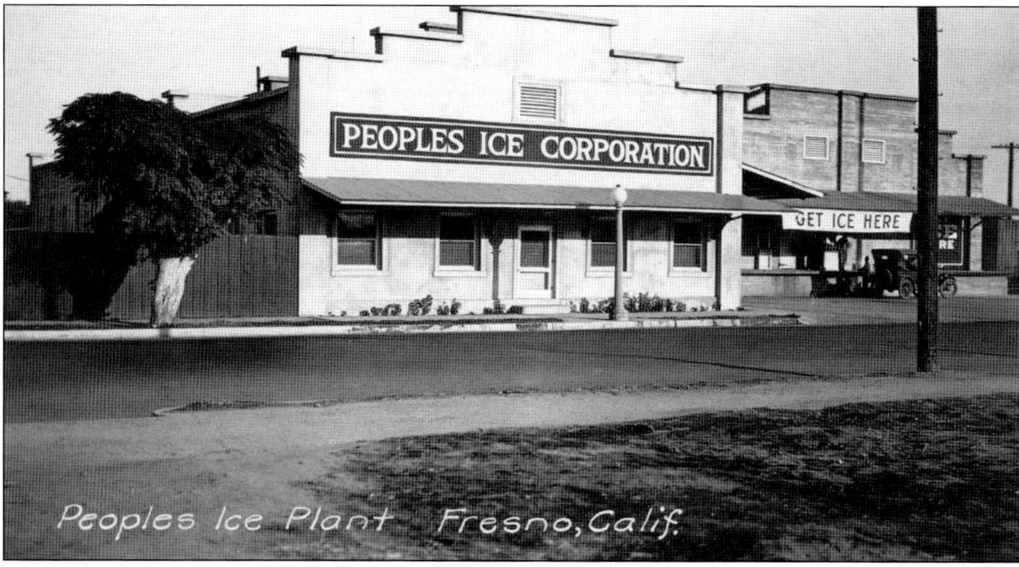

Pictured here is the office and warehouse of the Peoples Ice Corporation at 2035 S. Broadway. The ice service station was at 921 Belmont.

ICE SCHEDULE

Effective March, 15, 1920

10 lbs. to 150 lbs. each delivery,	- -	80c per cwt.
150 " " 300 " " "	- - -	70c " "
300 " " 600 " " "	- -	60c " "
600 " " 900 " " "	- - -	50c " "
900 " " 1500 " " "	- -	45c " "
1500 " " 2100 " " "	- - -	40c " "
2100 " " 4200 " " "	- -	35c " "
4200 " and over	- - - - -	30c " "

All coupon books 80 cents per cwt. On coupon books only, a discount of 5% will be allowed if paid for on delivery of book.

All butcher shops, groceries, etc , will be placed on a charge account payable Tuesday of each week for deliveries made during the previous week.

PEOPLES ICE CORPORATION

J. H. WOODEN, Manager

Phones 402, 403. Office and Factory 2035 South Broadway, Fresno, California
Ice Service Station at 921 Belmont, Phone 2294

Here is an ice delivery schedule from March 15, 1920. This schedule also details the payment terms allowed for businesses that purchased ice through Peoples Ice.

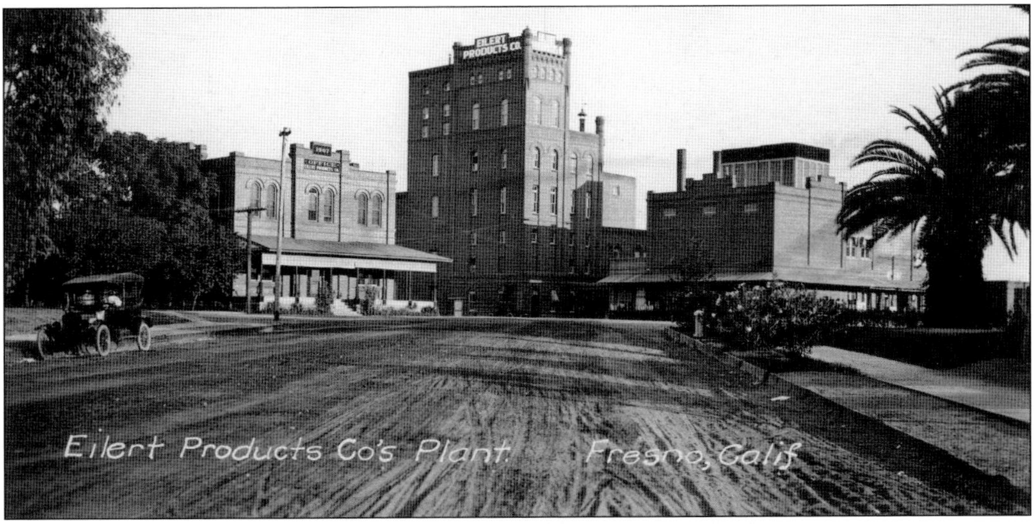

The Fresno Brewing Company was founded in 1900 by Ernest Eilert and was located at 100 M Street. The six-story brewery and surrounding buildings were designed by Eugene Mathewson in the Streetcar Industrial Brick style. At the peak of production, the brewery operated 24 hours a day, seven days a week, and employed 100 people. During Prohibition, the name was changed to Eilert Products Company, and they bottled soft drinks.

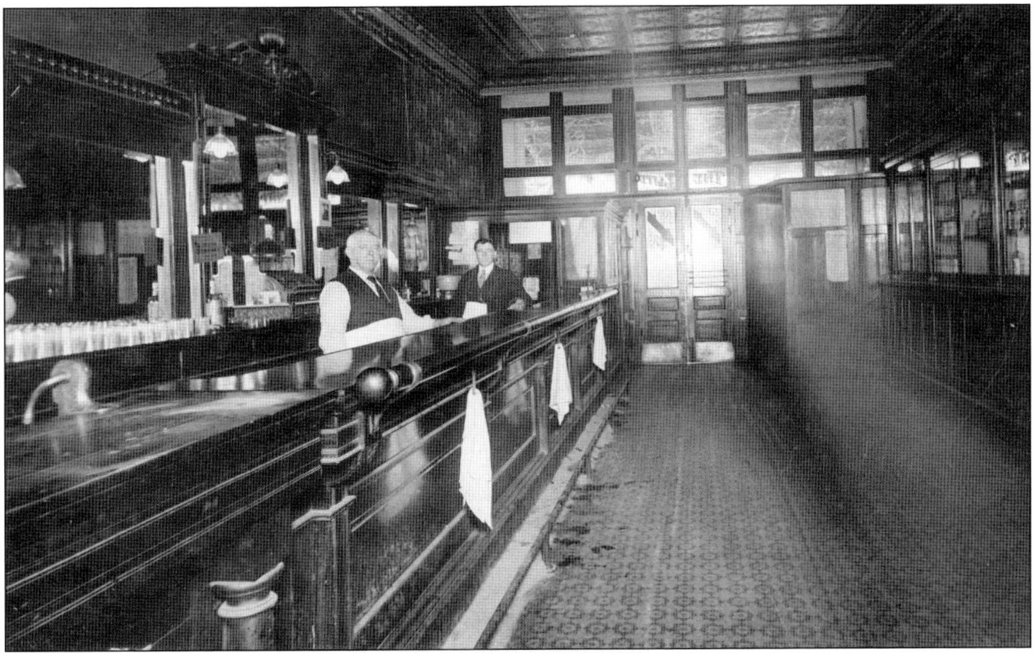

Pictured is the Elite Saloon, which was located at 1840 Mariposa Street (telephone no. 539). The proprietor was John A. Bratton. Except during Prohibition, Fresno never had a shortage of taverns or bars.

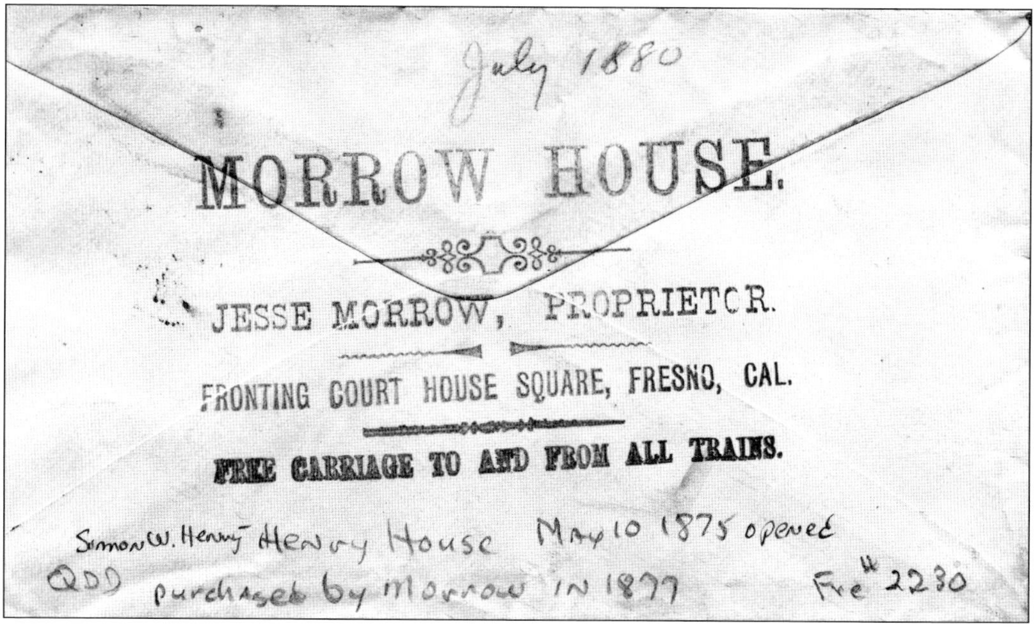

The Henry/Morrow House, built by Simeon W. Henry, a local blacksmith, opened on May 10, 1875. It was Fresno's first top quality hotel, with 35 beautifully carpeted rooms. In 1877, it was sold to Jesse Morrow. This image shows a rubber hand-stamped ad on the back of an envelope offered to guests for their use. Morrow House was located at Tulare and K (Van Ness) Streets.

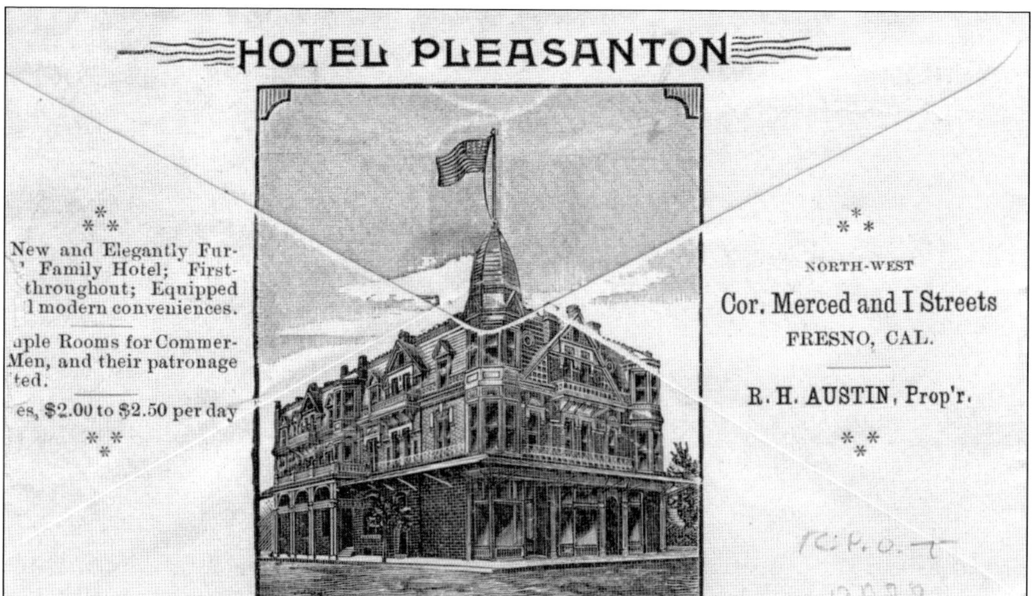

The Hotel Pleasanton, located on the northwest corner of Merced and Fulton Streets, was a 115-room luxury hotel. Rooms rented for $2 and $3 per night. R.H. Austin was the proprietor.

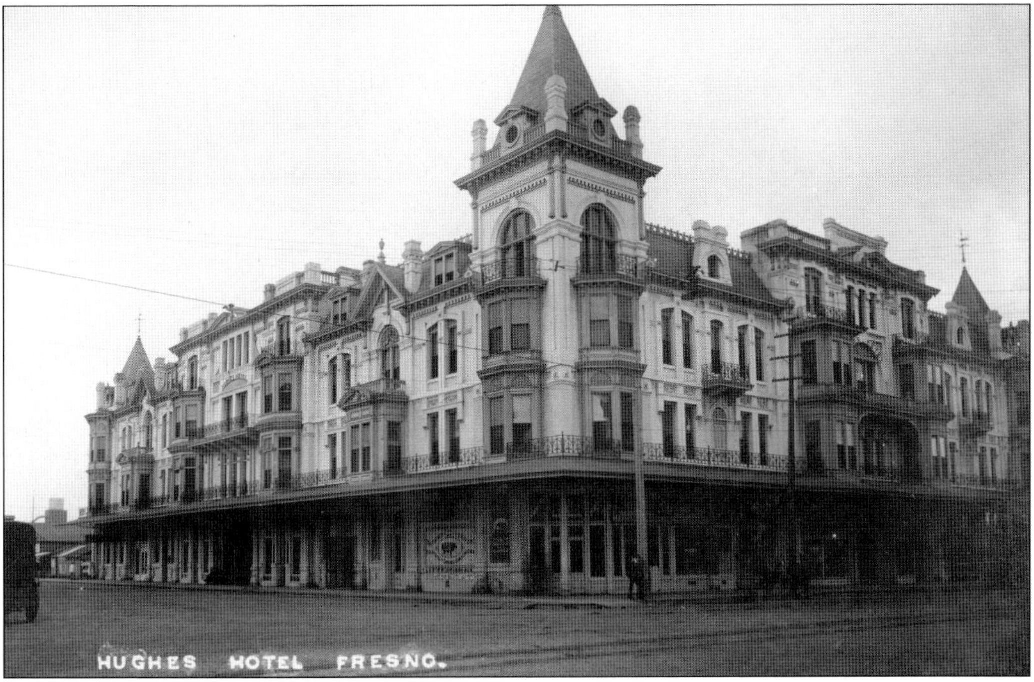

The Hughes Hotel was located on the southwest corner of Tulare and I (Broadway) Streets. It was built in 1888 at a cost of $300,000 by Thomas E. Hughes. The plush hotel had three great features: its own ice plant for cooling, its own electrical generator that lit all 145 rooms, and its own water supply, drawn from a 300-foot depth.

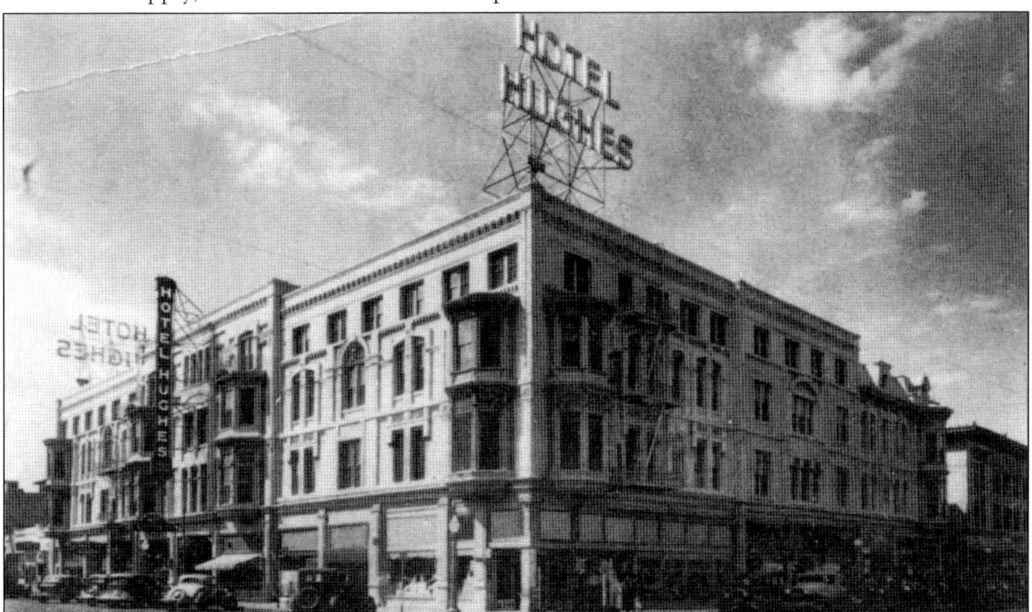

Fresno arsonists lit 13 fires in the downtown area on July 10, 1953. The Hughes fire was the first discovered, but still burned down the whole building. The hotel is remembered for its great service, outstanding meals, and a phone in every room. It faced US 99 and later offered free garage space.

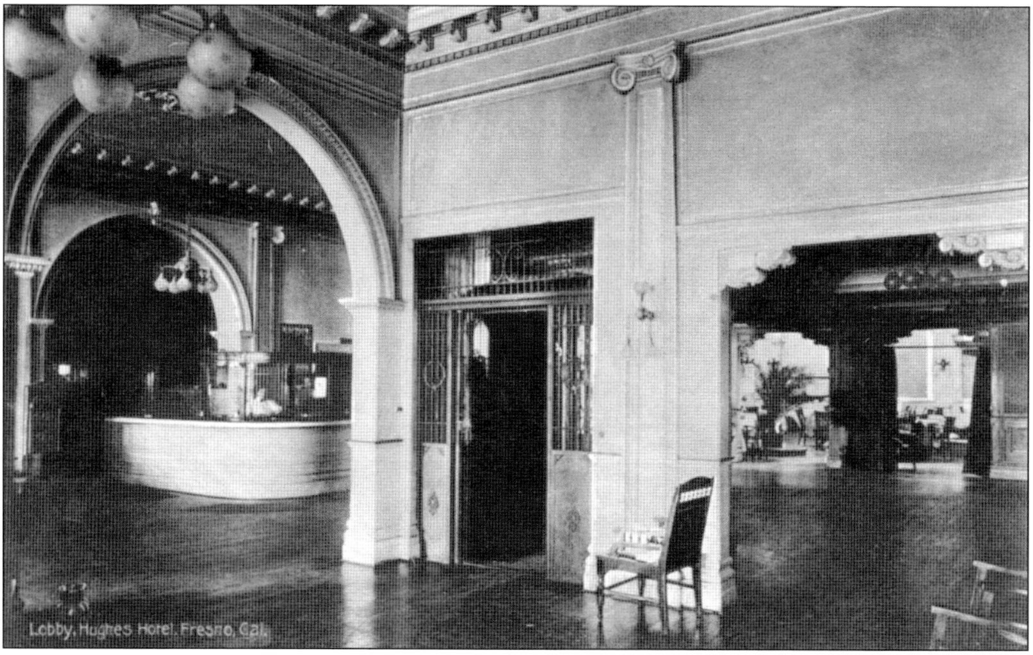

Pictured here are two views of the interior of the Hughes Hotel, with the reception desk above and a portion of the lobby below.

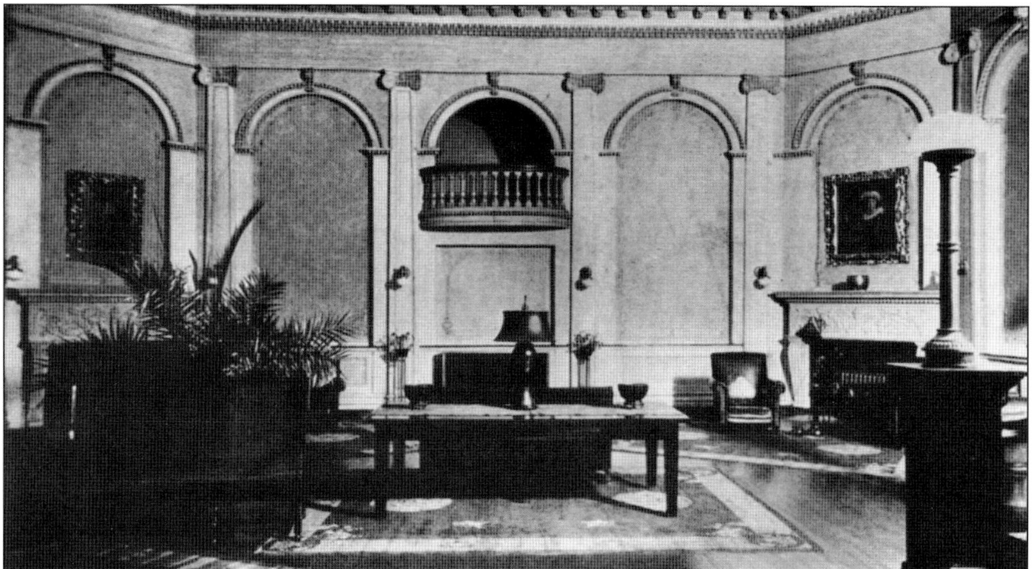

The lobby of *"The Hughes Hotel"* is comfortable on the warmest summer day. Our cooling system circulates 500 gallons of water and 45,000 cubic feet of air per minute.

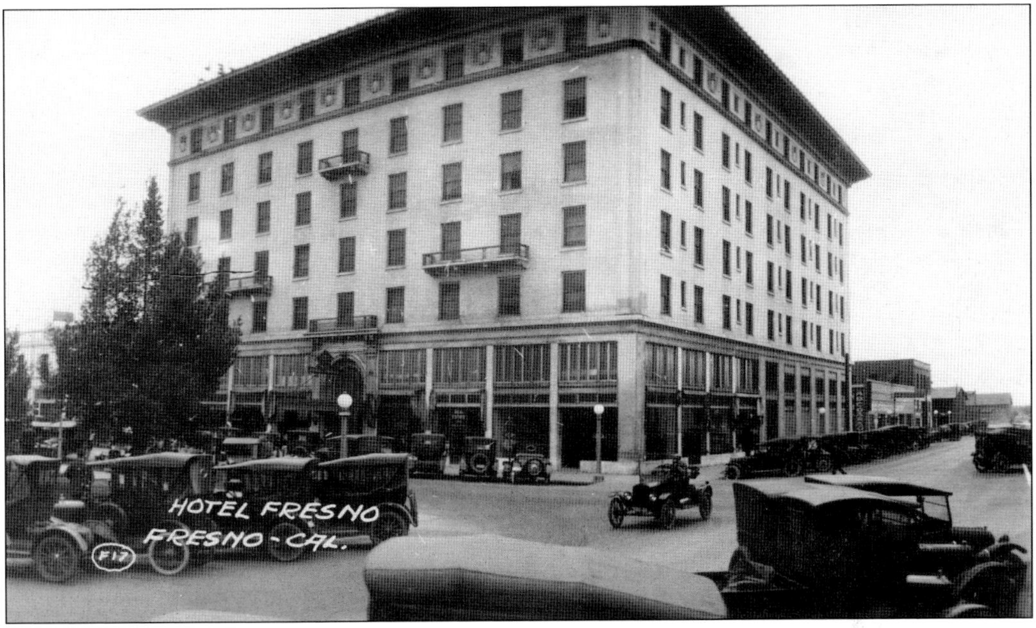

The Fresno Hotel was built in 1912 at the southwest corner of Broadway and Merced Streets. It was the center of Fresno social activities for over 15 years since it was the most plush hotel in town. It was opulently furnished and even had a pipe organ in the lounge. Celebrations were held in the hotel's Grand Ballroom or Colonial Dining Room.

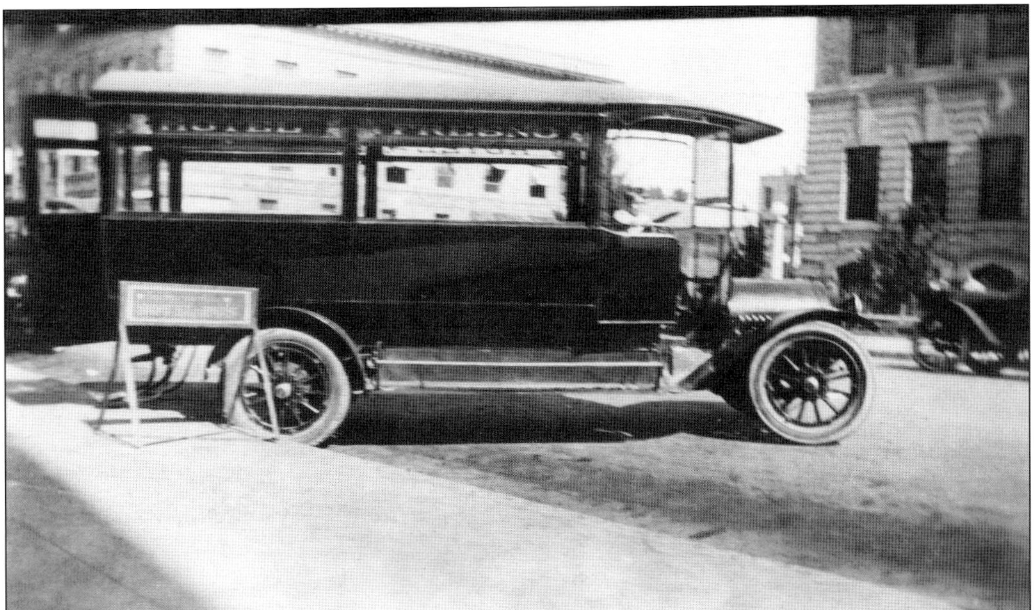

This early Fresno Hotel bus picked up and returned guests from the hotel and the two Fresno railroad stations. The guests were pleased to see fancy glittering chandeliers in the large Colonial Dining Room and Grand Ballroom. Dinner was several courses for only $1.25. Guests took two hours to dine and enjoyed fine wines, brandies, and desserts. (Fresno County Library.)

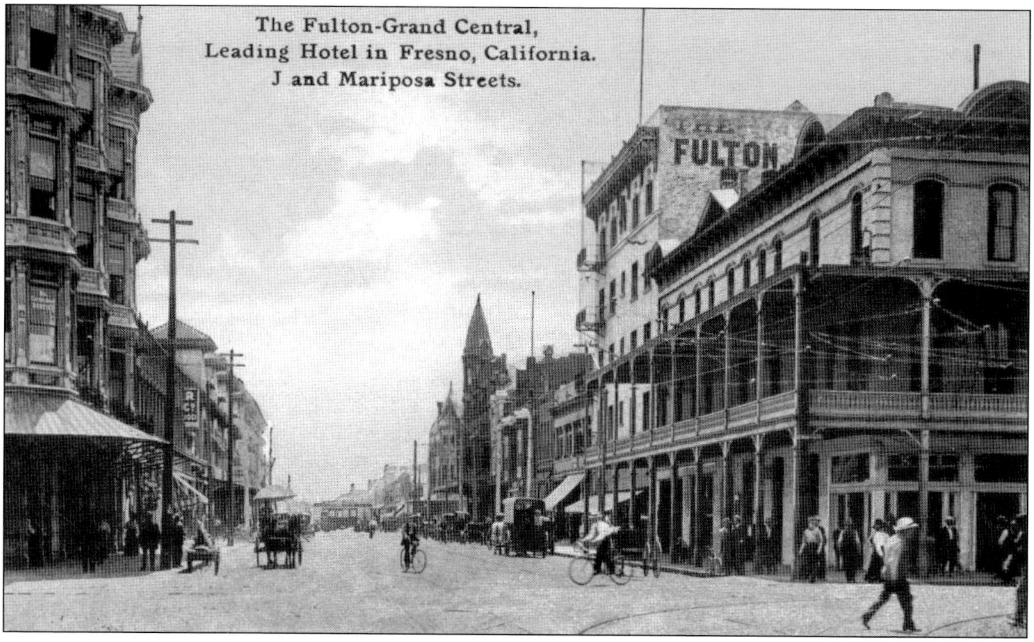

On the right side of this postcard view is the three-story Grand Central Hotel with veranda, located on the southwest corner of Fulton and Mariposa Streets. It was built in 1883 and sold to Fulton G. Berry, a San Francisco financier. He became a local character and Fresno booster and managed the Grand Central Hotel. He later had the five-story Fulton Hotel built next door for additional rooms.

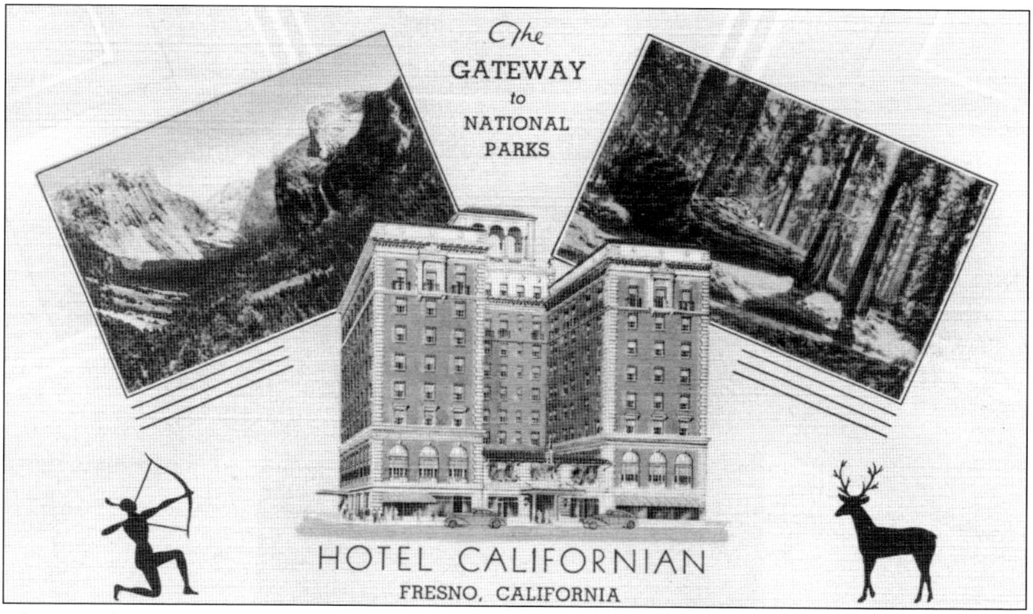

The Hotel Californian opened in 1923 on the southwest corner of Van Ness and Kern Streets. For the next 30 years, it was the city's largest and most important hotel. The banquet dining room seated 1,200, and the Grand Ballroom was available for large dances. From the late 1920s to the 1950s there was dinner and dancing on the weekends. The hotel's guest book was filled with all sorts of important people who stopped in Fresno, including presidents and movie stars.

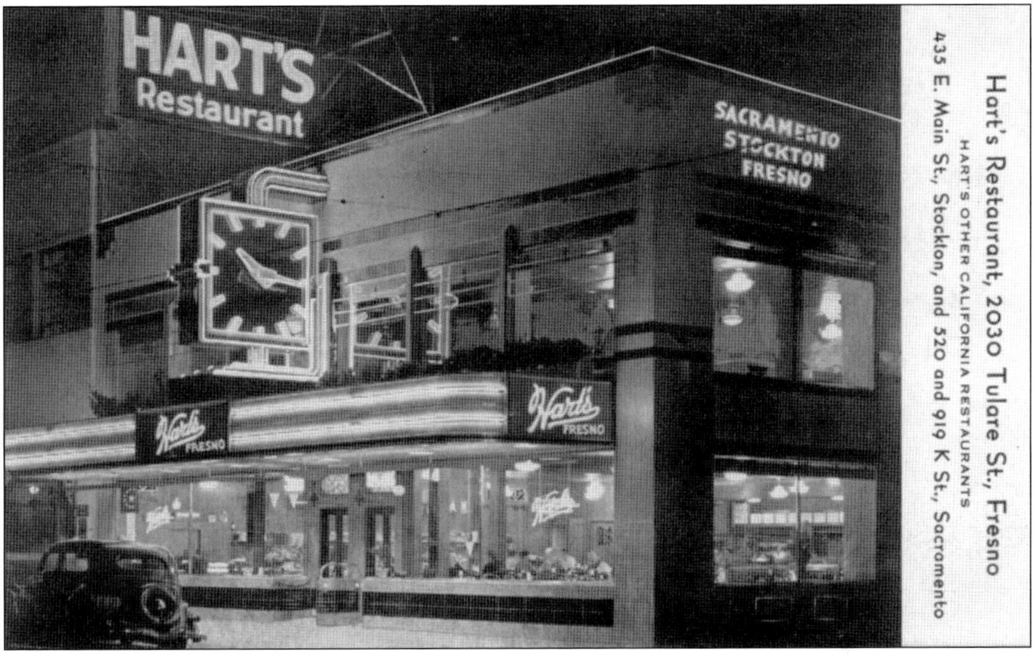

Fresno's most famous cafeteria was Hart's Restaurant. Originally located at 1014 J (Fulton) Street, it later moved to the south side of Tulare Street between Van Ness and Fulton Streets. The restaurant was part of a larger chain, with two locations in Sacramento and one in Stockton. Its most notable feature was its large neon clock.

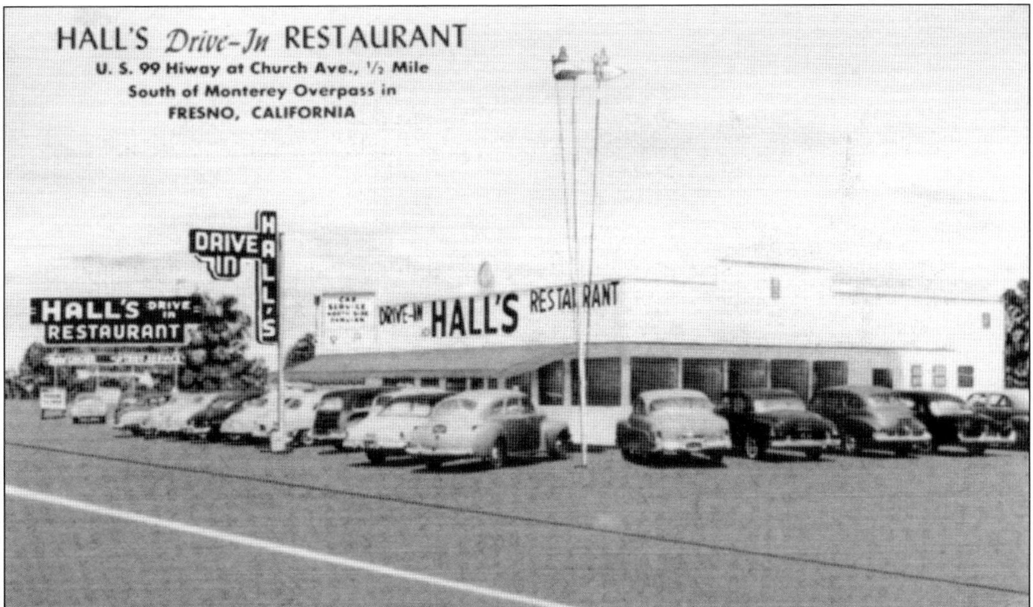

Hall's Drive-In Restaurant was a popular spot to stop on US Highway 99. It was located south of Fresno at US Highway 99 and Church Avenue, a half mile south of the Monterey Overpass. A restaurant operates at the location today.

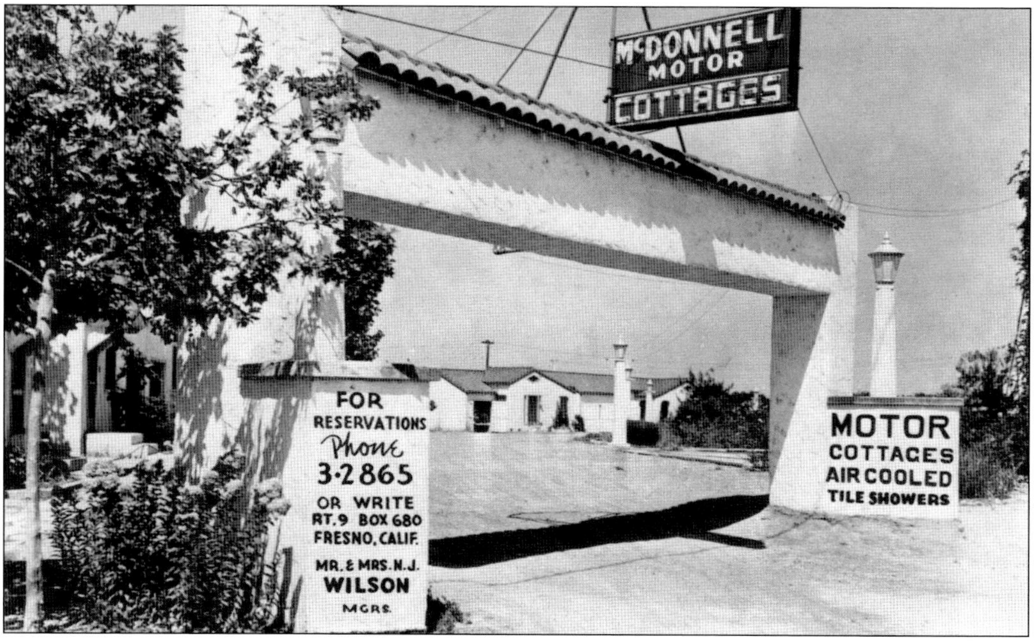

People hit the road after World War I with improved roads and increased access to cars. The need arose for reasonable accommodations along the major highways. McDonnell Motor Cottages is an example. The signs advertise air-cooled rooms, tile showers, a five-digit phone number, mailing address, and managers' names.

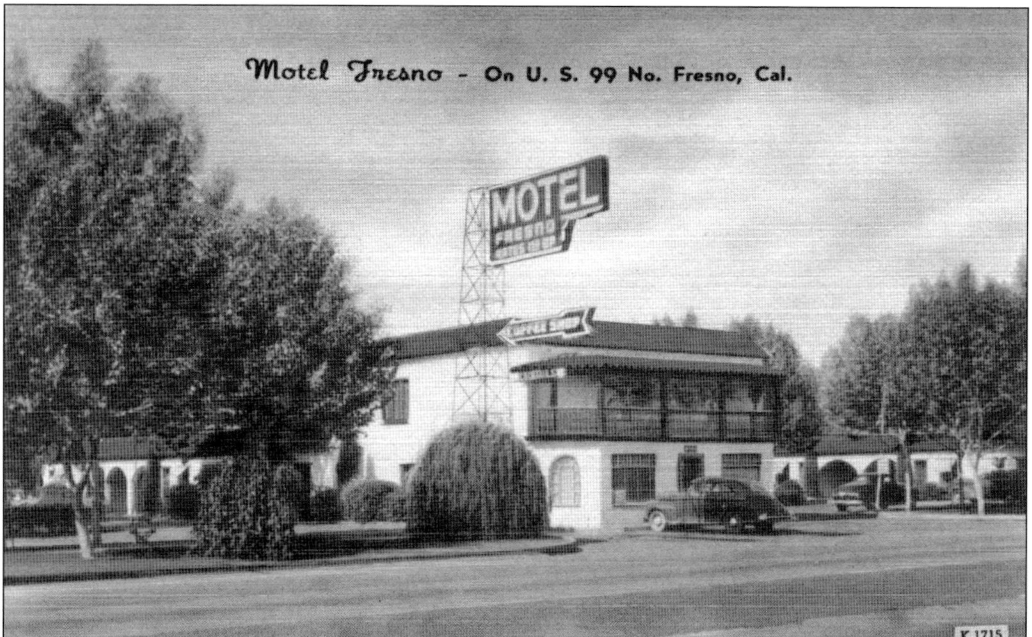

Motel Fresno was on US 99 north of the city (telephone no. 3-5104). It had 100 air-conditioned strictly modern units, tile baths, and radios. An excellent coffee shop and cocktail lounge drew people in for food and drink as well as lodging.

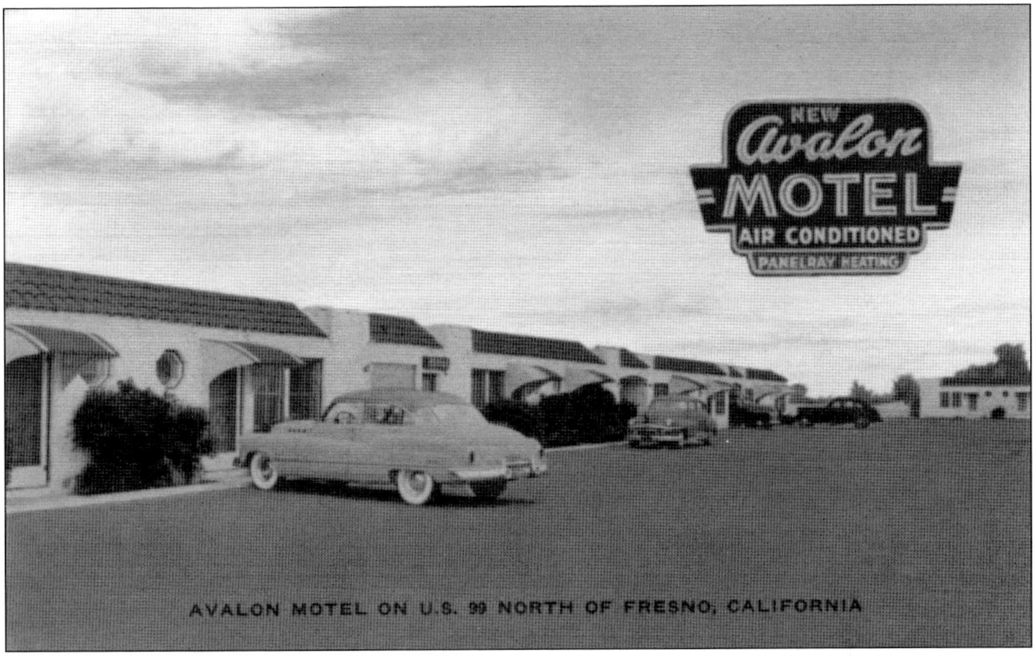

At the New Avalon Motel on US 99, four miles north of Fresno, the units had wall-to-wall carpets and radios. Family-sized units had kitchenettes, tile showers, air conditioning for summer comfort, and ray heat for winter enjoyment. The proximity of parking spaces to the rooms and some covered parking between rooms pleased travelers.

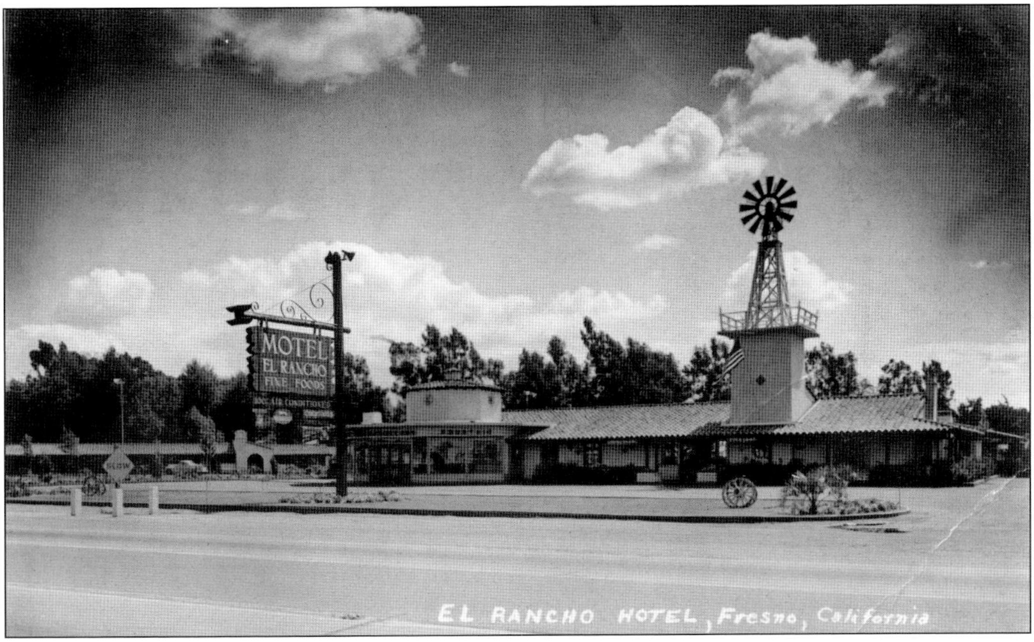

The Motel El Rancho was located at the north end of Fresno along US 99 (now Business 99). It was one of the two best motels along the strip. It had a popular restaurant and lounge. Its competition was The Hacienda Motel at US Business 99 and Clinton. The Hacienda is remembered for the glass-walled swimming pool facing the dining room.

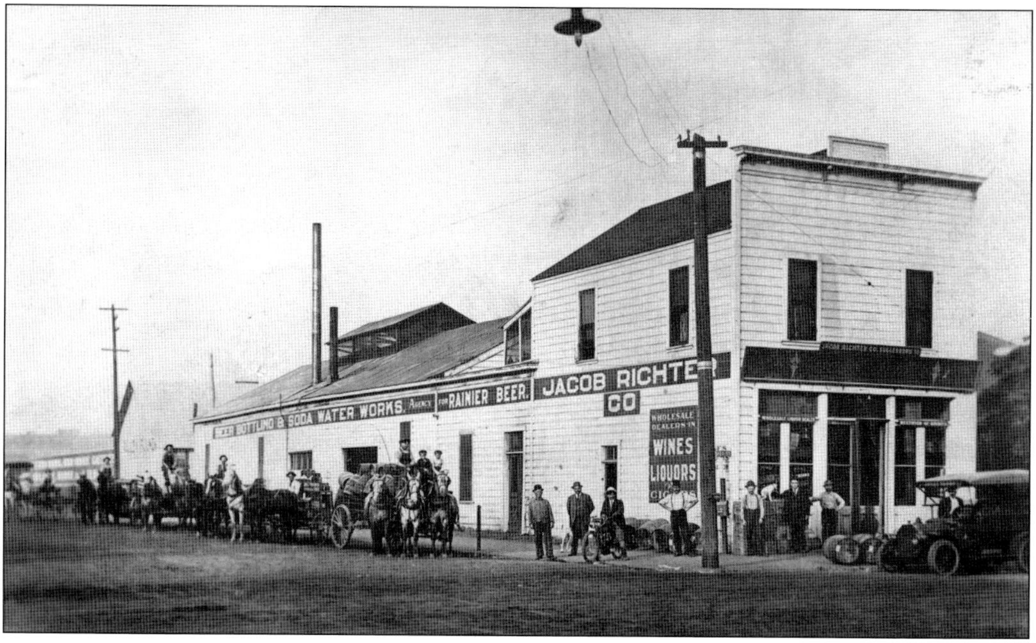

Jacob Richter Soda Works began in 1895 in the basement at Mariposa and I Streets (Broadway). By 1900, the company moved to 701 Broadway, at the corner of Broadway and Mono Streets. Richter bottled five different soda flavors and Rainer beer. The business is currently located at 1150 E. North Street, operating under the name of Pepsi Bottling Group.

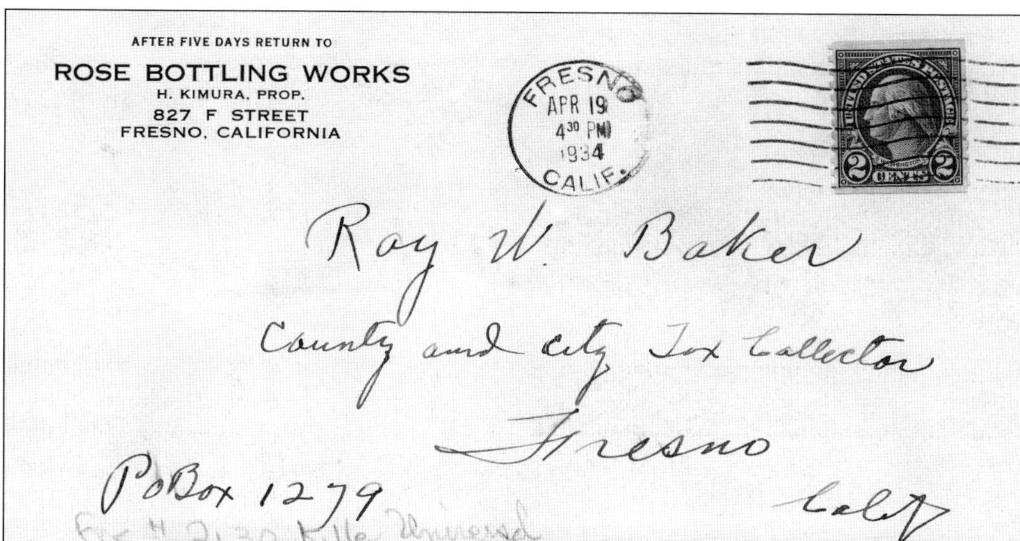

The Rose Bottling Works produced soft drinks at 827 F. Street with H. Kimura as proprietor. A major competitor was James Calandra Soda Works. This family ran various soda works for nearly 70 years in Fresno.

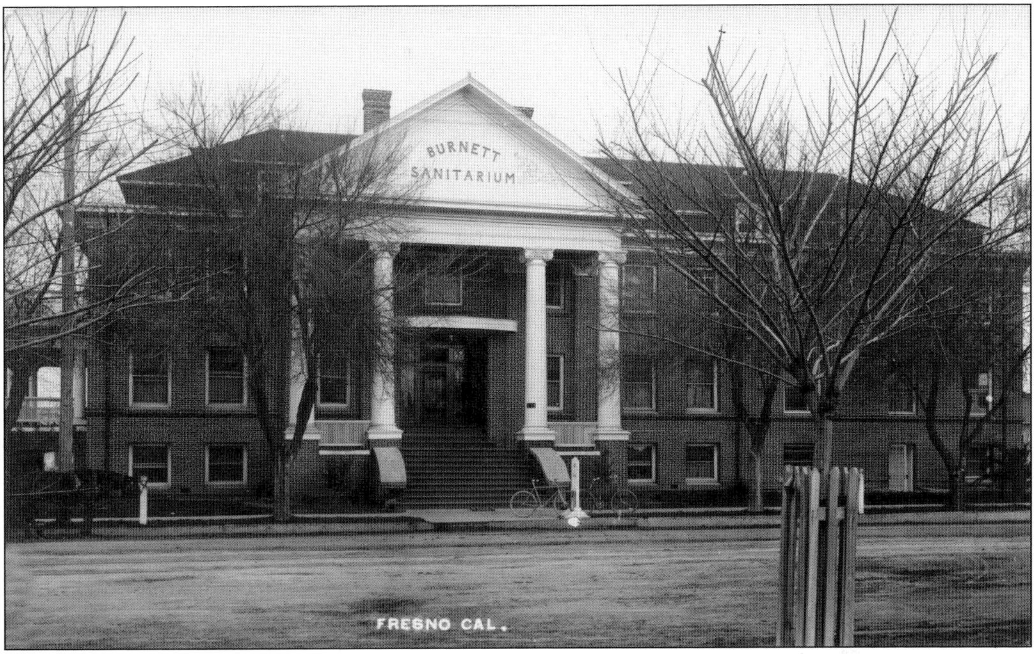

The Burnett Sanitarium started in 1902, along Fresno Street. It was a two-story brick building with 25 beds and a second floor dormitory for nurses. Early Fresno residents depended on this facility for all hospital services. By 1917, a new five-story building was constructed in order to meet the needs of the growing population.

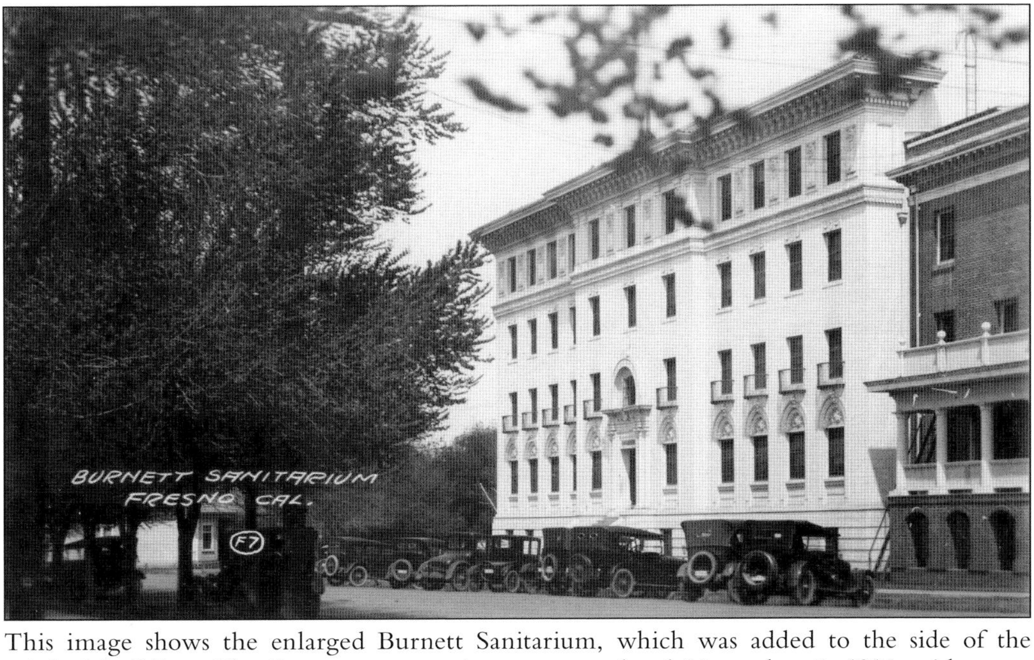

This image shows the enlarged Burnett Sanitarium, which was added to the side of the original building. The five-story expansion was completed November 5, 1917, with room for an additional 120 beds. In October 1945, the sanitarium's name was changed to Fresno Community Hospital.

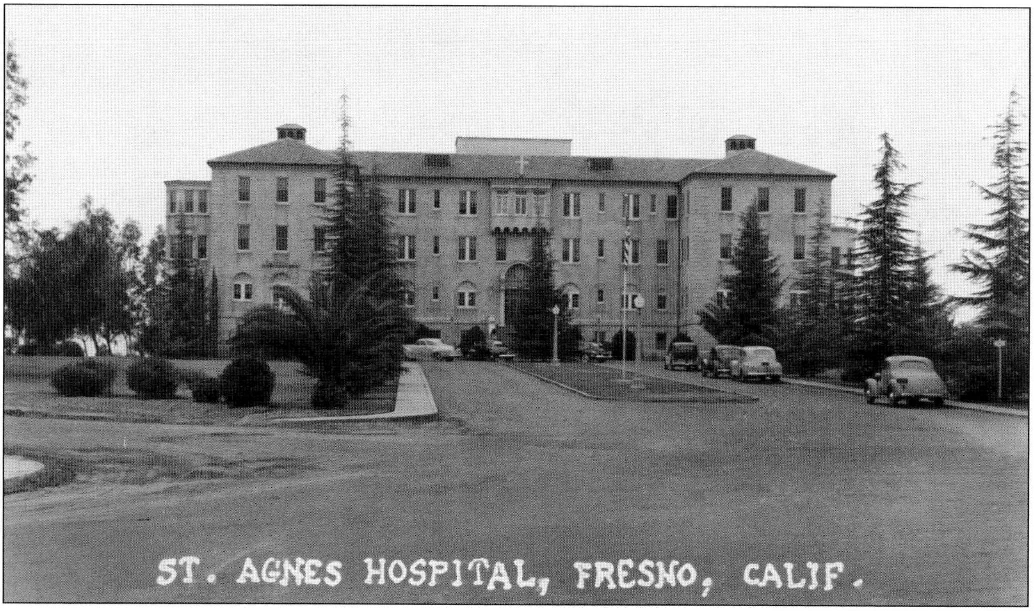

Saint Agnes Hospital was built in 1929 and was staffed by the Sisters of the Holy Cross. The facility had 75 beds and a staff of 32. Currently, Saint Agnes Hospital continues to grow and serve the area from a different location.

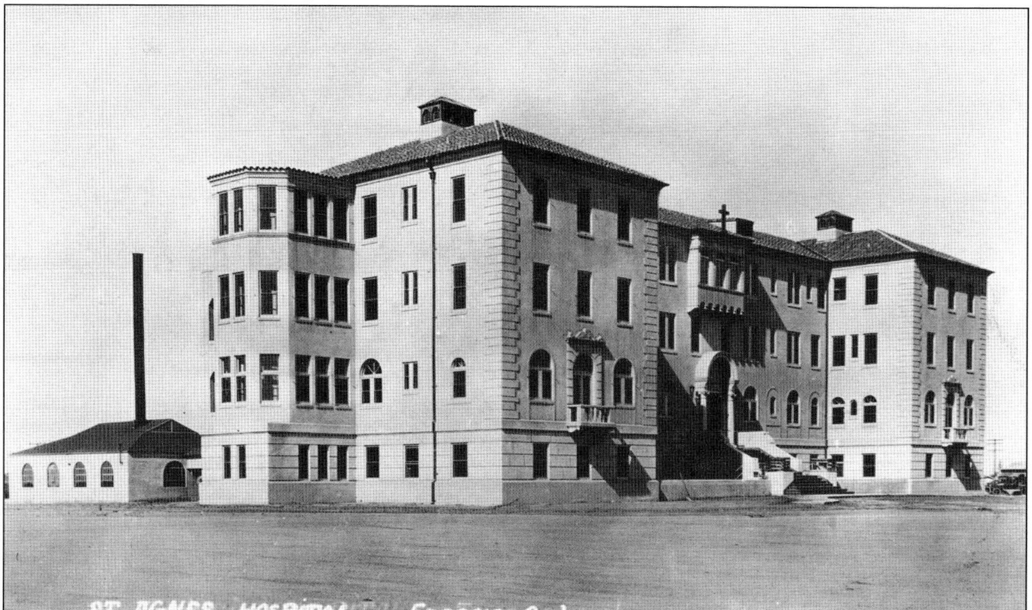

Here is a very early image of Saint Agnes Hospital with very little vegetation around the building.

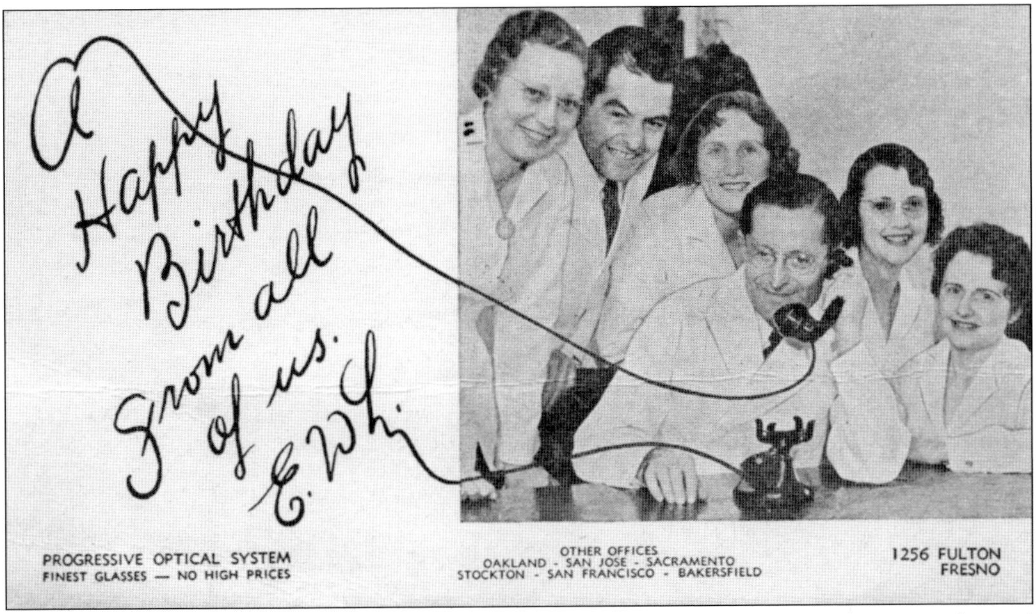

Eugene W. Laisne, optometrist, was in the Fresno office of Progressive Optical Systems, located at 1256 Fulton Street. Shown on the card is the entire office staff wishing a patient a happy birthday. This card was sent near the birthday of patients to remind them to get their eyes checked as needed. Stamped on the reverse of the card was "E.L. Laisne, Optometrist—Your House of Vision, using Progressive Eye Comfort Glasses."

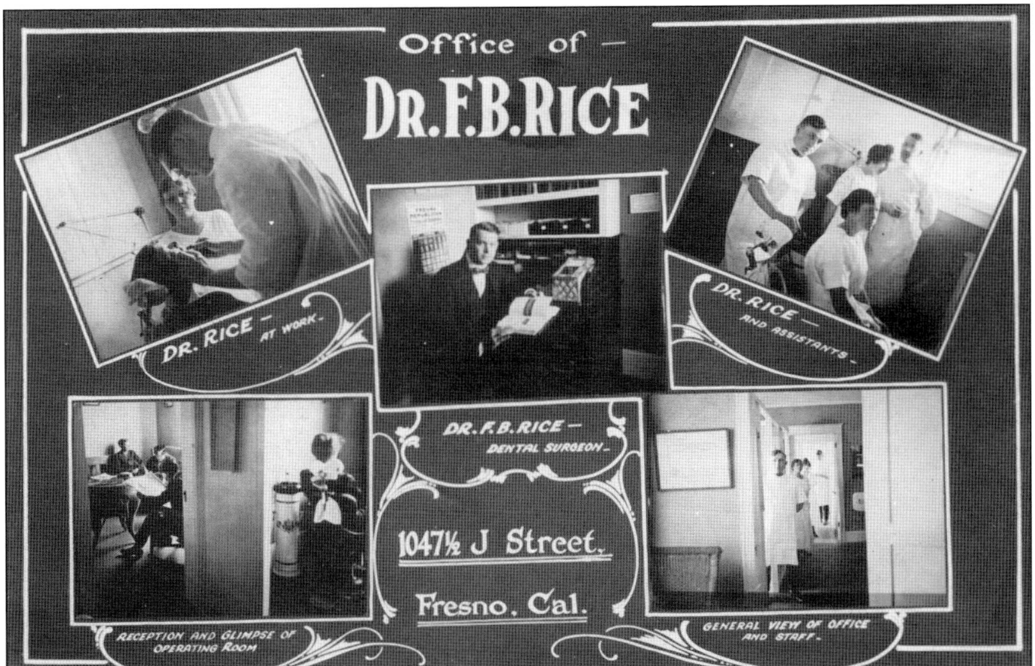

Most doctors did not advertise, but F.B. Rice, dental surgeon, did. Most of his patients were referred to him for specialized services. Doctor Rice's office was located at 1047 ½ Fulton Street. (Fresno County Library.)

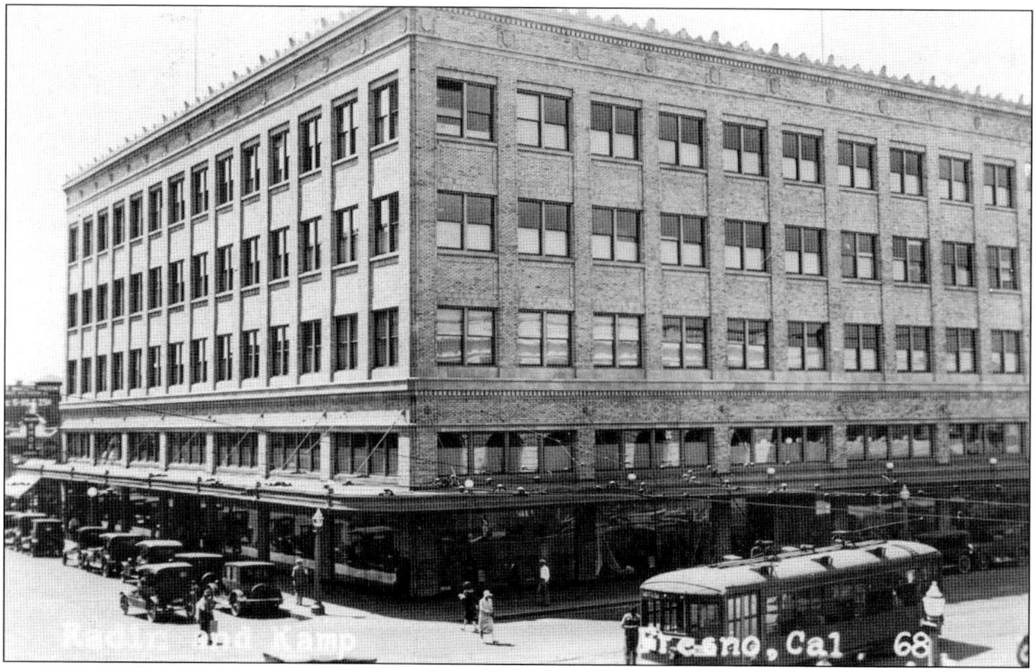

The Radin & Kamp Department Store operated in Fresno from 1889 to 1935 and is shown in this image at the southwest corner of Tulare and Fulton Streets. The grand opening of this location was on September 14, 1925. It was the first department store in Fresno to have escalators. Later tenants at this location were The Famous and J.C. Penney.

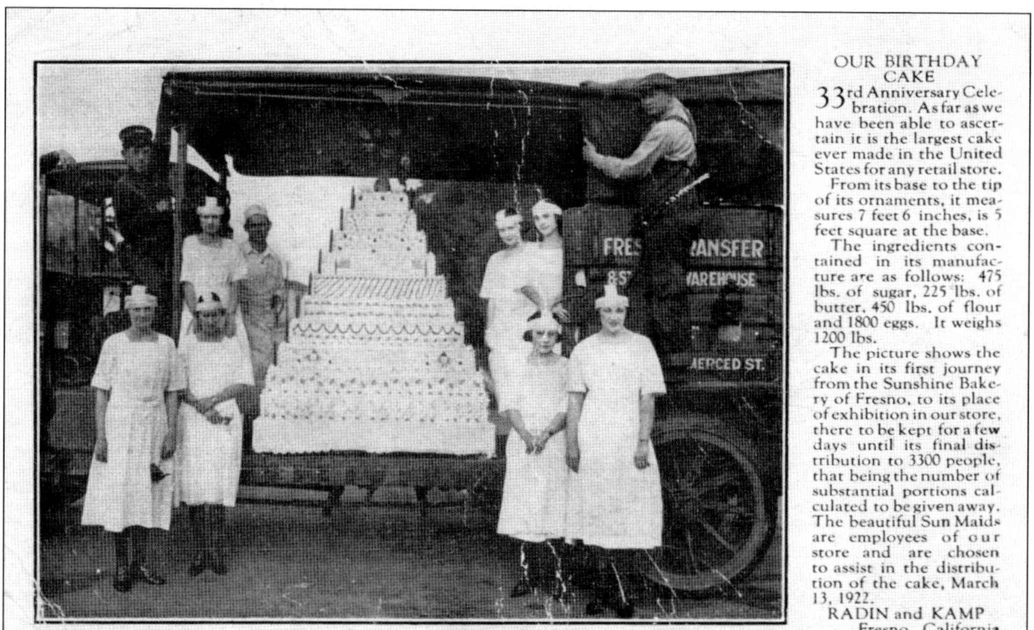

This image shows the Radin & Kamp Department Store receiving a birthday cake for its 33rd anniversary. Baked by Sunshine Bakery of Fresno and delivered by Fresno Transfer, the cake was cut on March 12, 1922, inside the store.

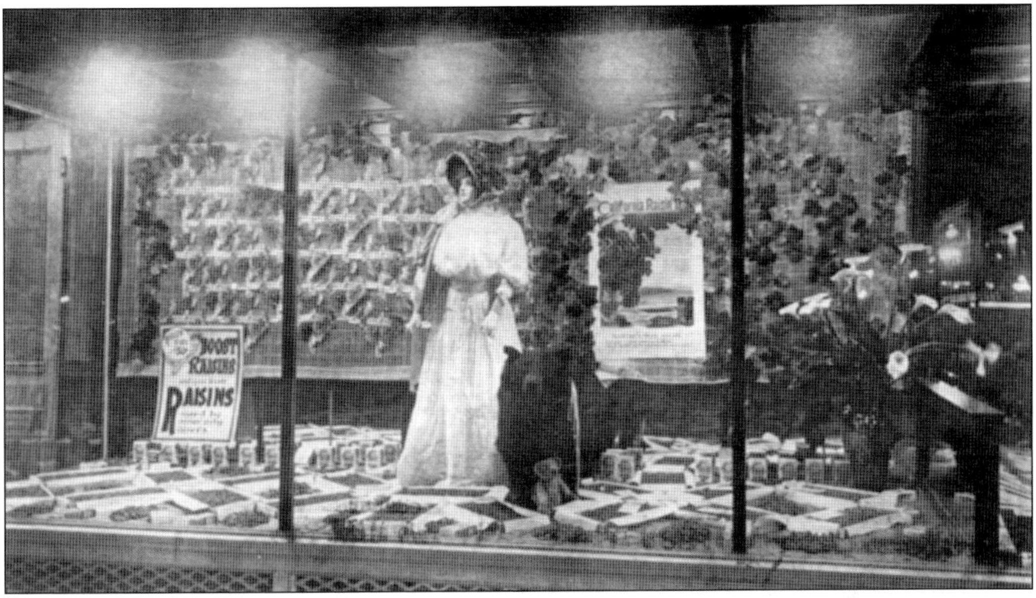

The H. Graff & Co. Raisin Day window display featured a mannequin wearing the Sun Maid dress and bonnet and many packages of raisins. Graff had three different locations: Inyo and H (Broadway), the northeast corner of Tulare & J (Patterson Block), and the southwest corner of Van Ness at Kern. In 1921, a major fire put it out of business.

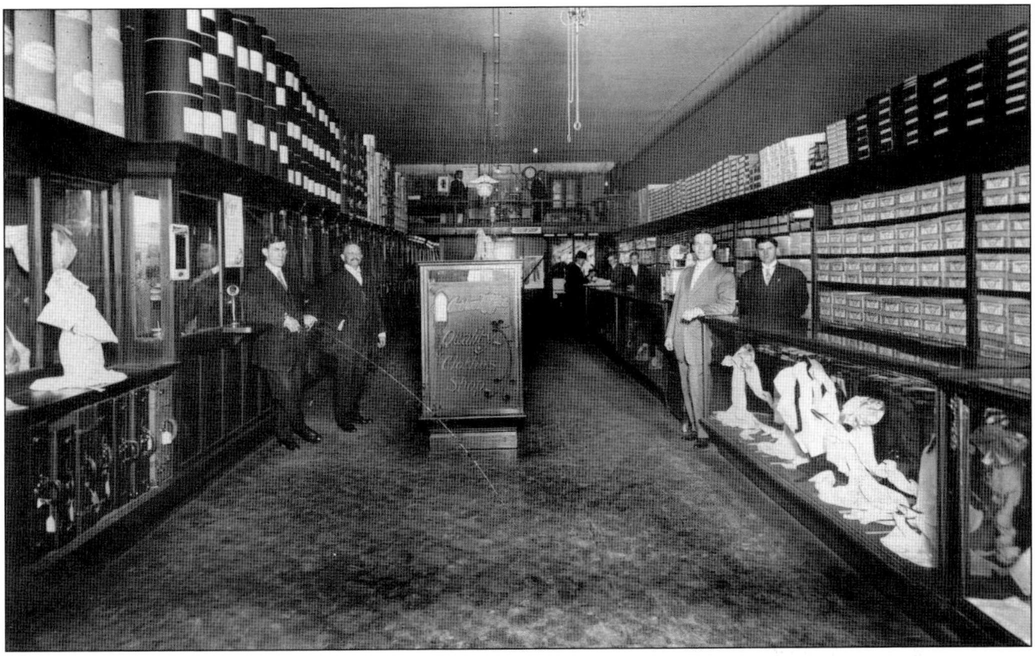

Here is an interior view of the Arthur McAfee Men's Clothing Store, located at 1027 Fulton Street. Postmarked March 11, 1909, the card was sent to W.O. Miles of 1228 F Street in Fresno. The message read, "We are ready with all the new styles" and was an advertisement card for their spring 1909 line of men's clothing.

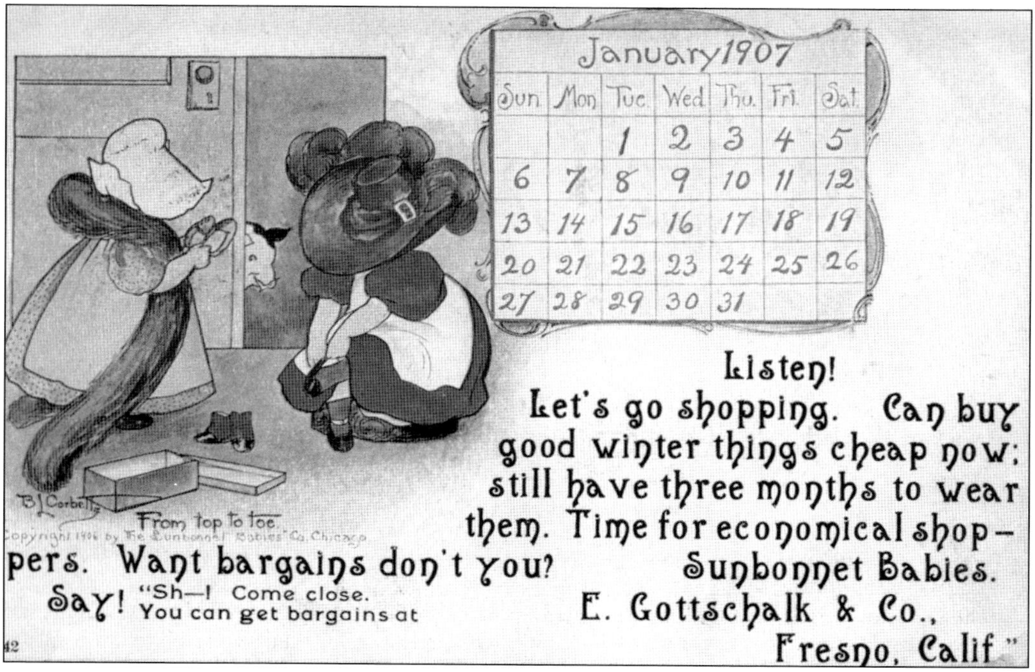

Shown here is an E. Gottschalk & Co. Sunbonnet Baby postcard. A different card was mailed each month for advertising purposes. Gottschalks began in 1904, and this postcard was issued while the store was located at the southeast corner of Tulare and Fulton Streets in the Forsythe Building. The company built its own building in 1914 at the southeast corner of Tulare and Kern Streets, where it remained until it ceased business.

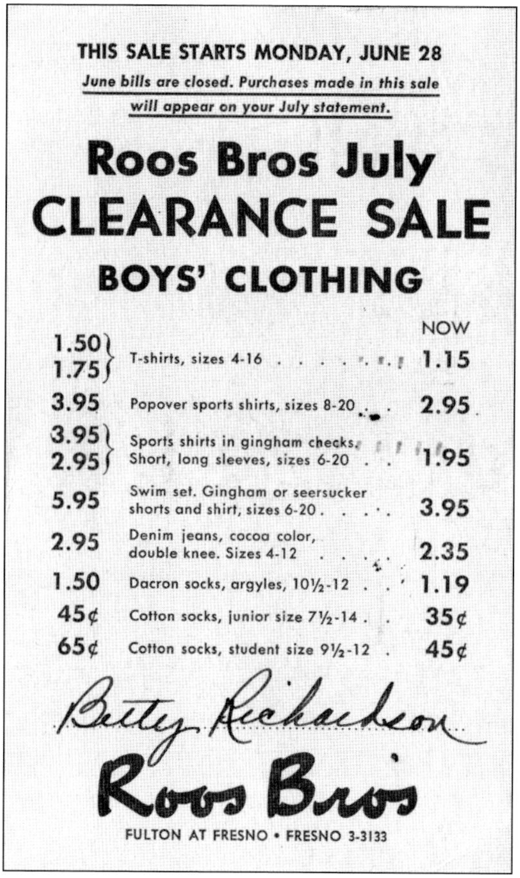

This postcard is from Roos Bros Men's and Boy's Store, which was located at Fulton and Fresno Streets. Roos Bros sold high quality clothing, even though the prices displayed seem inexpensive now. Betty Richardson, salesperson, addressed this card to a customer to inform him of the June 28, 1945, sale.

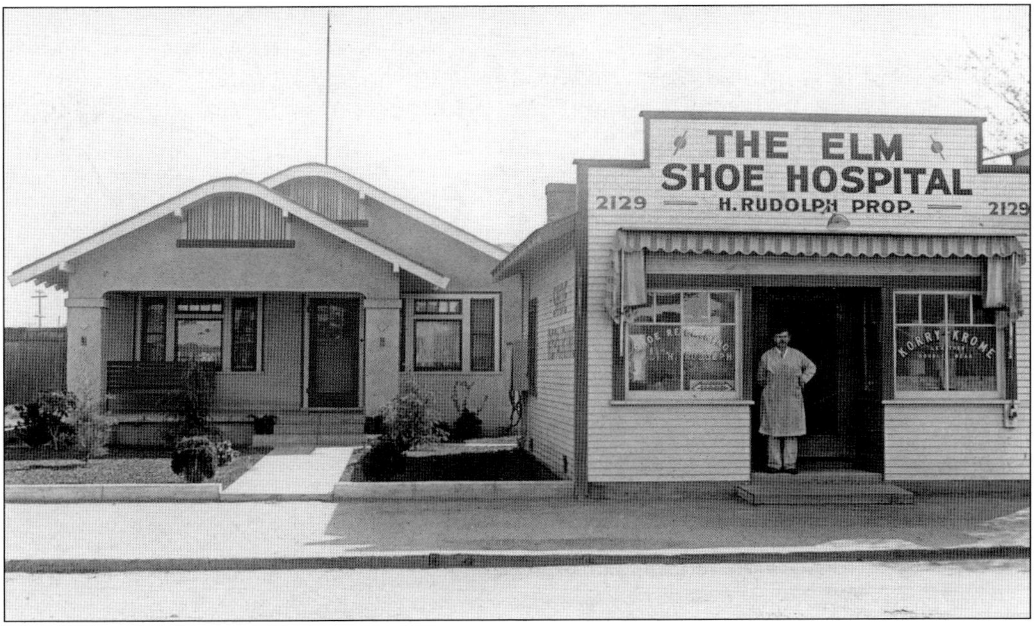

Here is an unusual business postcard for "The Elm Shoe Hospital." H. Rudolph, proprietor, is standing in the doorway of his business. Located at 2129 Elm Street, the home is of a style found all over Fresno in the 1930s.

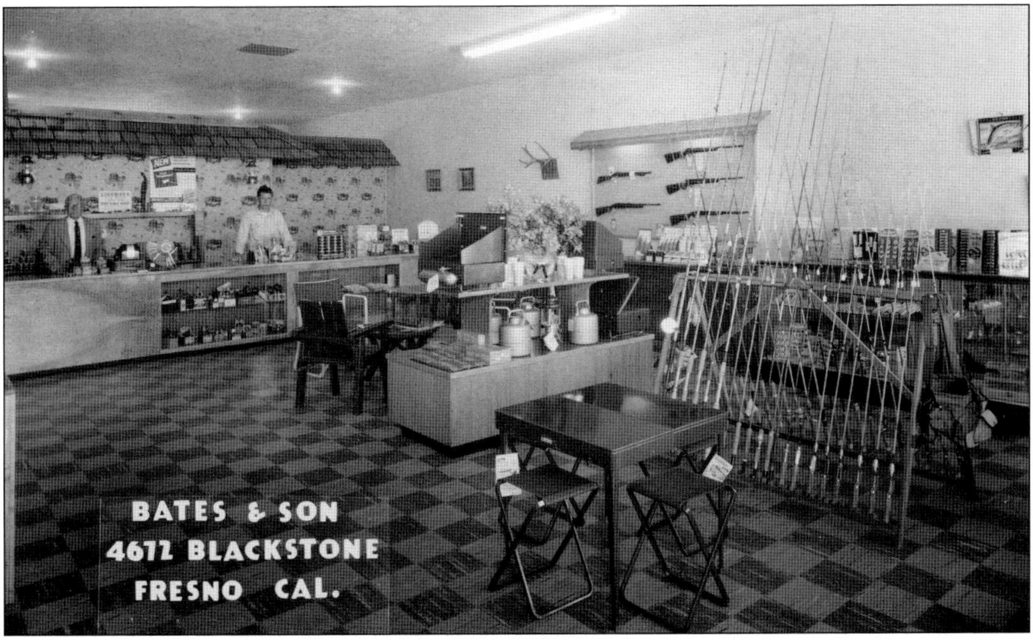

Shown here is an advertising postcard for Bates & Son Sporting Goods Store at 4672 Blackstone. Printed messages on the back of the card state "Trout season opens April 30—that's this Saturday" and "Open every nite this week to 9 PM" and "P.S. the 1955 fishing regulations are in now, come in and pick one up."

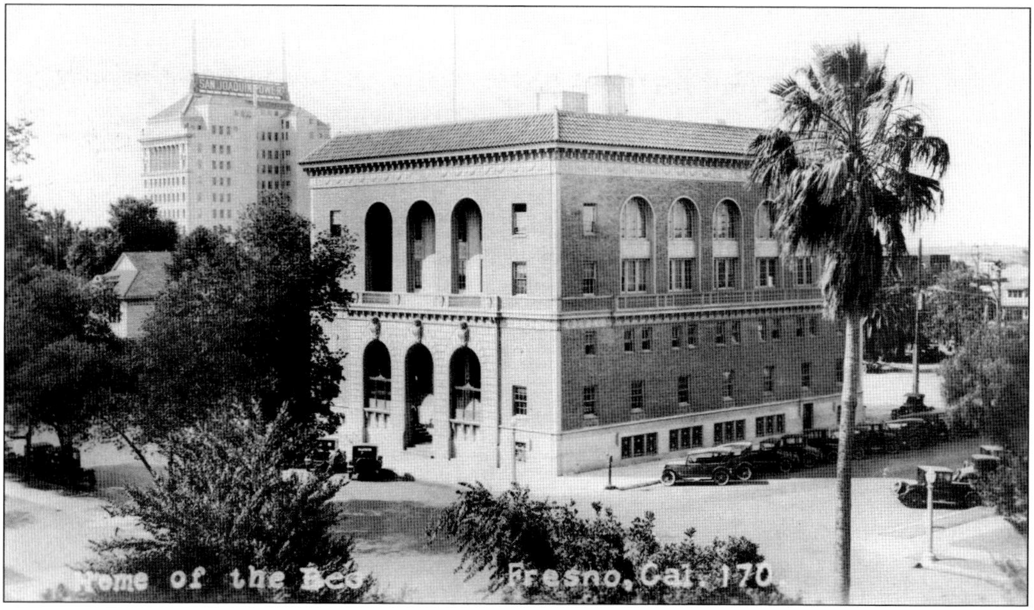

This postcard shows the Fresno Bee Building in the 1920s, located at the southwest corner of Van Ness and Calaveras Streets. The building was erected in 1922 and was later enlarged to add room for both the engraving department and the new KMJ Radio station.

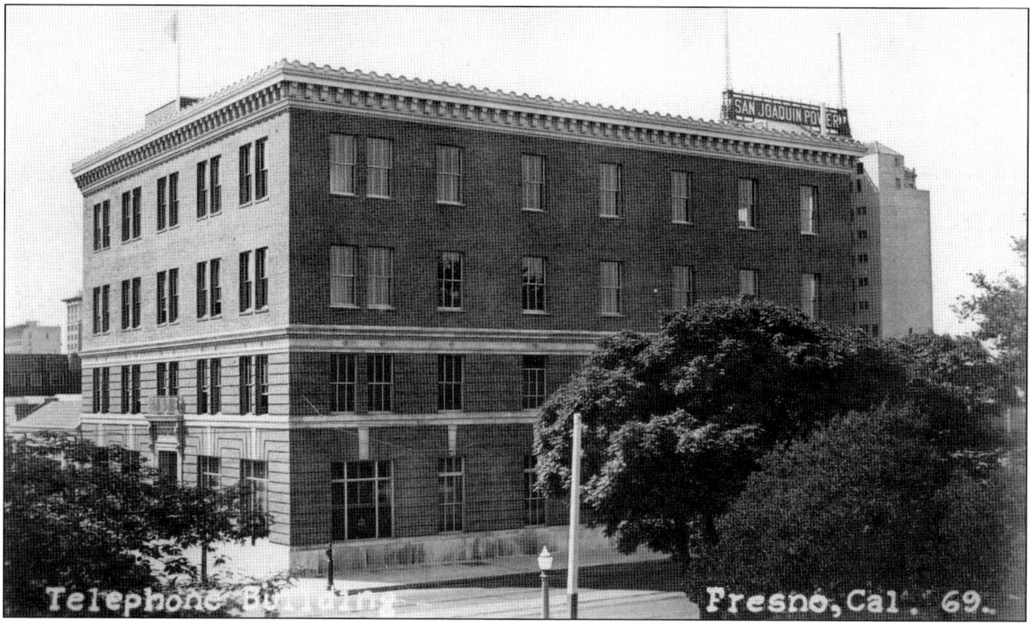

The Fresno Telephone Building was built in 1925 at 1455 Van Ness Street, where it still stands today. The original construction cost was $500,000. It opened for business in February 1926.

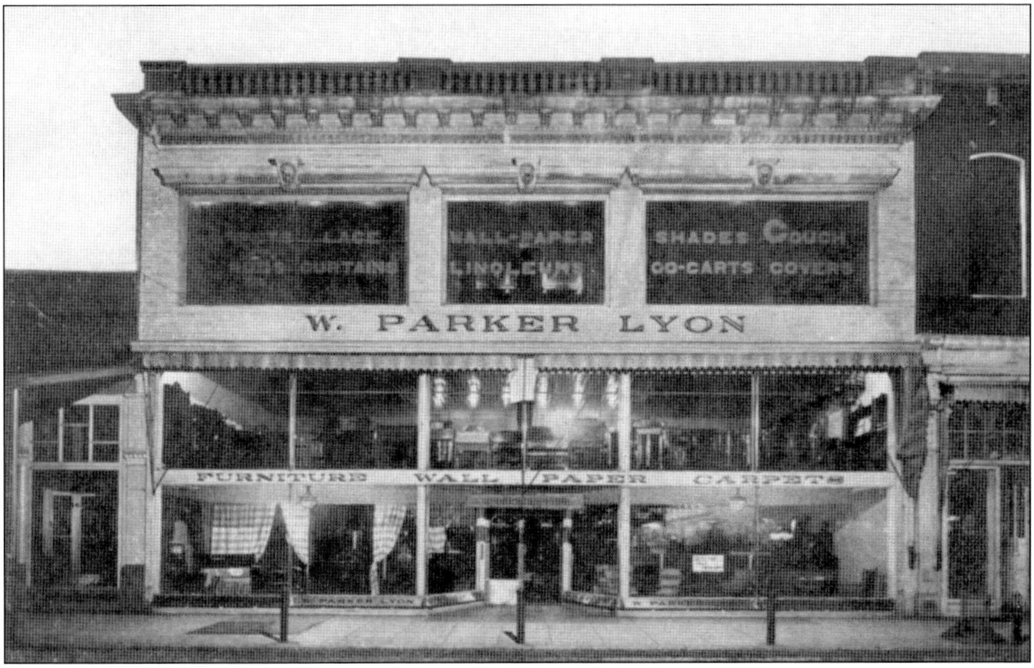

The caption on this card for the W. Parker Lyon furniture company of Fresno states that the store has a "50 foot front; 150 feet in depth; 3 floors and basement." (Fresno County Library.)

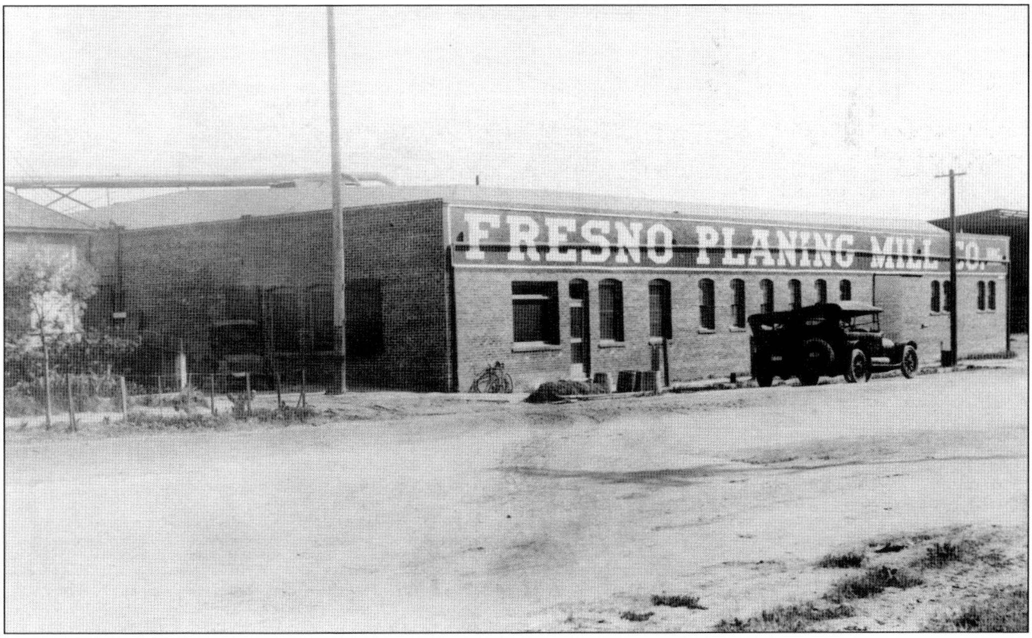

The Fresno Planing Mill began business in 1908 at 1820 Monterey Street, and is still in business at the same location today. The founders were A.W. Bernbauer, C.E. Bernbauer, and J.D. Craig.

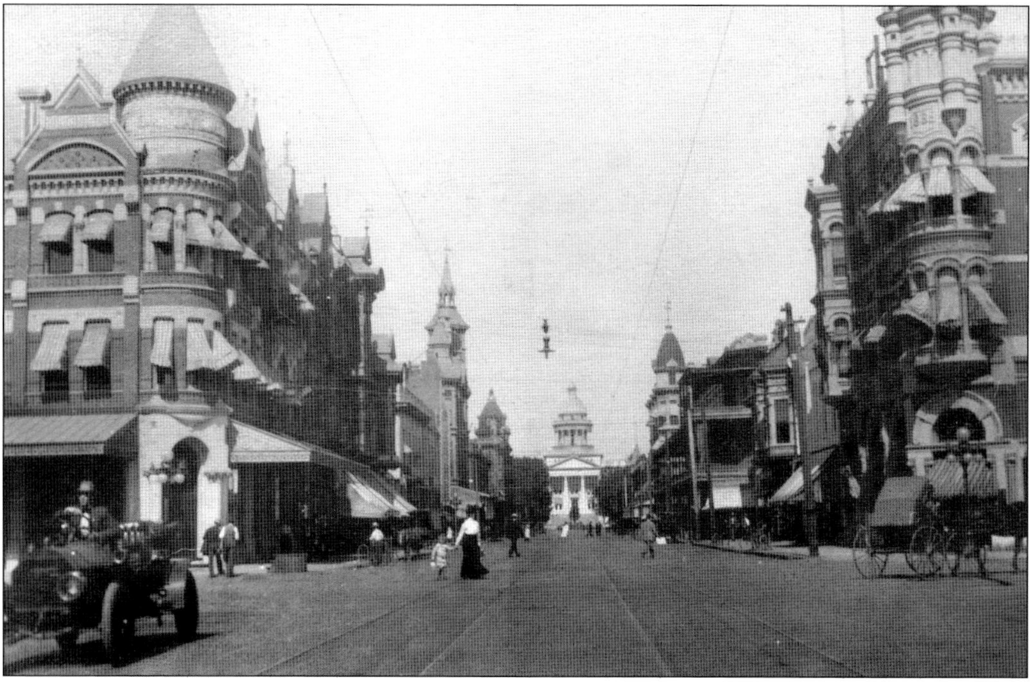

Shown in this image is the intersection of I Street (Broadway) and Mariposa Street, looking east along Mariposa Street toward the Fresno County Courthouse. The ornate building on the left is the First National Bank Building. On the right is the Farmers Bank Building.

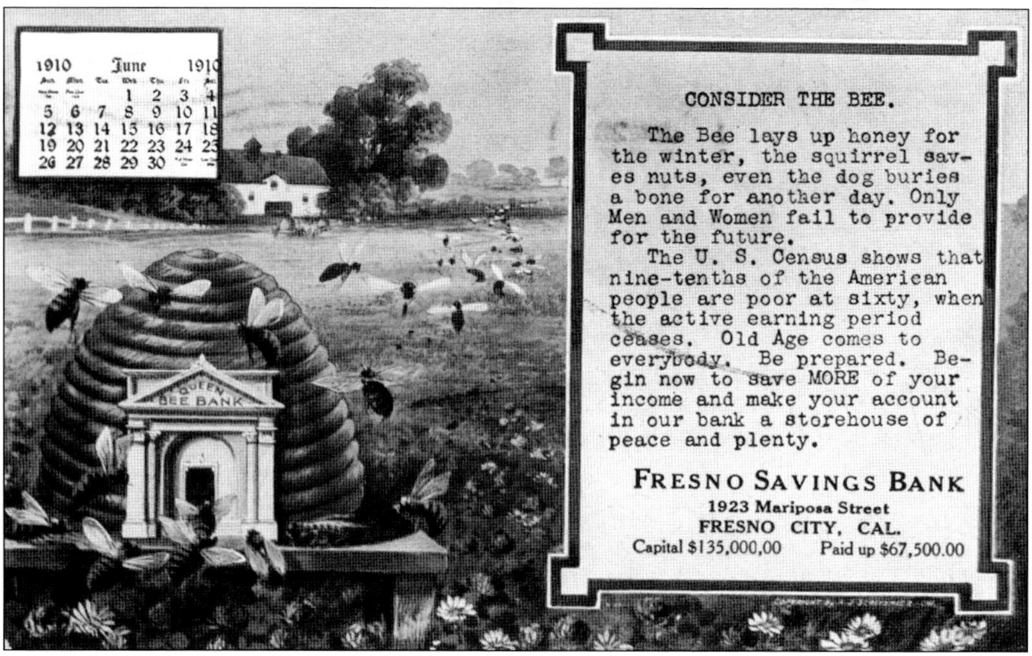

This postcard was used by the Fresno Savings Bank that was located at 1923 Mariposa Street. It was the sixth out of a set of 12 cards. These cards were an early form of junk mail sent out each month to new and potential customers. The message on the card was to entice residents to save money at the bank.

Six

Churches and Social Organizations

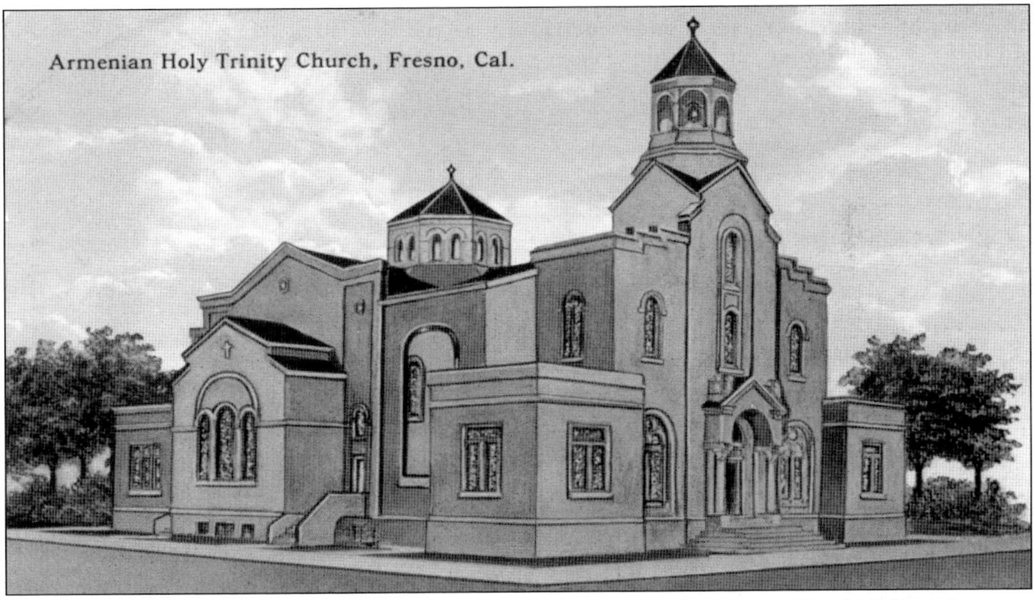

The Holy Trinity Apostolic Church was built in 1914 to replace an earlier building that was destroyed by fire. It was designed by Lawrence K. Cone (Condrajian) using a Period Revival design with Armenian influence. It was the first church built in the United States using such an influence in its design. The official ground breaking was November 1, 1914, when a handful of soil brought from the Monastery of St. Krikor the Illuminator in Erzeroum, Armenia, was placed in the foundation. It is still located at the southwest corner of Ventura and L Streets at the heart of Fresno's "Armenian Town."

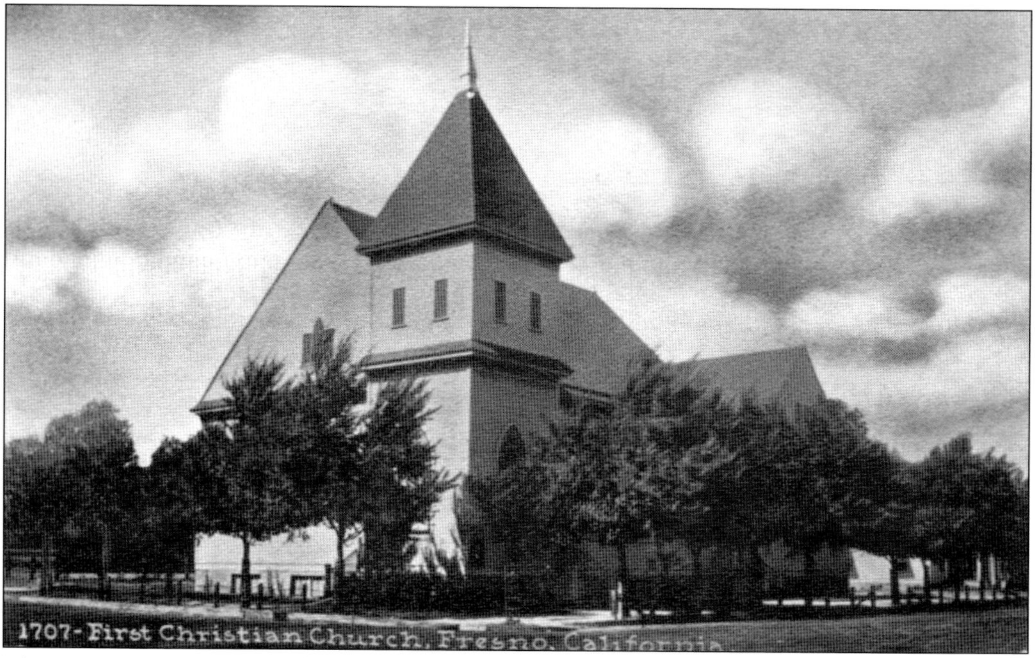

The Fresno Christian Church was organized in 1884 and its first church building was completed in 1886. Shown here is a view of the church between 1906 and 1910 at the northeast corner of N and Mariposa Streets.

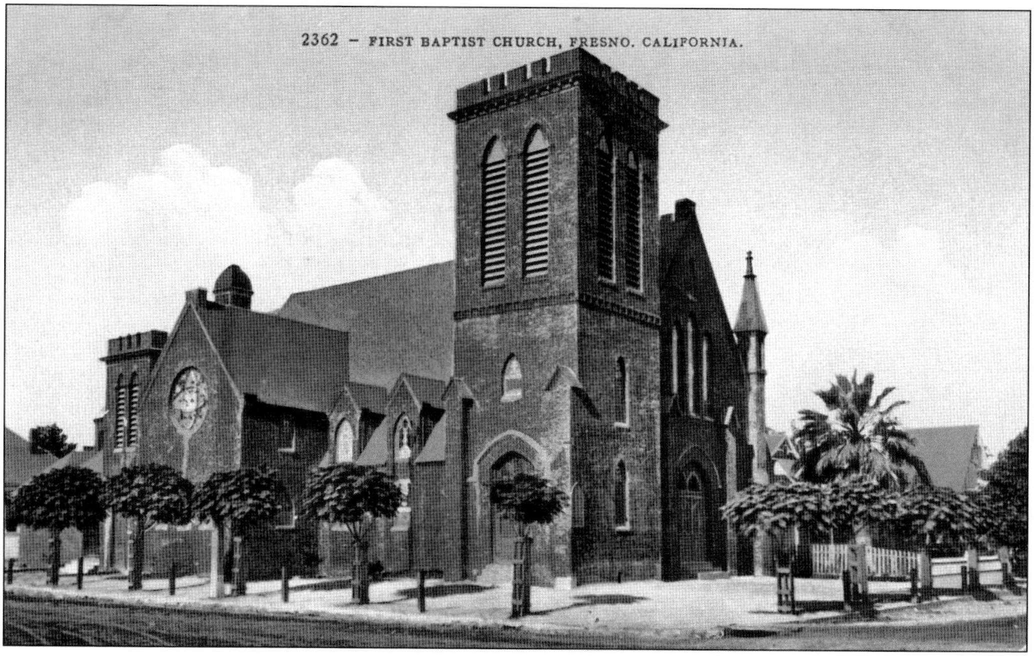

The First Baptist Church was organized in 1882 and its first building was completed in 1885. It was located on the northeast corner of Fulton and Merced Streets. Rev. T.T. Potter was the first pastor.

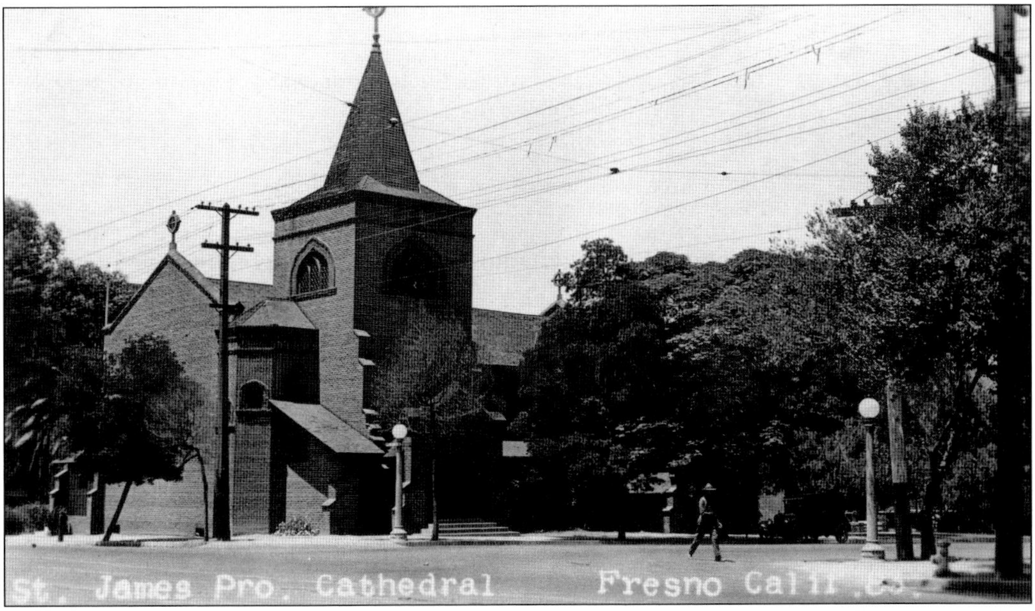

The St. James Episcopal Church was organized in 1881. Shown here is the St. James Protestant Episcopal Cathedral, which was located on the northwest corner of N and Fresno Streets. The building was demolished and replaced with the chamber of commerce building.

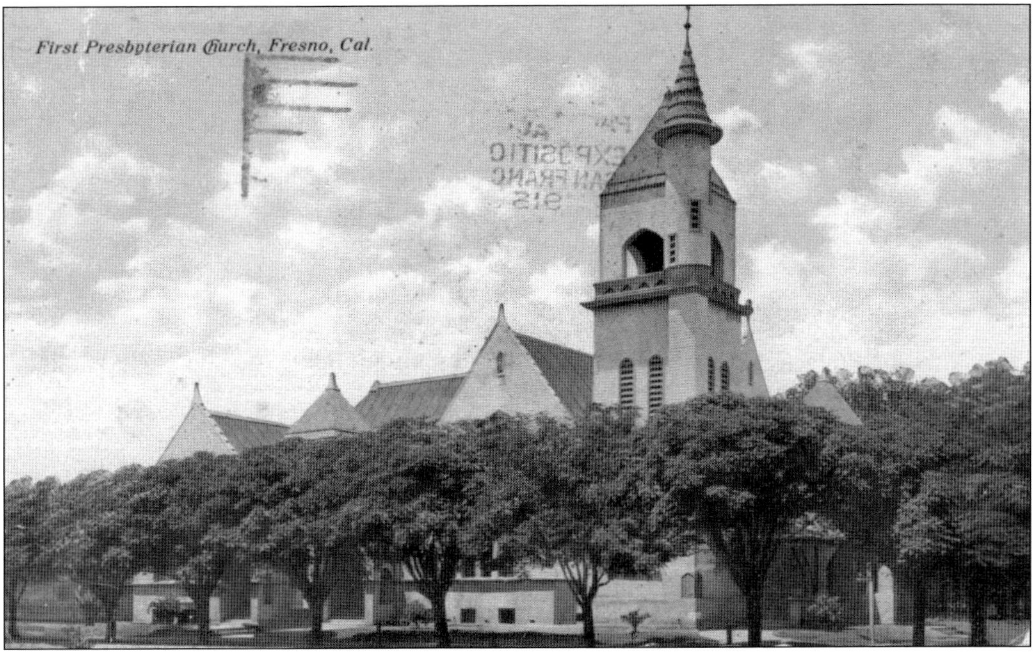

The First Presbyterian Church was organized in 1885. The first building was erected in 1888 on the northwest corner of Van Ness and Merced Streets. This postcard shows the building around 1910.

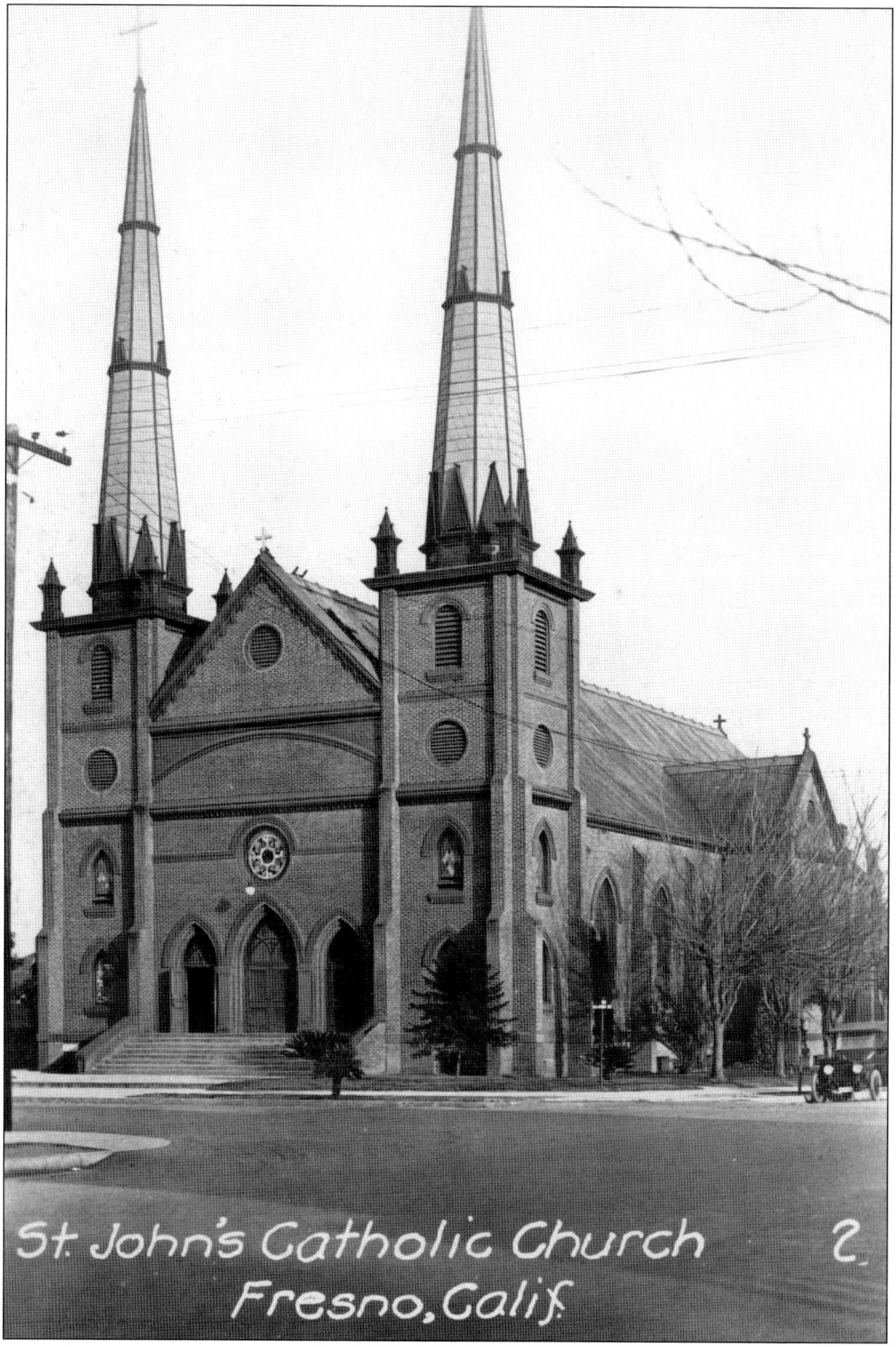

Fresno's first Catholic church was built on the southeast corner of M and Fresno Streets. Rev. Fr. Valentine Aguilera was the first resident priest. Shown in this image is the second location of the St. John Catholic Church currently on the southeast corner of R and Mariposa Streets.

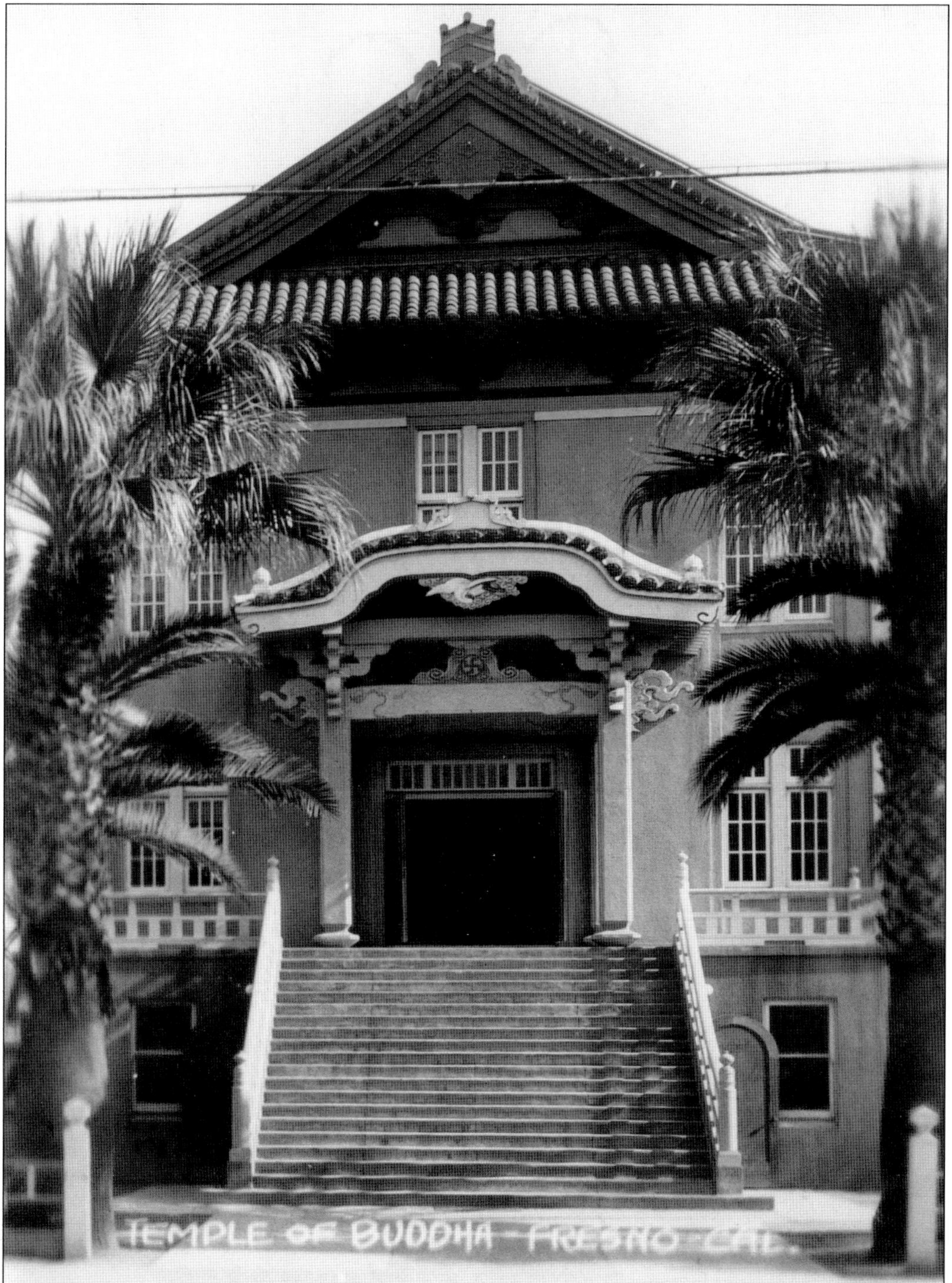

This postcard shows The Temple of Buddha, which is still located at 1340 Kern Street. The first temple gathering was held in 1899, led by Rev. Kakuro Nishiyima from San Francisco. The first church leader was Rev. Fukiyo Asaeda, who conducted the first official church service on January 24, 1901. The building shown here was constructed in 1902 by the Japanese community.

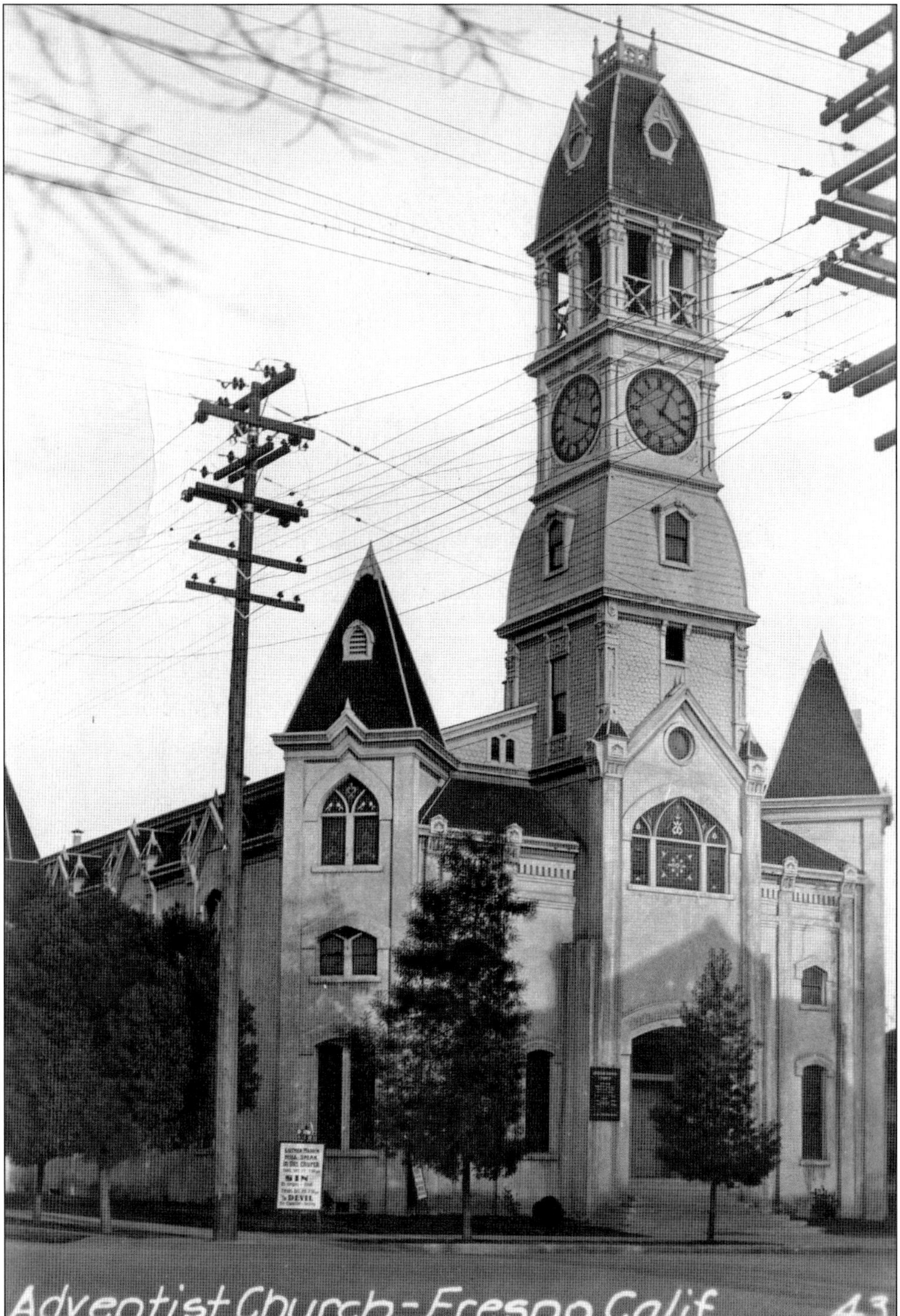

The Seventh Day Adventist Church, shown here, was built in 1888 and was located on the southeast corner of O and Mariposa Streets. It was one of the most ornate of the early churches, with its prominent spire that held a 300-pound bell and clock that chimed on the hour.

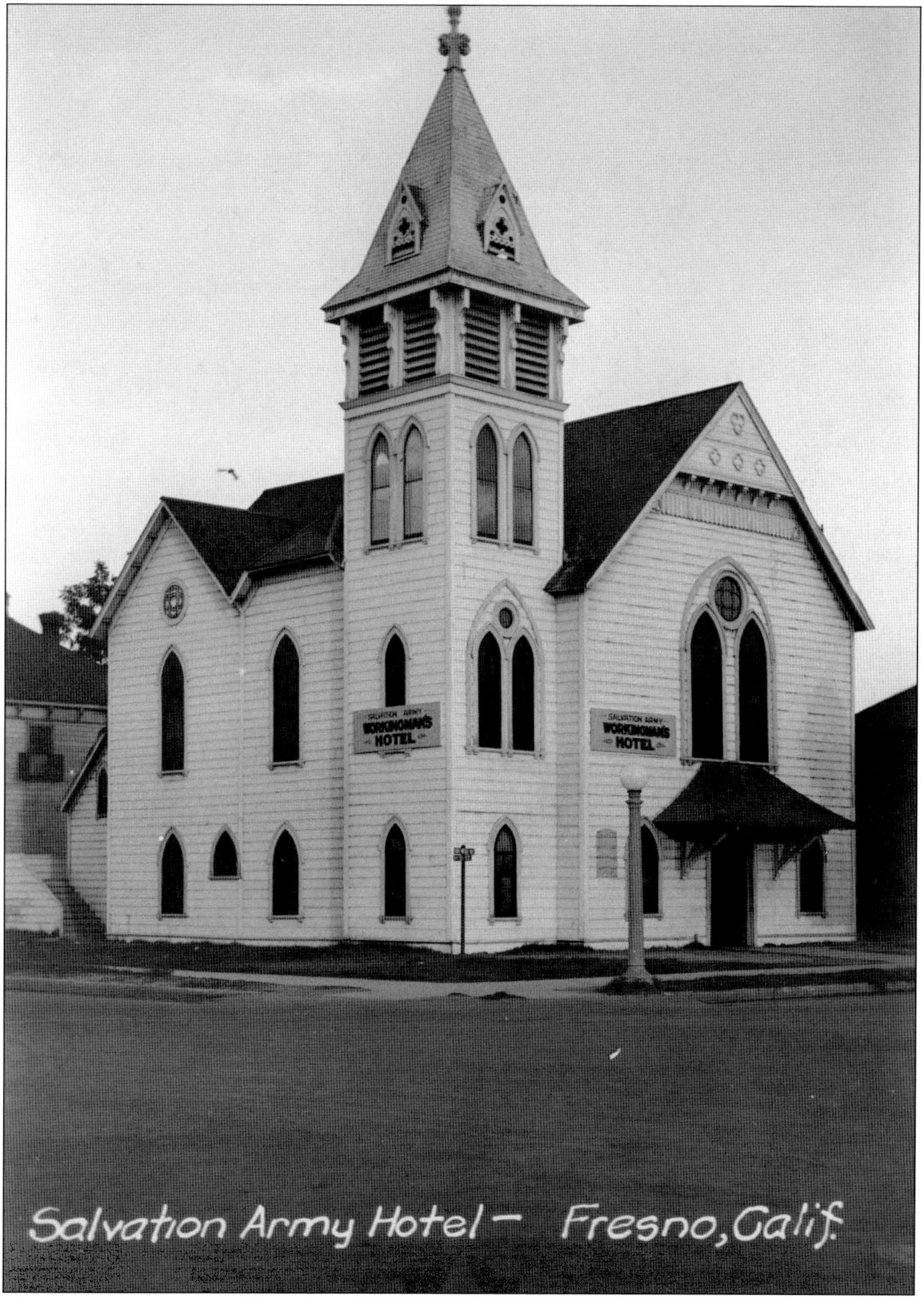

The First Congregational Church was built in 1884 and was located on Van Ness Street between Inyo and Mono Streets. The building was later converted to the Salvation Army Hotel.

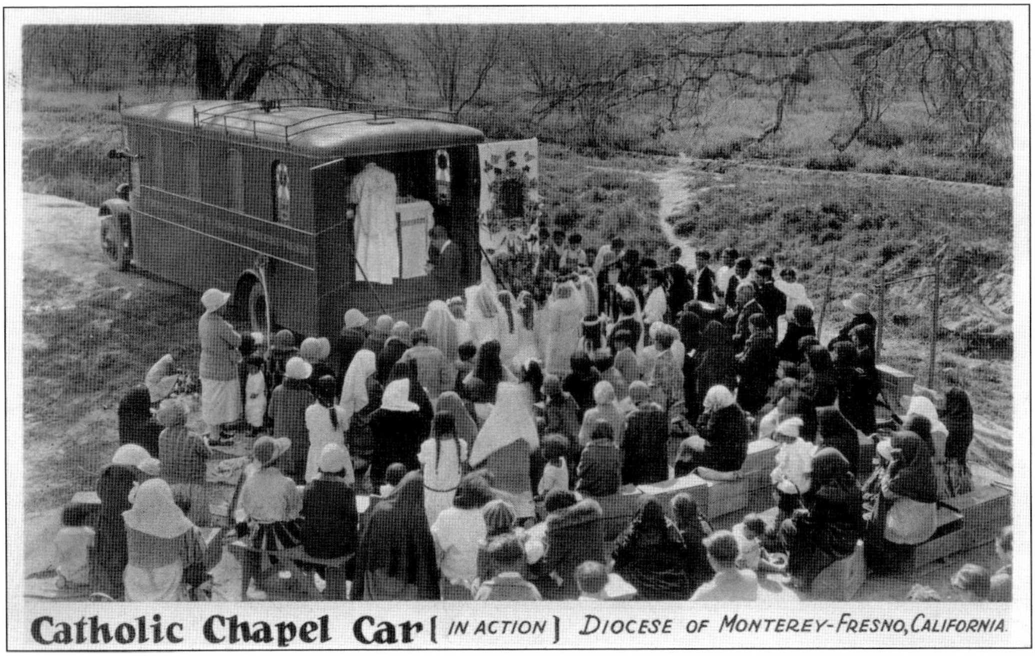

The Catholic Chapel Car was used by the Diocese of Monterey-Fresno to serve outlying communities that were unable to provide a fixed location for worship. Shown here is Mass being celebrated from the back of the car. (Fresno County Library.)

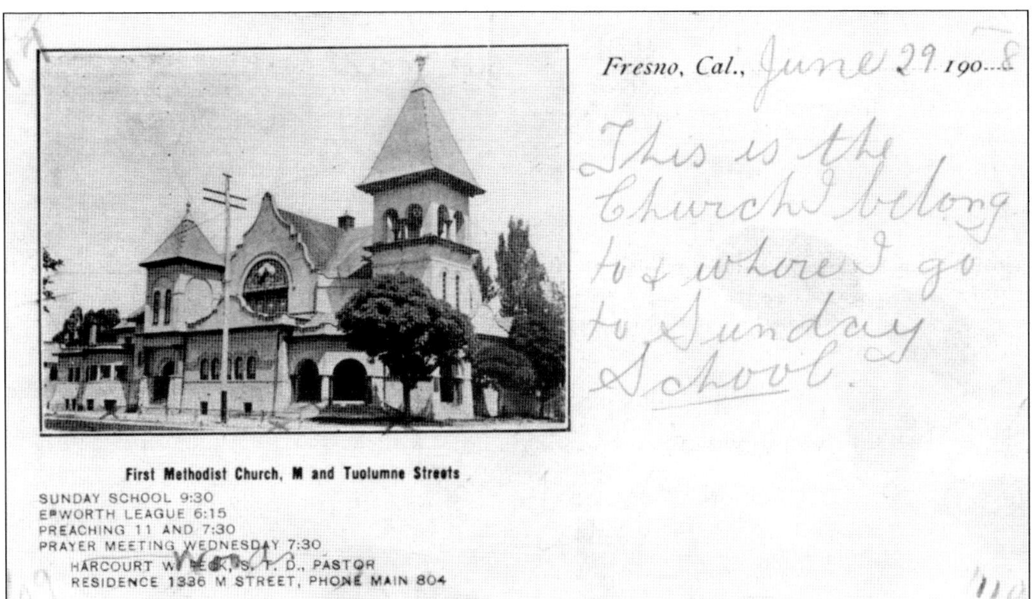

There were numerous Methodist churches formed in Fresno's early history. Shown in this postcard image is the First Methodist Church located at M and Tuolumne Streets.

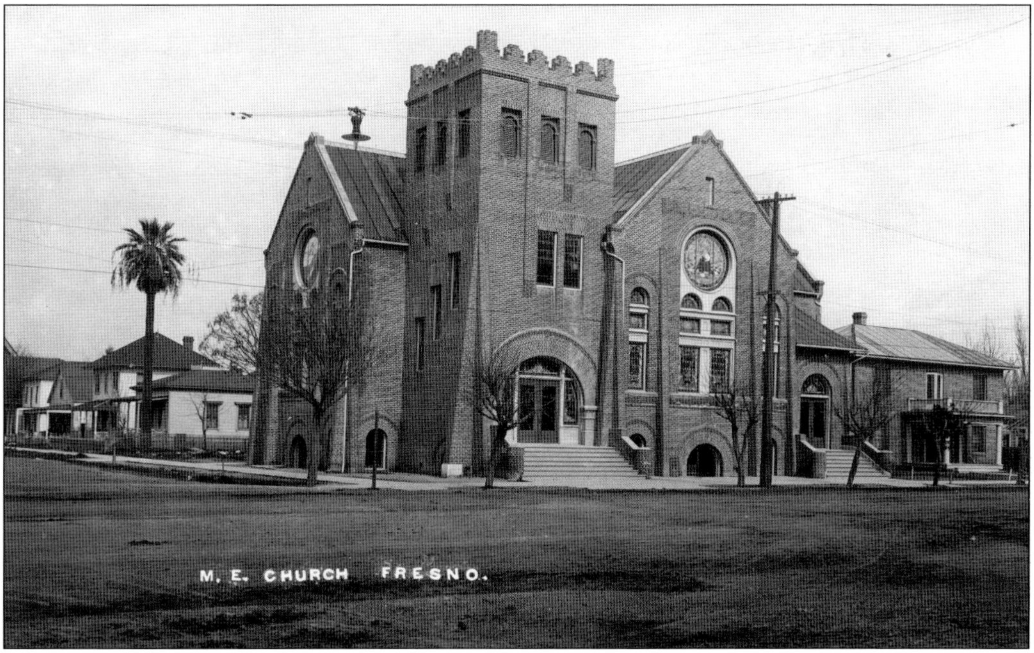

Many of the early settlers in Fresno after the Civil War were of the Methodist Episcopal faith. In 1874, barely two years after Fresno was founded, the first church in the city was Methodist Episcopal. In 1876, a small church was built on the northeast corner of Fresno and L Streets. After this building was destroyed by fire, a new church was built at the same location and is pictured here.

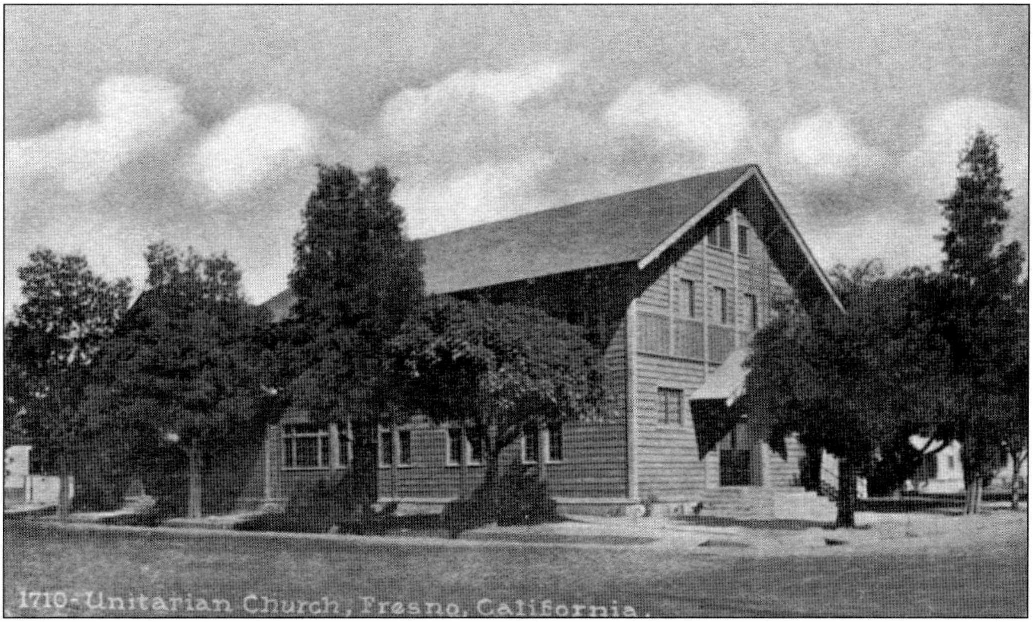

The First Unitarian Church was organized in the 1890s with Dr. Chester Rowell as one of its founders. Its first church building was built in 1910, and its first pastor was Rev. Thompson Clayton. The church was disbanded in the 1920s. In 1954, the Unitarian Universalist Church was organized and was located at 4144 Millbrook Avenue. In 2007, the church moved to Clovis.

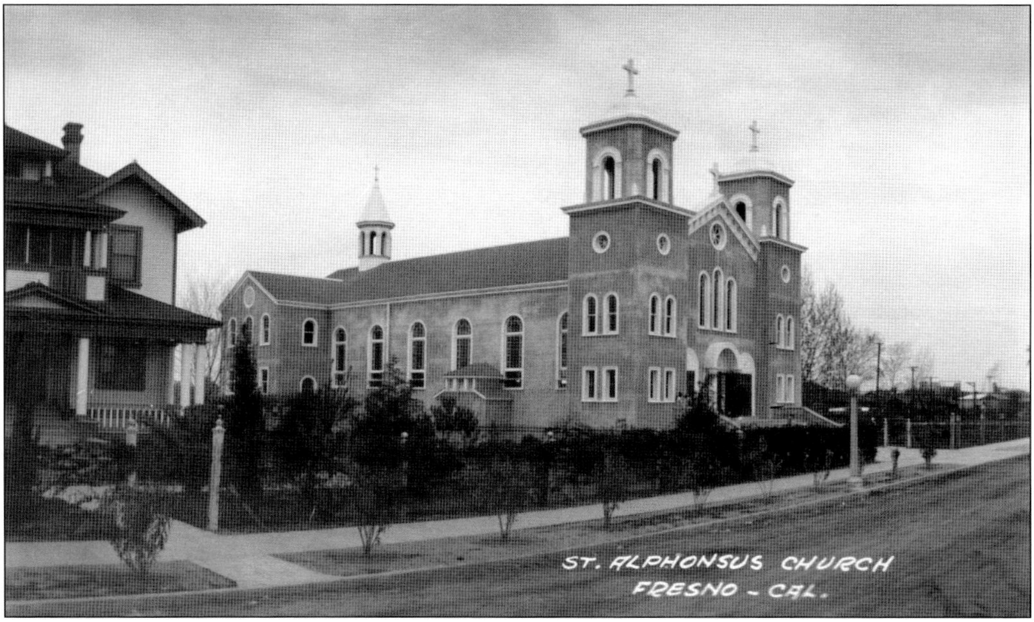

St. Alphonsus Catholic Church is pictured here at 351 East Kearney Boulevard. It was the home parish for many generations of the Fresno Italian community. The parish was founded in 1908 by Italian immigrants. Ground breaking for the church was held May 14, 1909. The first priests were Fathers Weber and Carroll. Today the building is listed in the National Register of Historic Places.

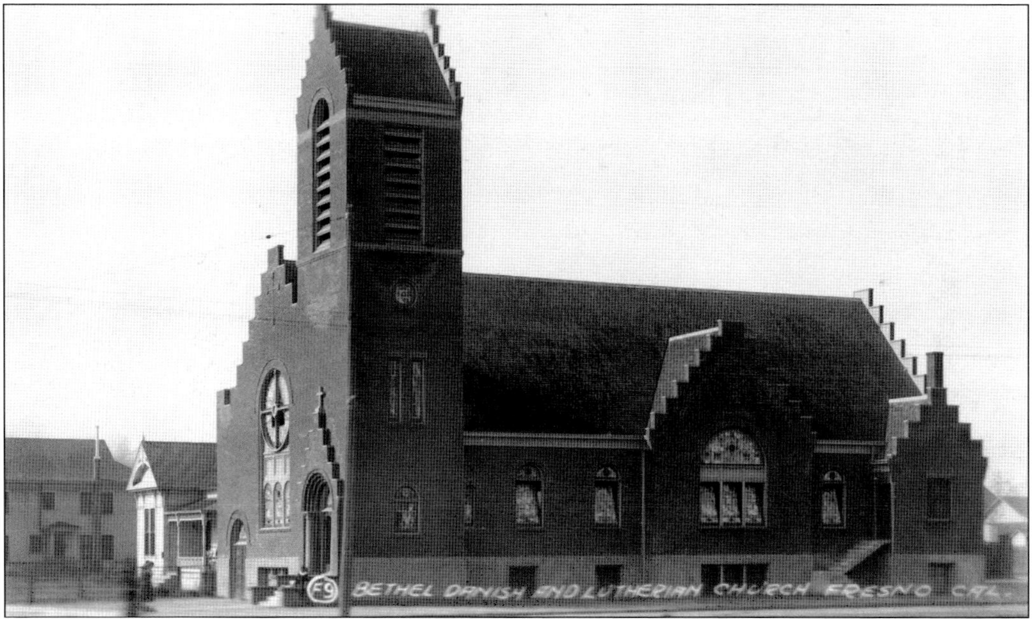

The Bethel Danish Lutheran Church was organized by Danish immigrants in 1915. The brick church shown here was built in 1917 and is still an active church at 183 N. Broadway. Until 1947, all services were in Danish. Today, the church is known as the Bethel Evangelical Lutheran Church.

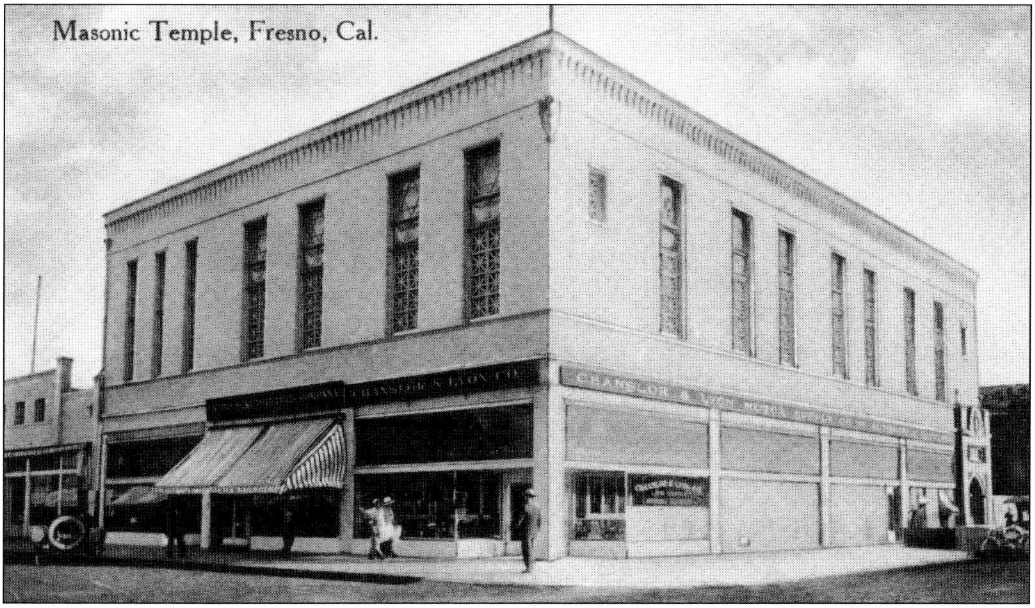

The Masonic Temple pictured here was built in 1910 after the previous lodge burned down at its location at Tulare and Broadway Streets. This new lodge was located at the southwest corner of Van Ness and Merced Streets. Lodge no. 247, Free & Accepted Masons, was chartered on October 10, 1878.

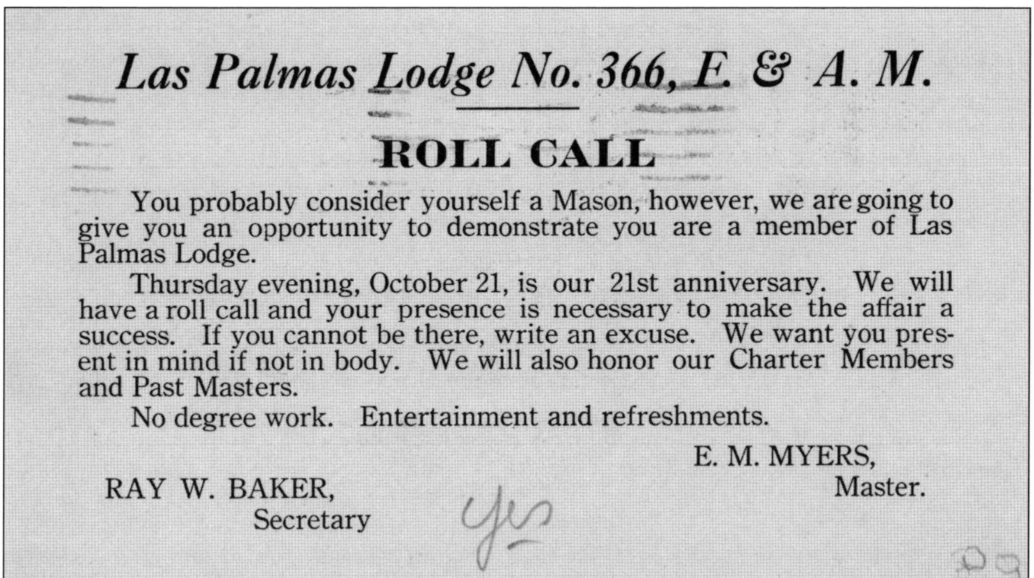

Las Palmas Lodge No. 366, F. & A. M.

ROLL CALL

You probably consider yourself a Mason, however, we are going to give you an opportunity to demonstrate you are a member of Las Palmas Lodge.

Thursday evening, October 21, is our 21st anniversary. We will have a roll call and your presence is necessary to make the affair a success. If you cannot be there, write an excuse. We want you present in mind if not in body. We will also honor our Charter Members and Past Masters.

No degree work. Entertainment and refreshments.

E. M. MYERS,
Master.

RAY W. BAKER,
Secretary

Las Palmas Lodge no. 366, F. & A.M. was chartered in 1905 and is still an active Masonic lodge, located at 2992 E. Clinton Avenue. This postcard notifies the member of a "Roll Call" to celebrate the organization's 21st anniversary. The card ends with "No degree work. Entertainment and refreshments."

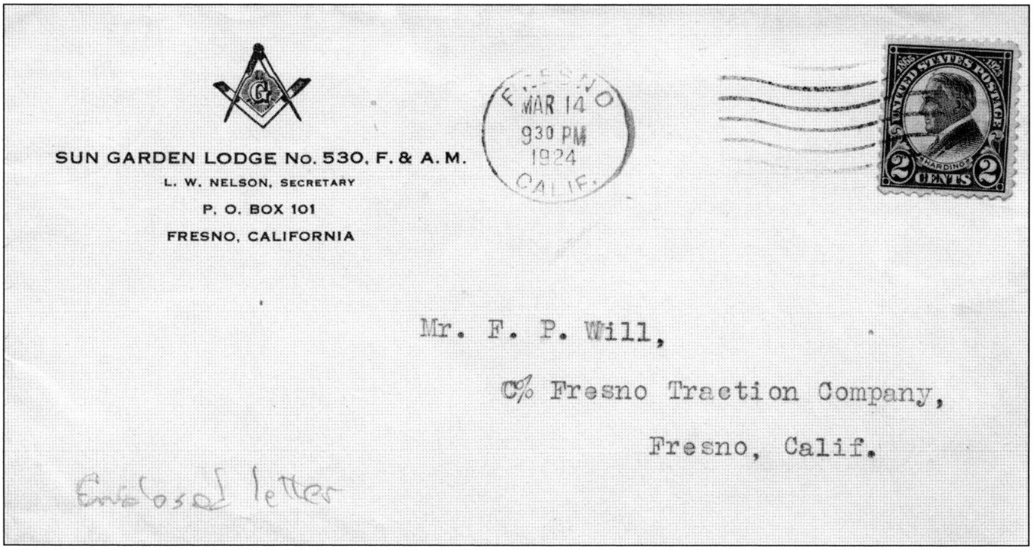

The Sun Garden Lodge no. 530, F. & A.M. was chartered in 1923, and its last meeting was in 1993. This business envelope was addressed to the Fresno Traction Company, which operated the streetcars for the city.

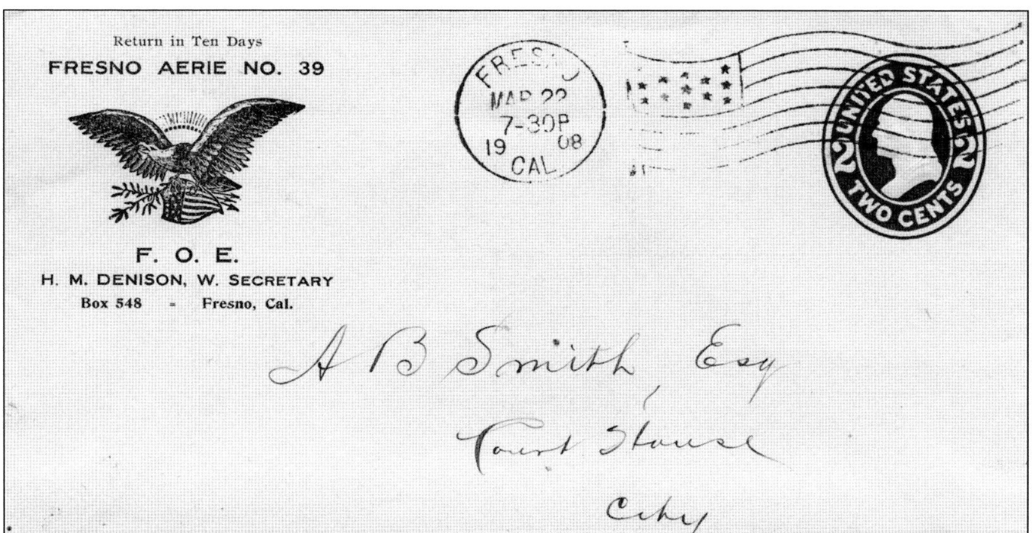

The Fraternal Order of the Eagles, Fresno Aerie no. 39 was formed in 1899 and was a social organization of individuals engaged in one way or another in the performing arts. This early envelope was postmarked March 22, 1908. The Fresno chapter disbanded in 2010.

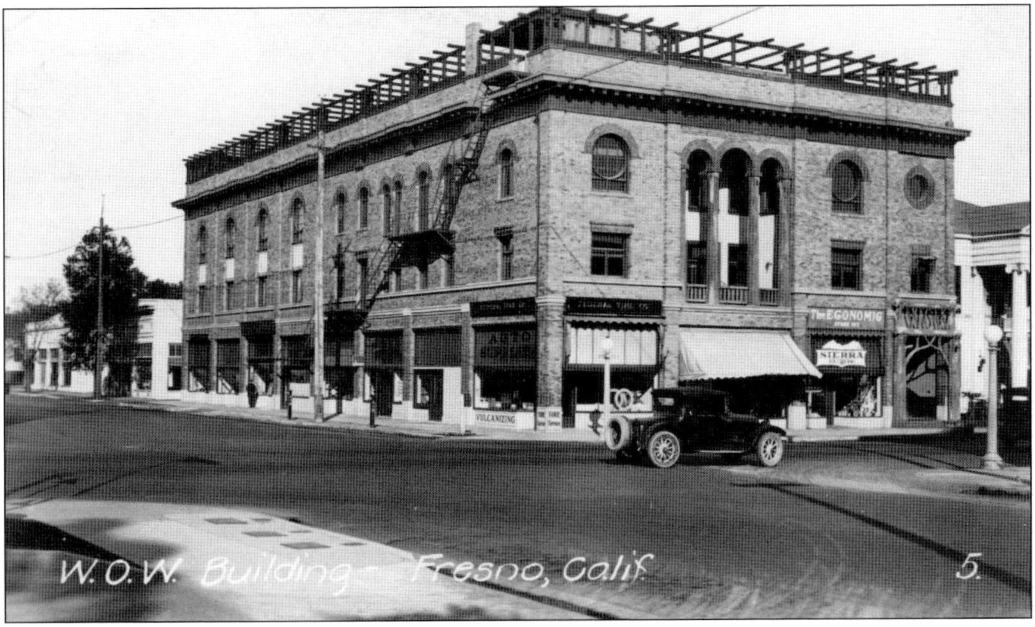

Located at the southeast corner of Van Ness and Tuolumne Streets was the Woodmen of the World Building. WOW was a life insurance benefit and recreation group that was very active in early Fresno.

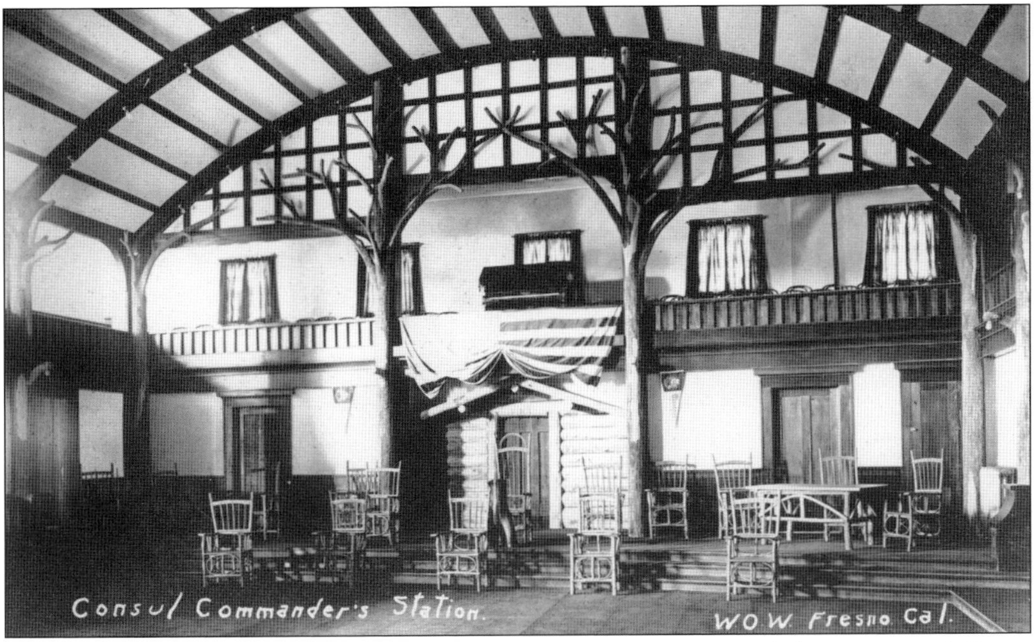

Shown here is an interior view of the Woodmen of the World's second-floor meeting hall.

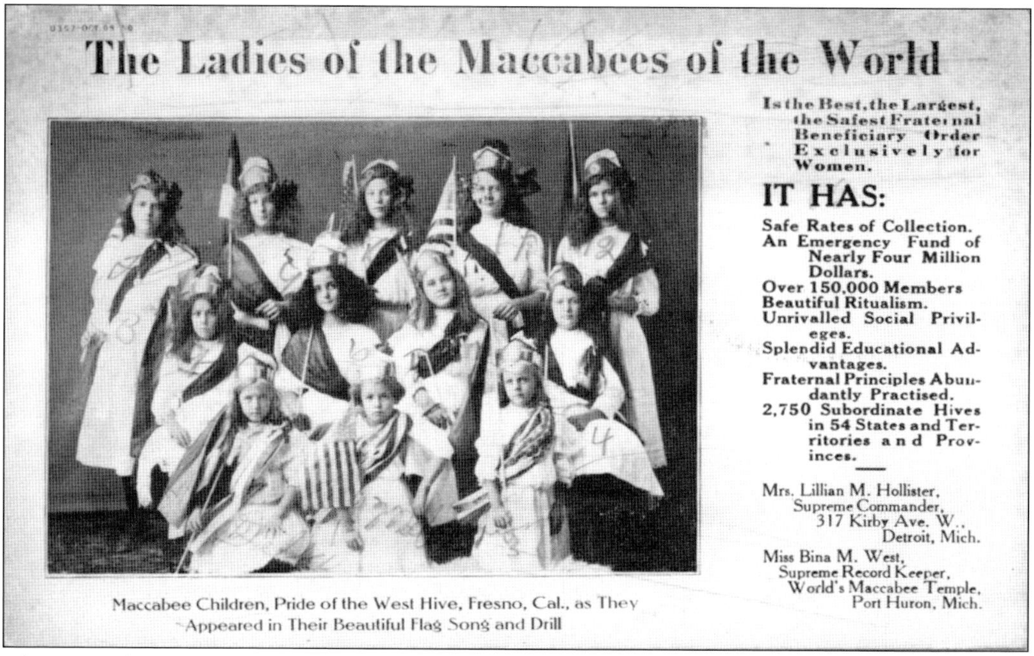

The Maccabees of the World was a major insurance lodge. Local chapters were called "hives," and men's and women's groups were organized separately. Shown here is the Maccabees Children Pride of the West Hive of Fresno.

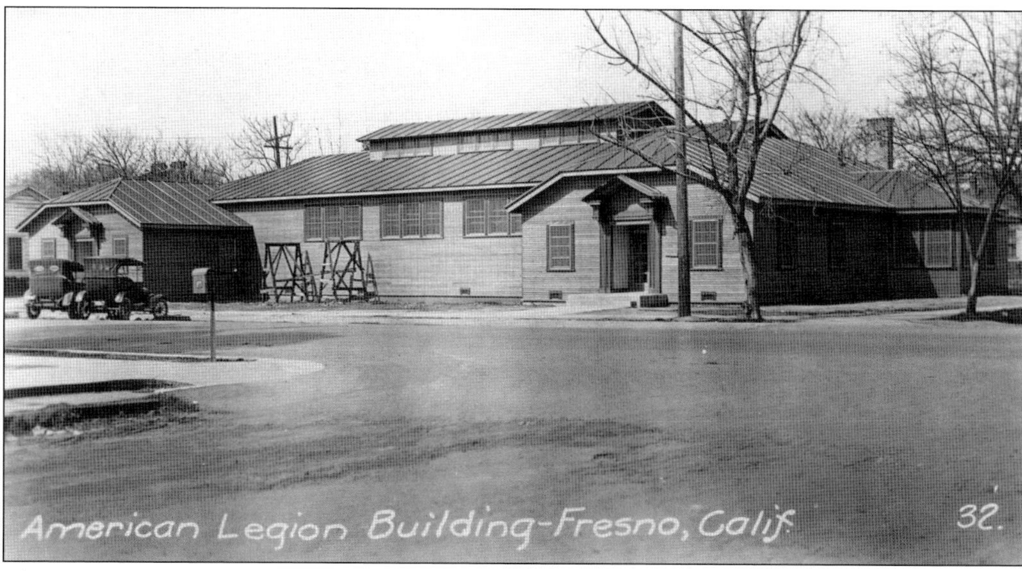

The American Legion Hall no. 4 was located at 2345 Mariposa Street from the 1930s to the 1950s, when the city acquired the property to build a police station. The Legion had an earlier hall at 1022 Broadway, but was forced to close it in the 1930s after a ban on slot machines.

Seven

SCHOOLS

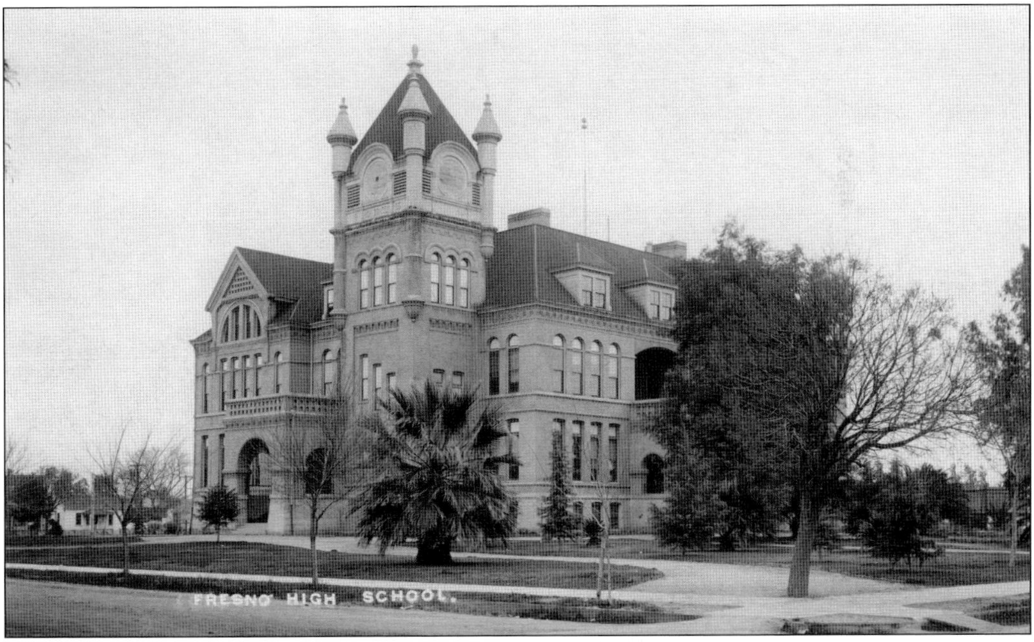

The building in this image was the first permanent high school in Fresno. Contractor F.W. Hickox built the school in 1895–1896 at a cost of $53,100. The building was located in the city block bound by P, Stanislaus, O, and Tuolumne Streets. The school was designed for 400 students and had a gymnasium, theater-style lecture room, a chemical laboratory, and a library.

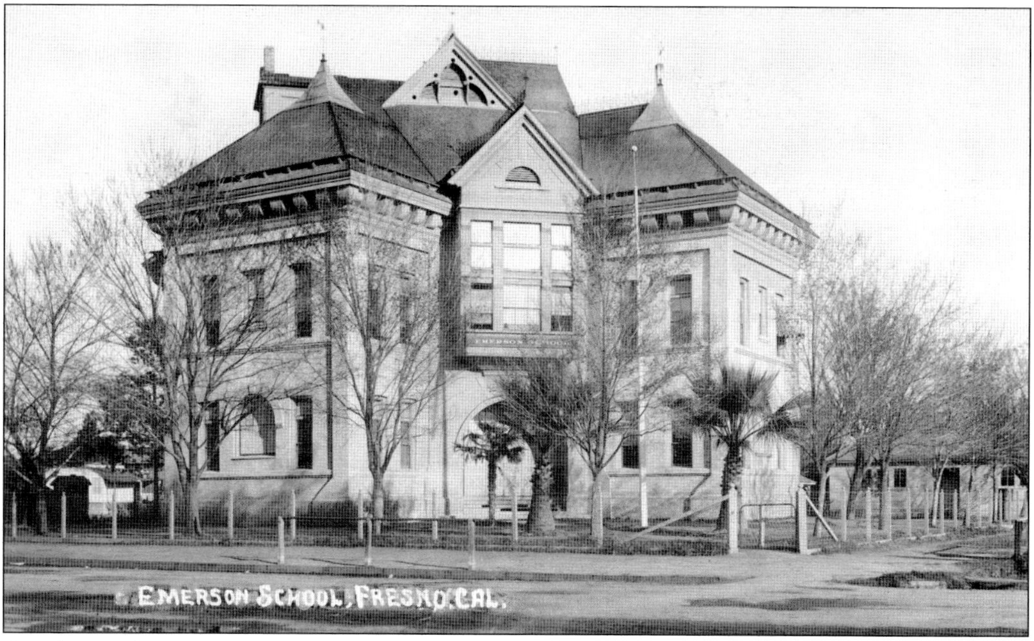

Another early grammar school was known as the K Street or Emerson School. It opened in September 1889 on the southeast corner of K (Van Ness) and Santa Clara Streets in an area known as "Armenian Town." Its most famous student was William Saroyan.

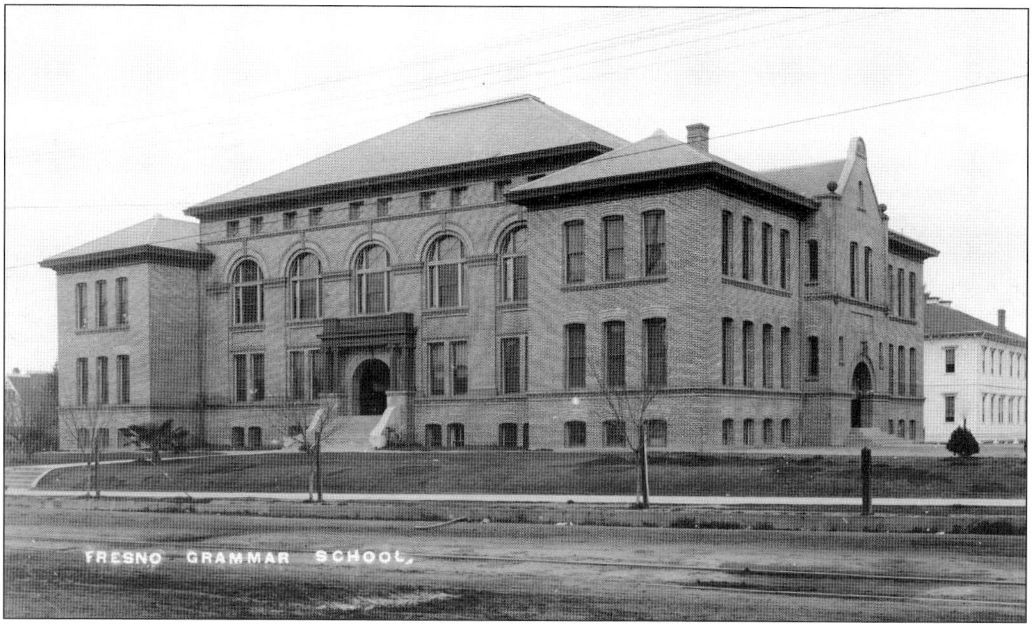

The Fresno Grammar School, which opened in 1902, occupied the site where the Memorial Auditorium stands today. The building was later named the Luther Burbank Grammar School. The building to the right was Central or White School. It was opened in 1897 and had seven rooms for 400 students. (Fresno County Library.)

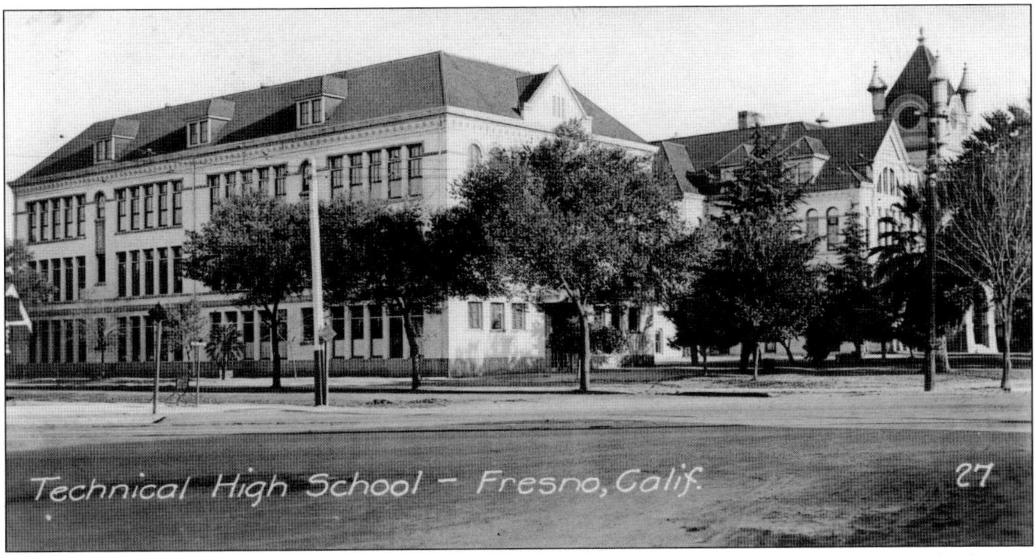

Next to the Fresno High School building was the Fresno Polytechnic Annex, which was completed in 1911. The Annex was the home of the Fresno Normal School, a two-year teacher training school. These facilities were used at different times by students of Fresno High, Fresno Tech, Junior College, and Fresno Normal School.

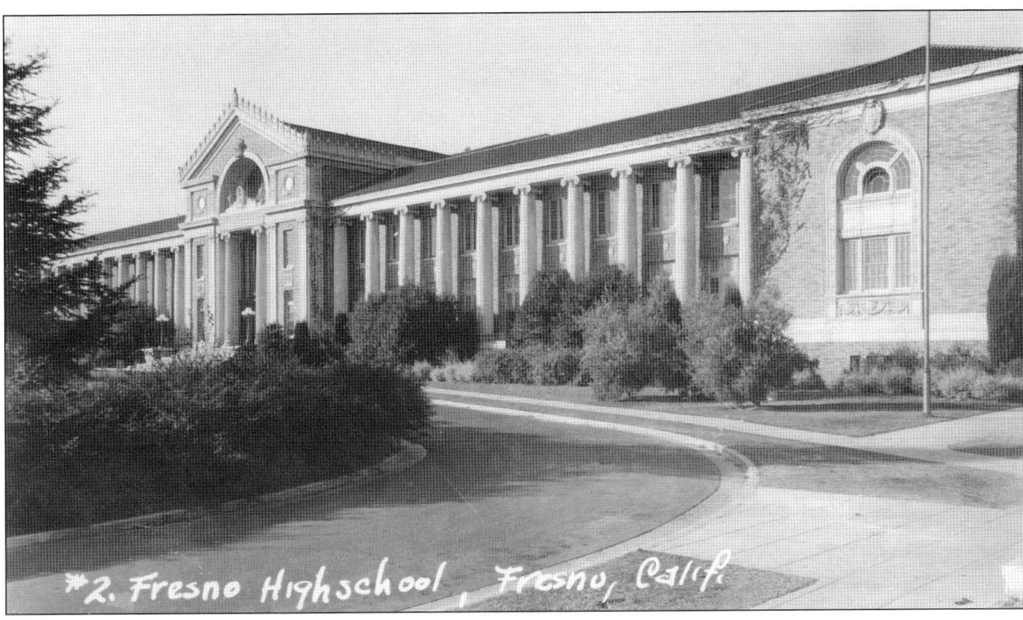

By 1919, Fresno High School had an enrollment of 1,732 students. To relieve overcrowding, a new Fresno High School was built in 1921 on Echo Street between University and Weldon Streets. Shown here is the first building there, which is still being used today.

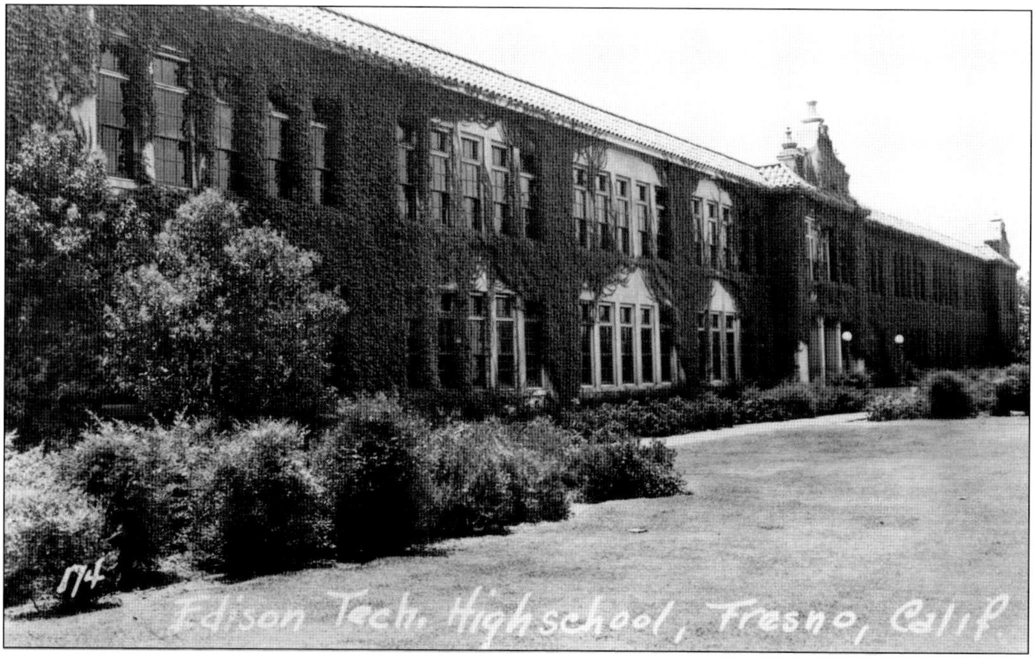

In 1926–1927, Edison Technical High School was built at Jones and California Streets. Edison High School is still at the same location, but all the original buildings were torn down in 1967 when an extensive rebuilding was done. Today, Edison High School is a magnet school, housing the district's computer-tech program, emphasizing math, science, and computers.

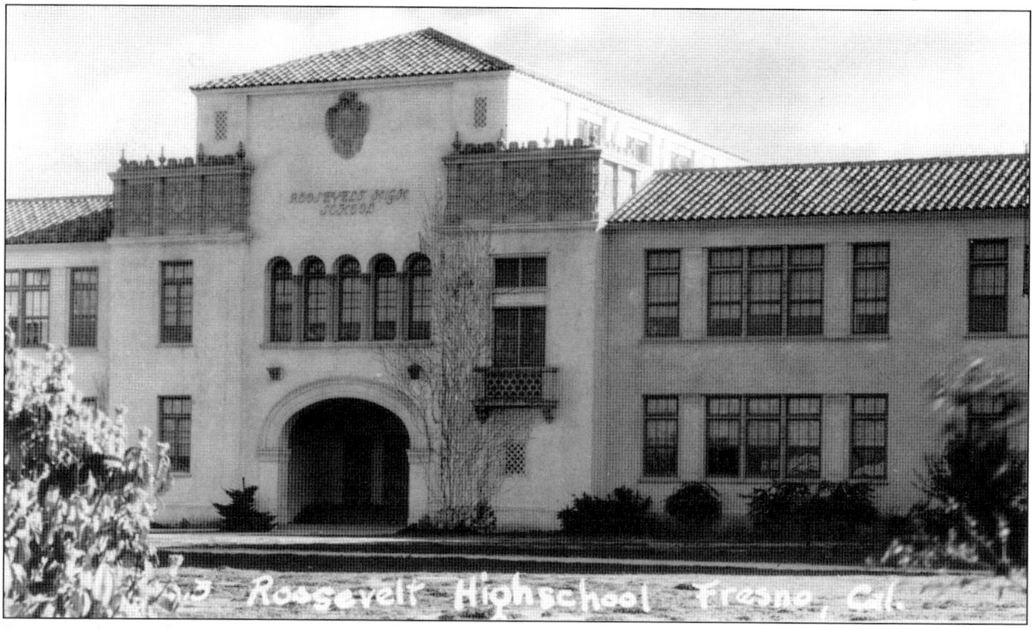

Roosevelt High School began operation on September 10, 1928. The main building was constructed in 1927 on the southeast corner of Cedar and Tulare Streets where it is still located today. In 1972, a large remodeling program was completed, adding a new administration building and science facilities. The high school served seventh to twelfth grades until 1978–1979, when it became a ninth-to-twelfth-grade high school.

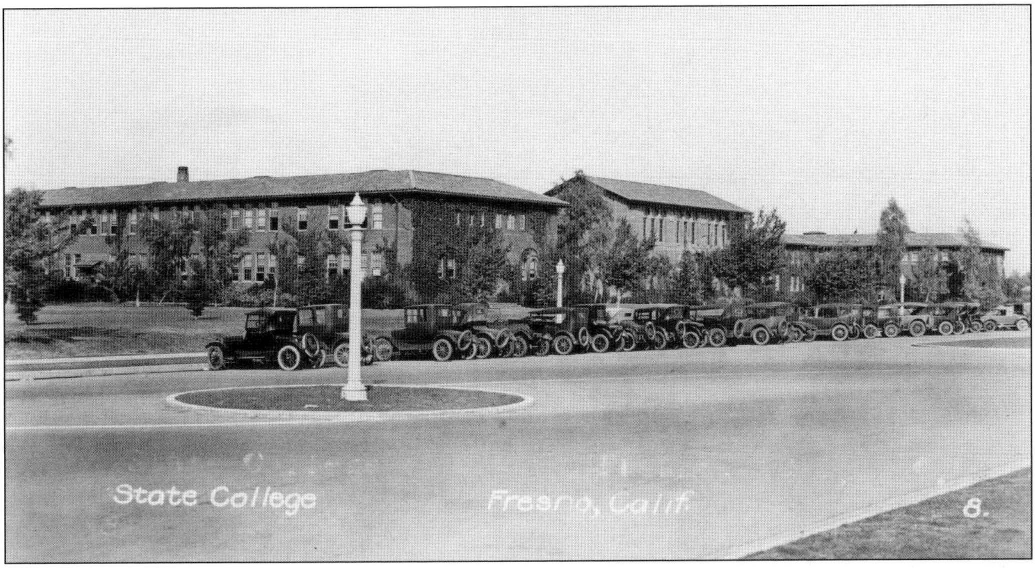

Fresno State Teachers' College came into existence in 1921 as a name change from the earlier Fresno State Normal School. The normal school left its Fresno High location and moved to Van Ness and McKinley Streets in 1913. The building shown was designed by Charles McDougal and was completed in 1915. (Fresno County Library.)

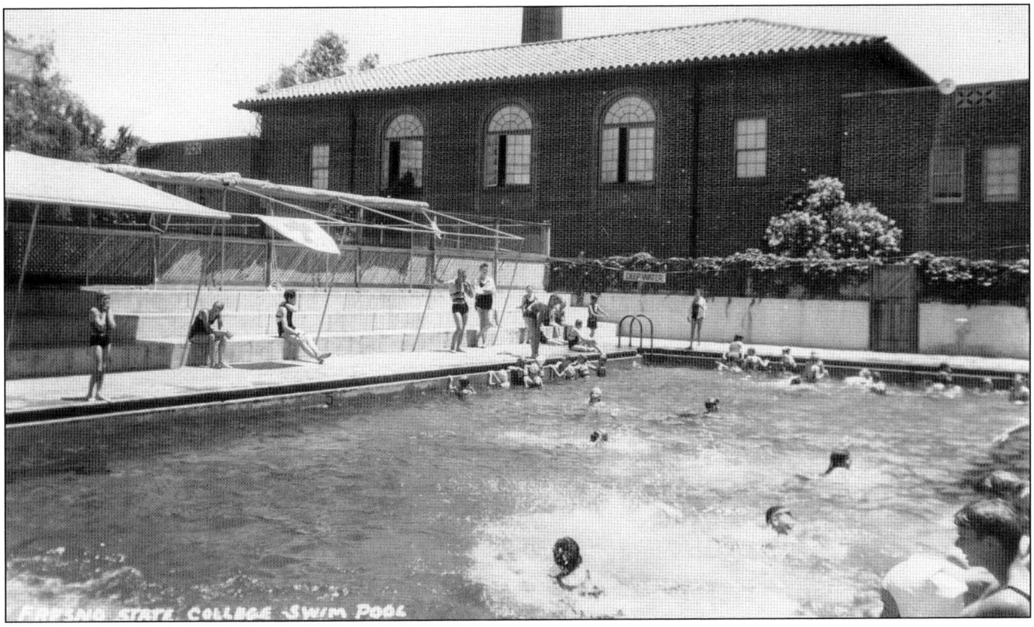

Fresno State College later came into existence in 1935 as a name change from Fresno State Teachers' College. Shown here is the swimming pool that was located on the north side of the main building. Today, the school is known as Fresno City College.

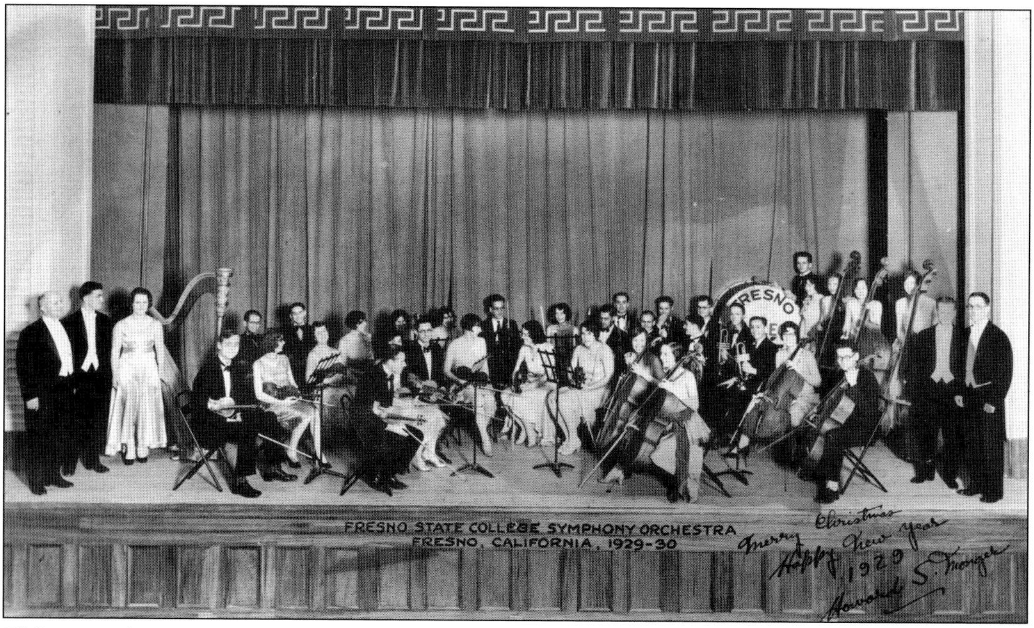

This season's greetings card, showing the Fresno State Symphony Orchestra, was sent in 1929 by Howard Monger. The name "Fresno State College" was being used instead of "Fresno Teachers' College" although the name was not formally changed until 1935.

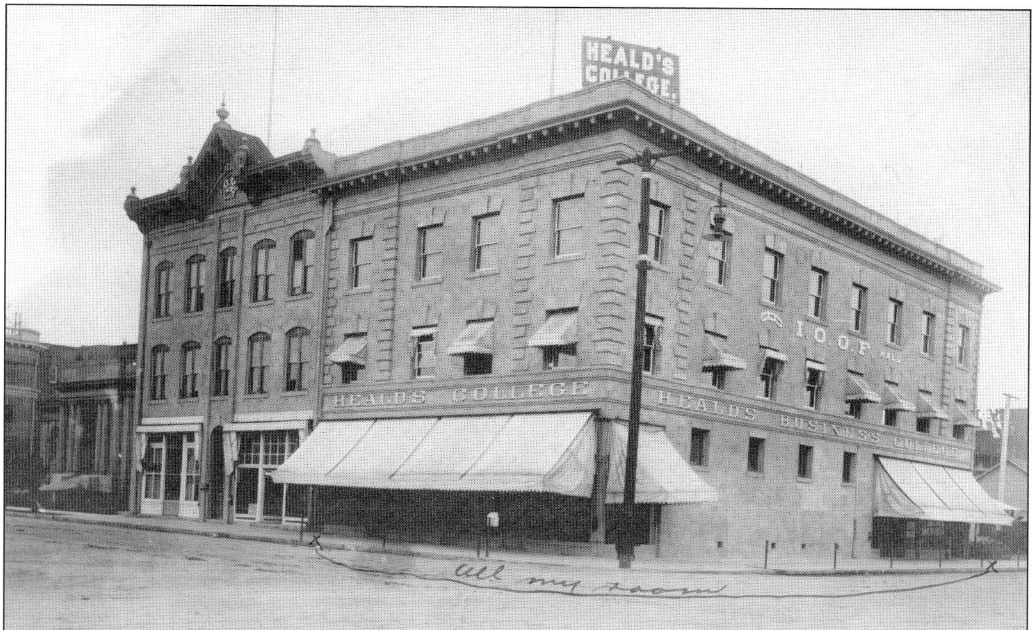

In 1916, Heald's College was located on the northeast corner of Merced Street and Broadway. The second floor of the building was shared by the business college and the IOOF Hall. The ground level was occupied by Smith-Walsh Auto Supply. (Fresno County Library.)

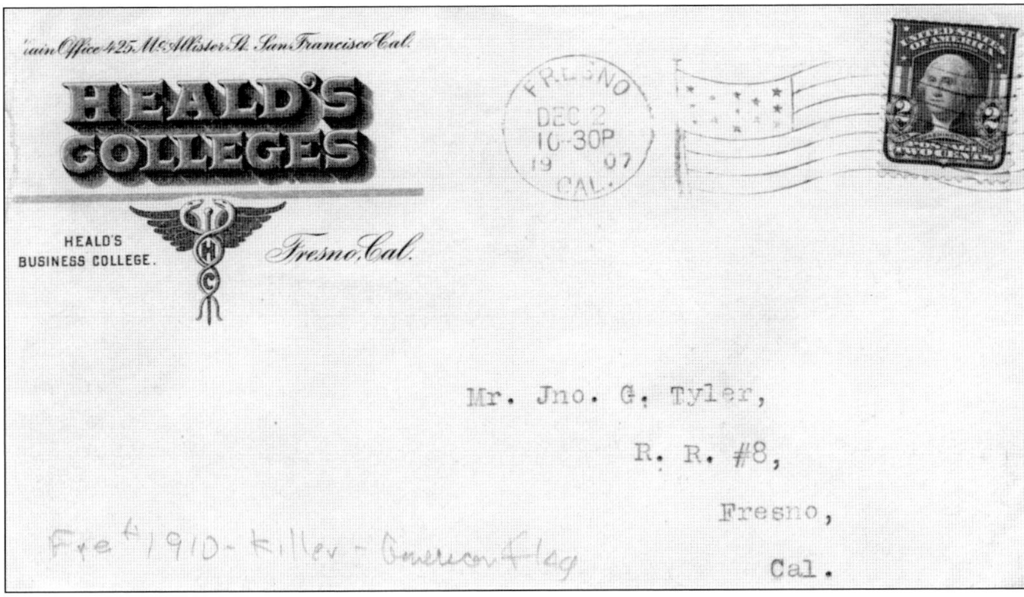

Heald's College began September 1, 1891, as Fresno Business College at the southeast corner of Tulare and Fulton Streets. Later the college was named Chestnut Wood Business College, then Heald's College, and finally Central California Commercial College, or "4 C's College." It has been in continuous operation for over 120 years.

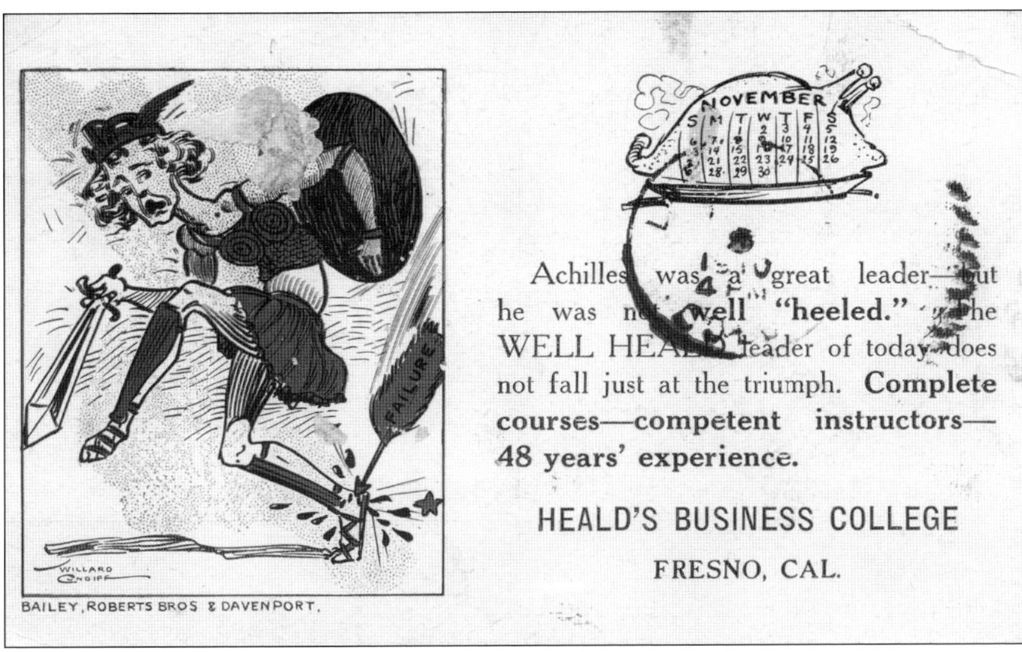

Calendar for 1907-1908

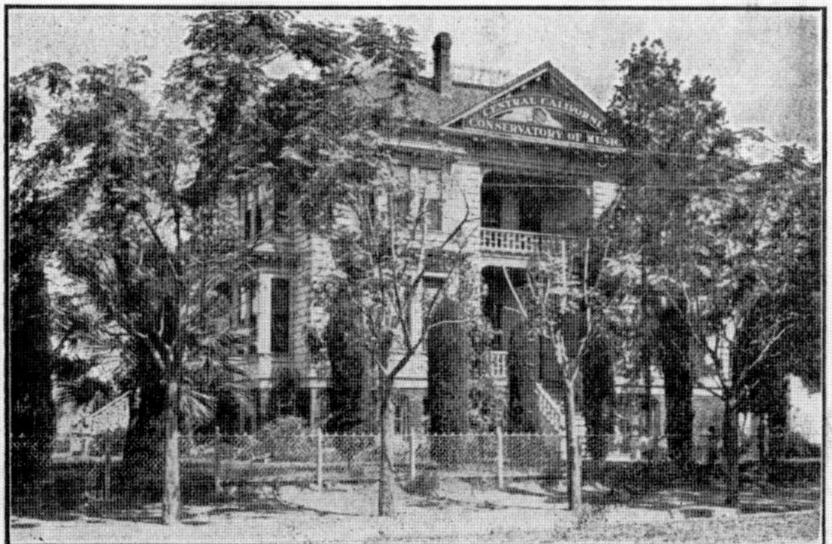

FALL TERM	SUMMER TERM
Begins Monday, Sept. 9, 1907	Begins Monday, June 1, 1908
Ends Saturday, Nov. 30, 1907	Ends Saturday, July 11, 1908
WINTER TERM	**CHRISTMAS VACATION**
Begins Thursday, Dec. 2, 1907	Begins Monday, Dec. 23, 1907
Ends Wednesday, March 4, 1908	Ends Wednesday, Jan. 1, 1908
SPRING TERM	**RECITAL WEEK**
Begins Thursday, March 5, 1908	Begins Monday, May 25, 1908
Ends Wednesday, May 27, 1908	Ends Saturday, May 30, 1908

Central California Conservatory of Music

Piano and Theory

1104 O Street, Fresno, California

Telephone Main 384 PAUL FAST, Director

The Central California Conservatory of Music was formed in 1896. The first director was Paul Fast, whose music education had been in Germany. As the college grew, the sounds of several musical instruments could be heard. Shown here is an advertising card from the early 1900s.

Eight

Agriculture

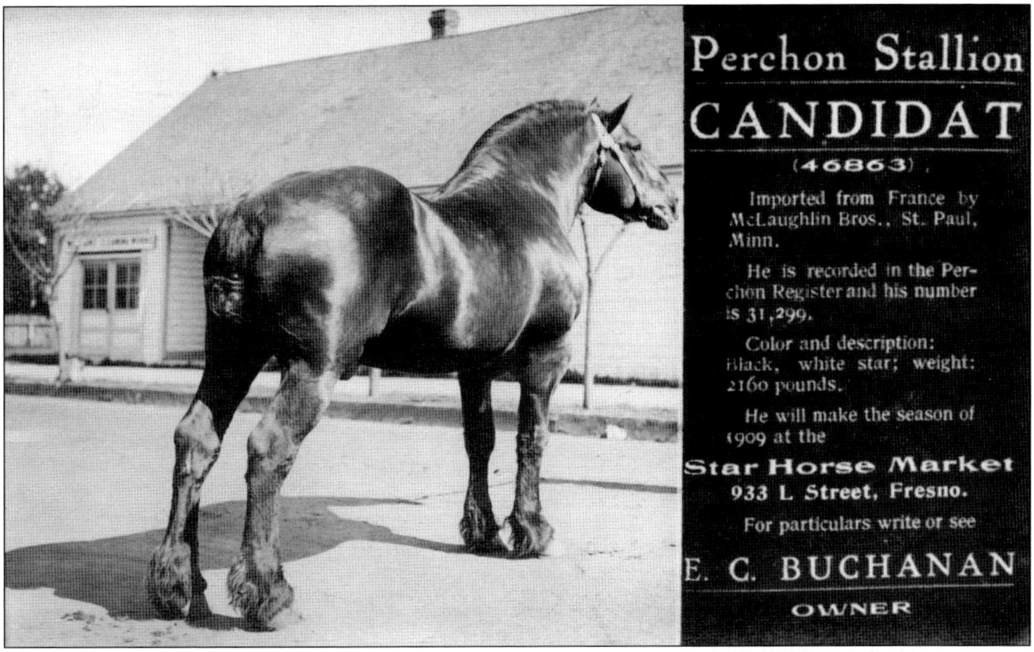

This postcard announces the stud service being offered by E.C. Buchanan for the Perchon stallion "Candidat." Horses of this size were highly desirable for their ability to pull farm equipment and livery wagons. Candidat was available at the Star Horse Market on 933 L Street. All you had to do was bring your mare for a visit. (Fresno County Library.)

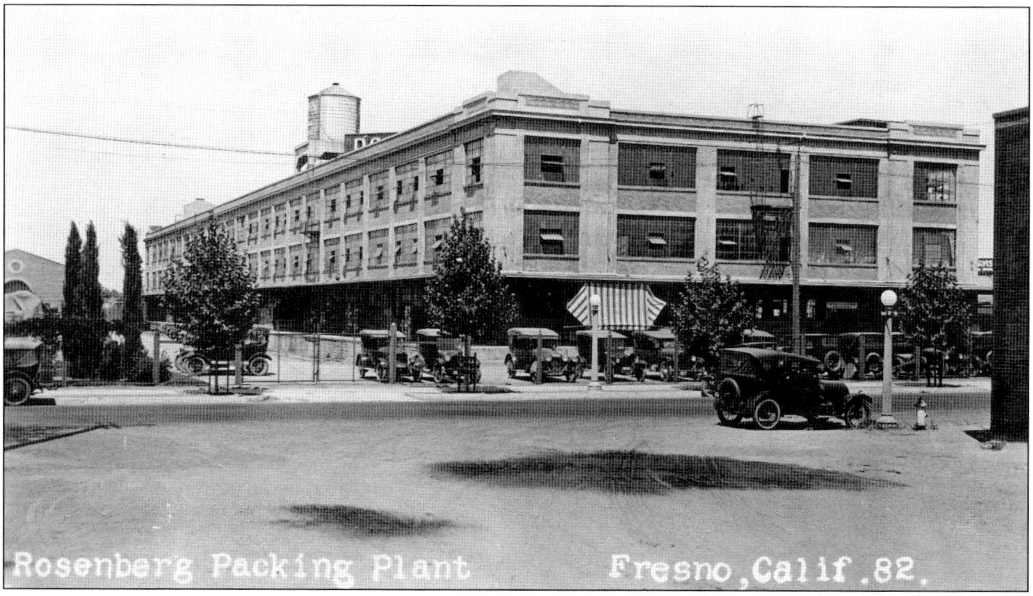

This postcard shows the "new" Rosenberg Packing Plant that was located at the south end of Broadway Street in the 1920s. The Rosenberg Brothers had the largest raisin packing operation in the world at that time.

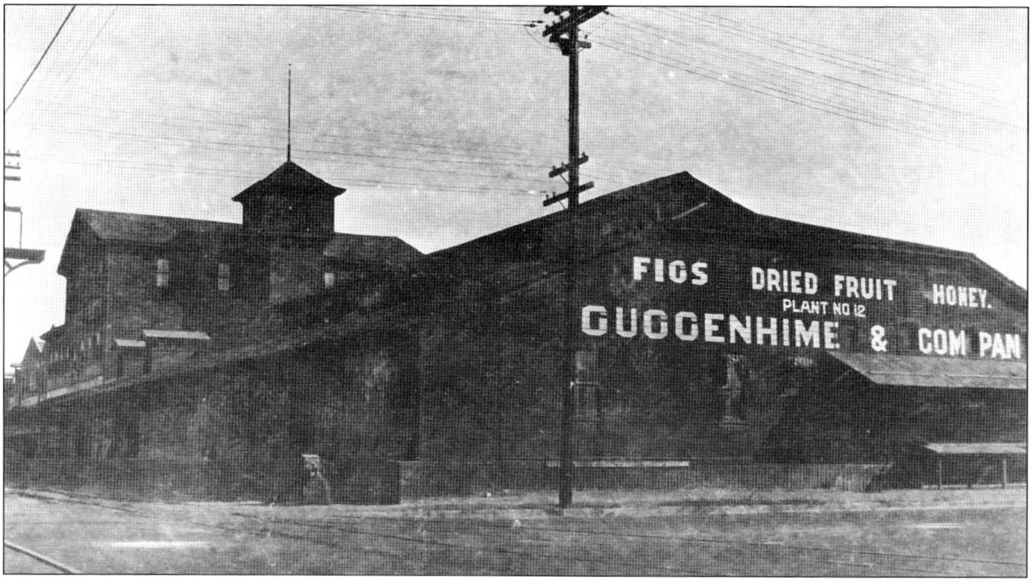

The Guggenhime & Company packing plant was located along the east side of Santa Fe Avenue along the Santa Fe railroad tracks and covered several blocks south of Tulare Street. After the decline of the Rosenberg Brothers packing operation, Guggenhime took the position as the largest independent packer.

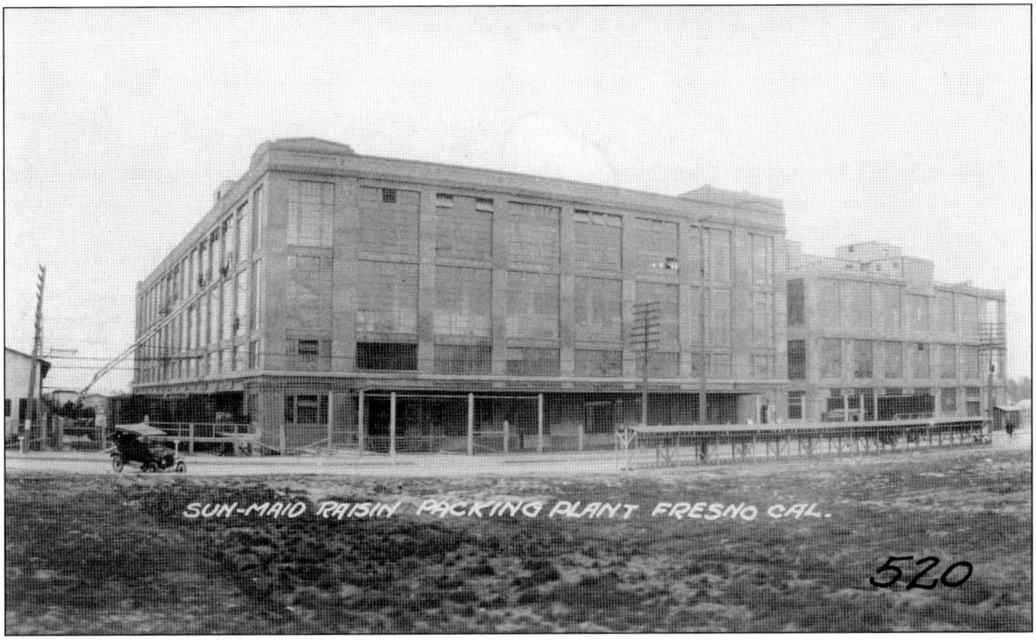

One of Fresno's most successful agricultural operations was Sun Maid Raisins. Originally formed under the name California Associated Raisin Company, it adopted the Sun Maid name in 1915. Shown here is the new Sun Maid packing plant no. 4, which was located on Hamilton and East Avenues.

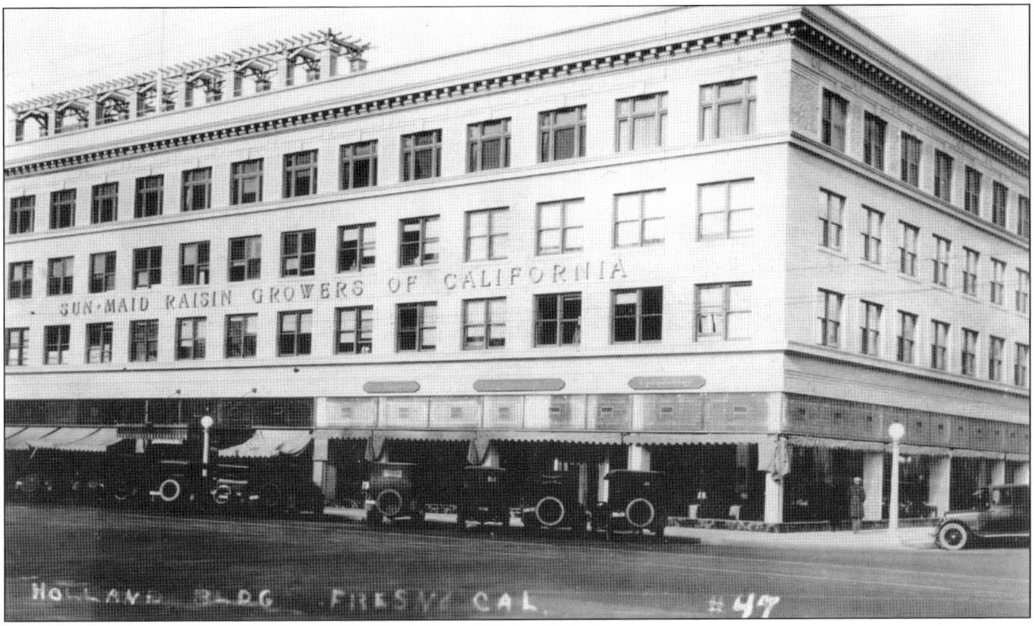

The Holland Building was located at the northwest corner of Fresno and L Streets and was the headquarters of the Sun Maid Raisin Growers of California in 1918.

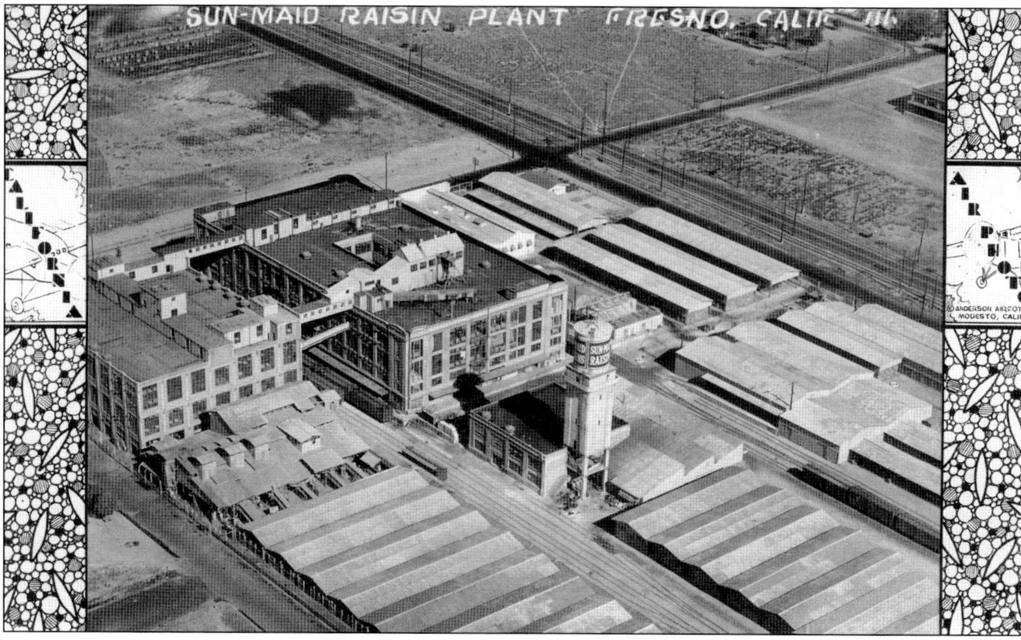

Here is an aerial view of the Sun Maid packing plant. The demand for raisins was so great that the company ran out of operating room. In 1964, the operation was moved to Kingsburg, California.

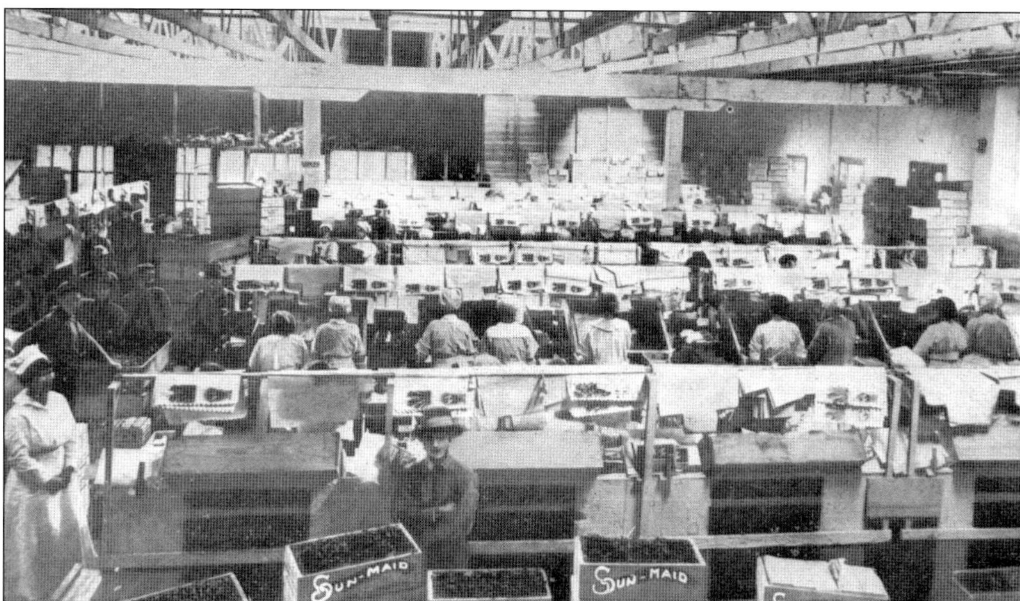

Here is a view of the interior of the Sun Maid Raisin packinghouse in Fresno. Workers were employed to fill the cartons by hand, as well as hand sorting the product to remove defective raisins. (Fresno County Library.)

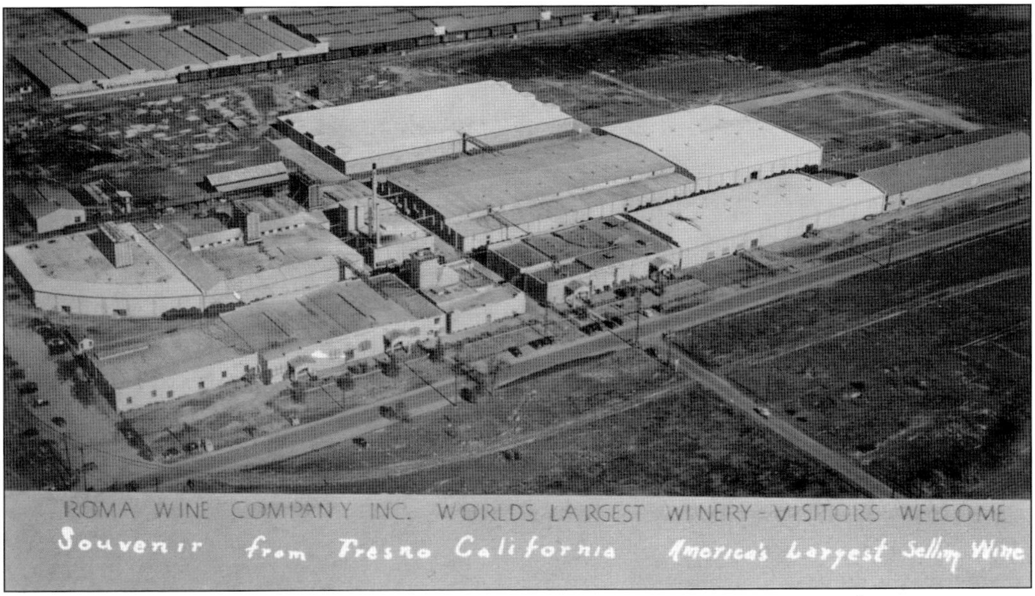

Pictured here is the Roma Wine Company, which at one time was the world's largest single winery. It was owned by John B. Cella, who had two other wineries in Lodi and Healdsburg. His plan was to produce only sweet wines and brandy at the Fresno operation. At its peak, the facility produced 10 million gallons of wine per year and bottled 8,500 cases of wine per day.

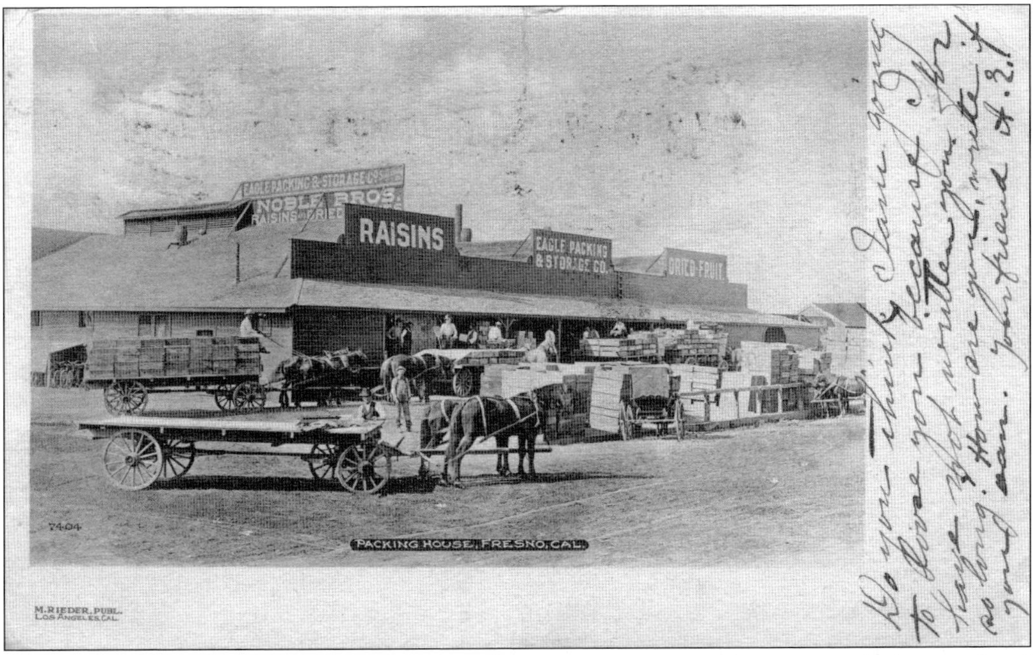

Here is an exterior view of the Eagle Packing & Storage Co packinghouse, which specialized in raisins and dried fruit. This card was postmarked November 6, 1905, and was sent to Miss Sparks of Brooklyn, New York. The message reads, "Do you think I am going to leave you because I have not written you for so long? How are you. Write if you can. Your Friend A.S."

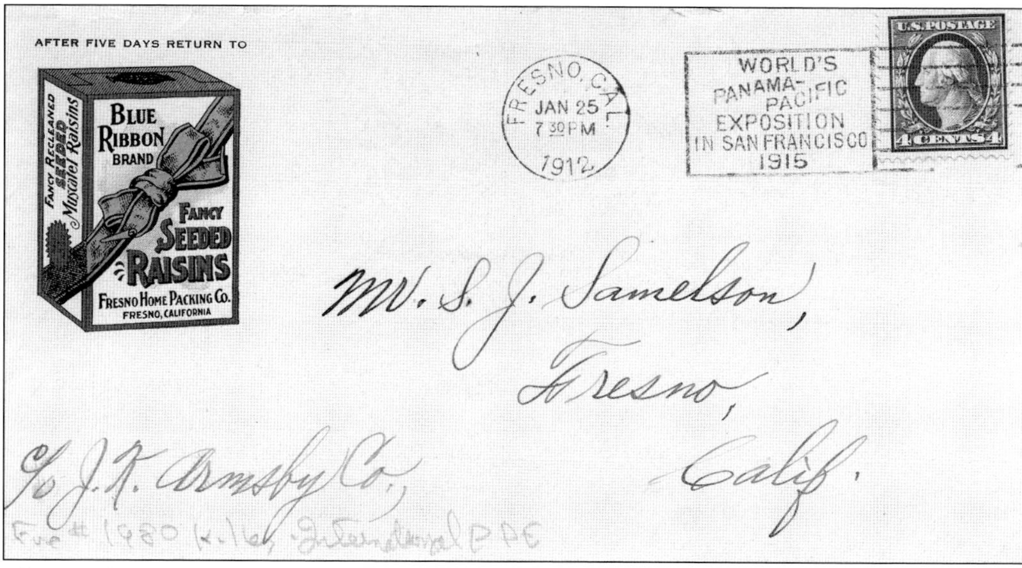

The envelope shown has an illustrated advertisement for Blue Ribbon Brand Fancy Seedless Raisins, which were packed by the Fresno Home Packing Company. The company was one of the first to employ a mechanical peach peeler, which revolutionized the packing industry.

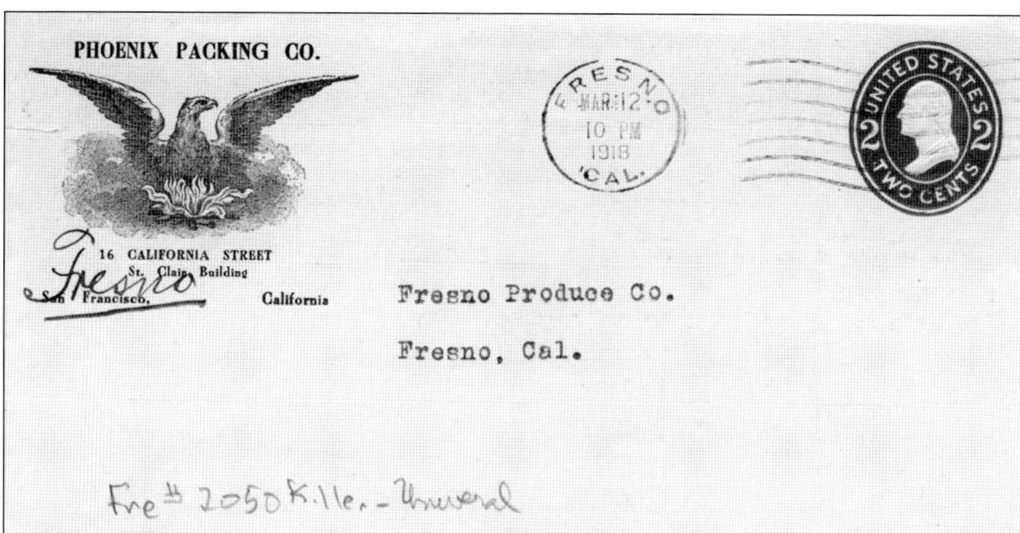

The Phoenix Packing Company was headquartered at 16 California Street in San Francisco, but had a packinghouse in Fresno between Mariposa and Tulare Streets. Shown here is an envelope with the company logo.

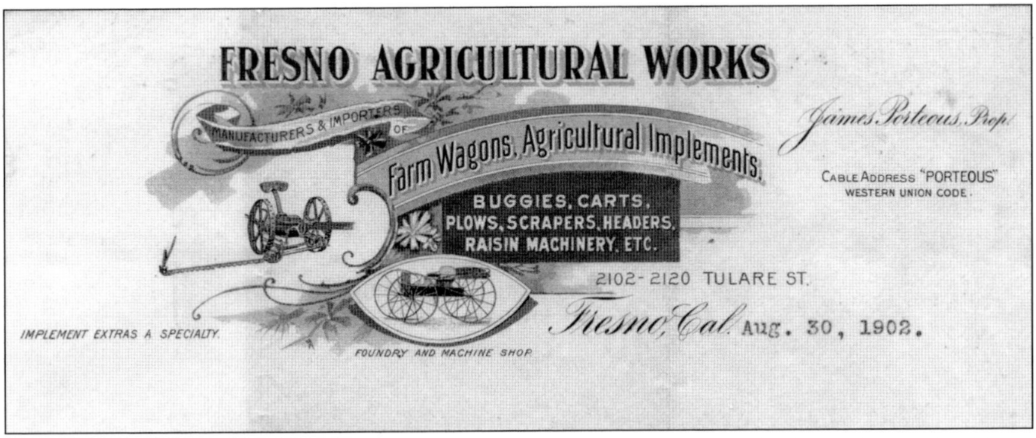

The Fresno Agricultural Works was started by James Porteous in 1876 on the south side of Tulare Street, across from the county courthouse. The company developed The Fresno Scraper, a farm implement that easily moved dirt. The scraper was sold all over the United States and the world. In 1991, The Fresno Scraper was listed by the American Society of Mechanical Engineers as an International Historic Engineering Landmark.

By 1933, the Fresno Agricultural Works manufactured and sold many kinds of farm implements, from pumps to harrows. In 1952, the hardware portion of the business was sold to John Rosetta, and the store was renamed Fresno Ag Hardware. The store continues to operate today.

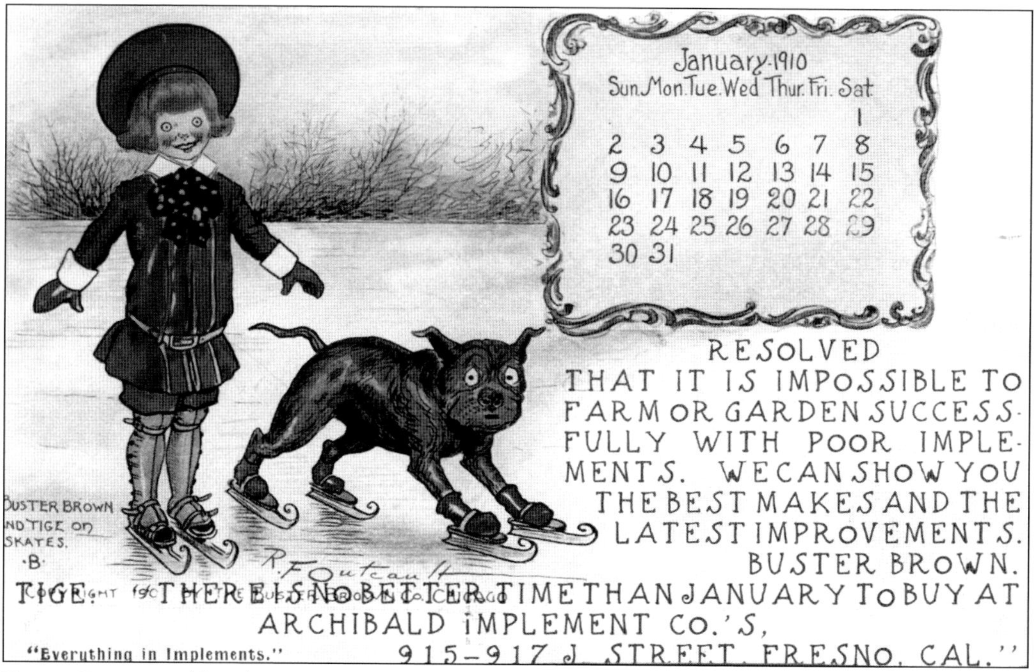

Buster Brown and his dog Tige were common advertising trademarks utilized in early publicity. Shown here is a January 1910 postcard for the Archibald Implement Company, which was located at 915–917 J Street (Fulton). Archibald Implement would set up an annual display at the Fresno County Fair so that farmers could see the latest in farm machinery.

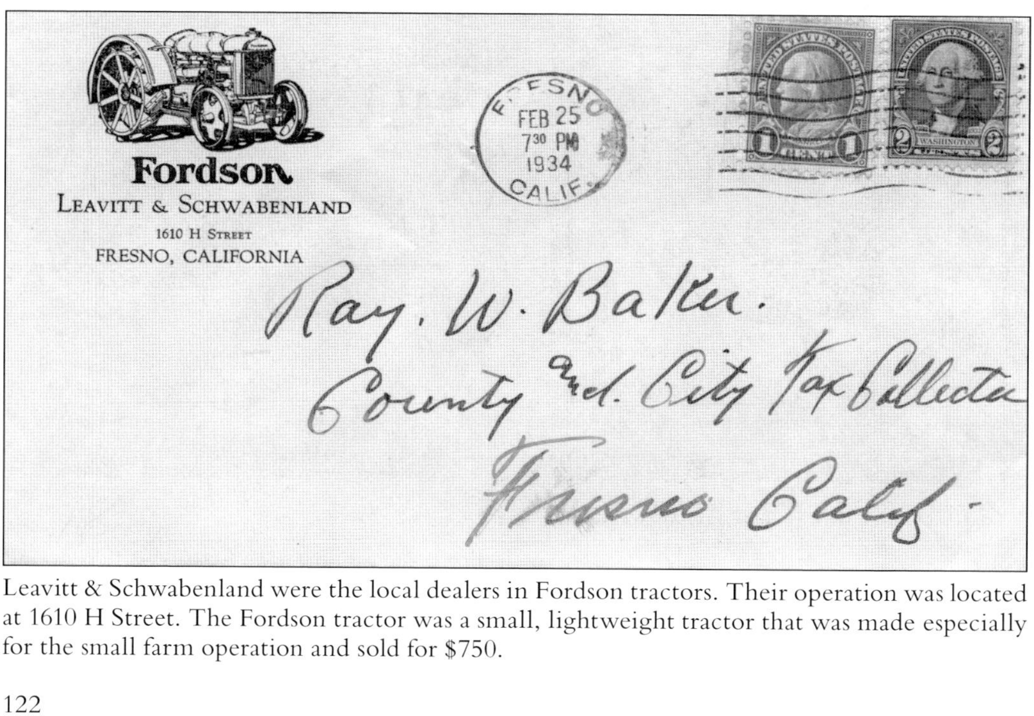

Leavitt & Schwabenland were the local dealers in Fordson tractors. Their operation was located at 1610 H Street. The Fordson tractor was a small, lightweight tractor that was made especially for the small farm operation and sold for $750.

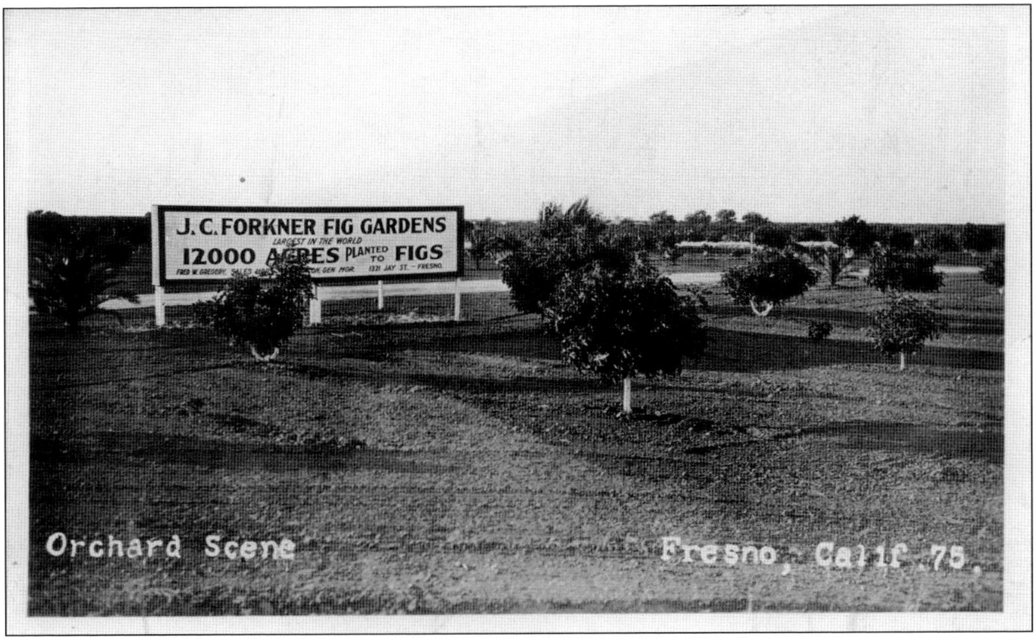

In 1912, James Clayton Forkner set out to develop 12,000 acres of "hog wallow land" situated between the northern city limits and the San Joaquin River into fig orchards. Using a fleet of Fordson tractors pulling Fresno Scrapers, he prepared the land for irrigation and built a 25-mile canal that ran from the Kings River to his property. This postcard advertises the sale of land in the "Fig Gardens."

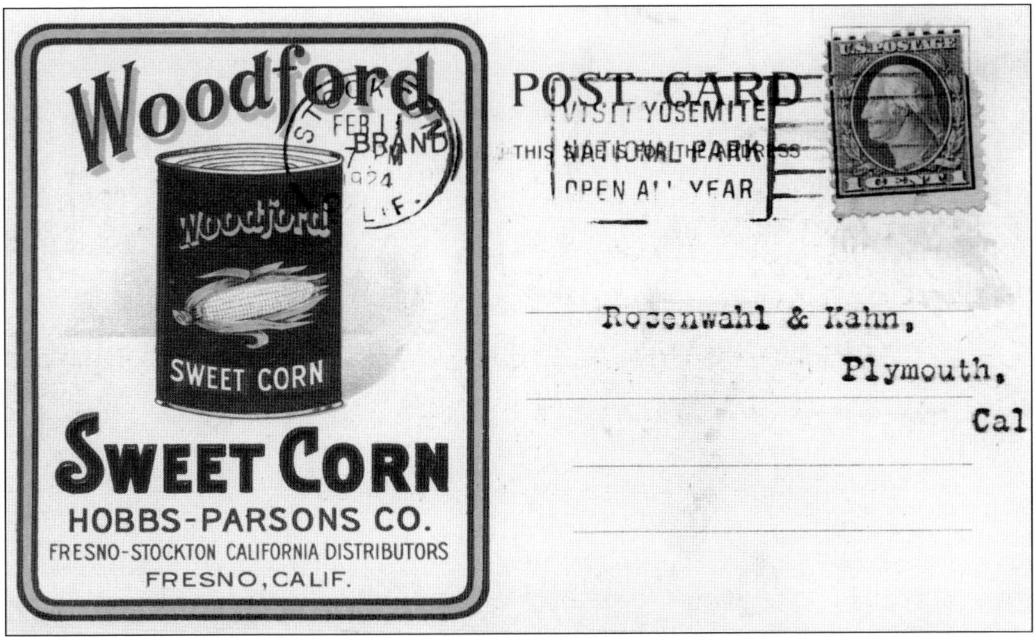

Hobbs-Parsons Company was a major wholesale produce supplier for local markets and was located at 951 H Street, between Tulare and Inyo Streets. It was founded in 1892 by Albert L. and Samuel S. Parsons. The business changed hands and was owned by the Powell and Munger Family for over 70 years. The original long building still stands on H Street.

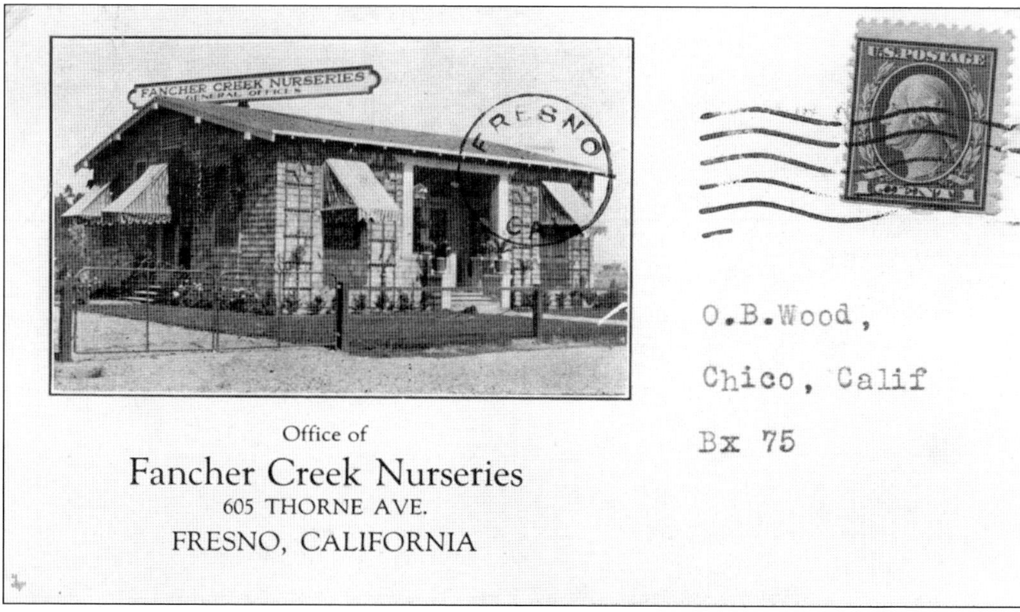

Fancher Creek Nurseries was located at 605 Thorne Avenue and was owned and managed by George C. Roeding, a trained horticulturist. George was the son of Frederick C. Roeding, who donated 118 acres of land, which became Roeding Park, Fresno's first major park. George was responsible for nurturing the park in its infancy and brought it to life.

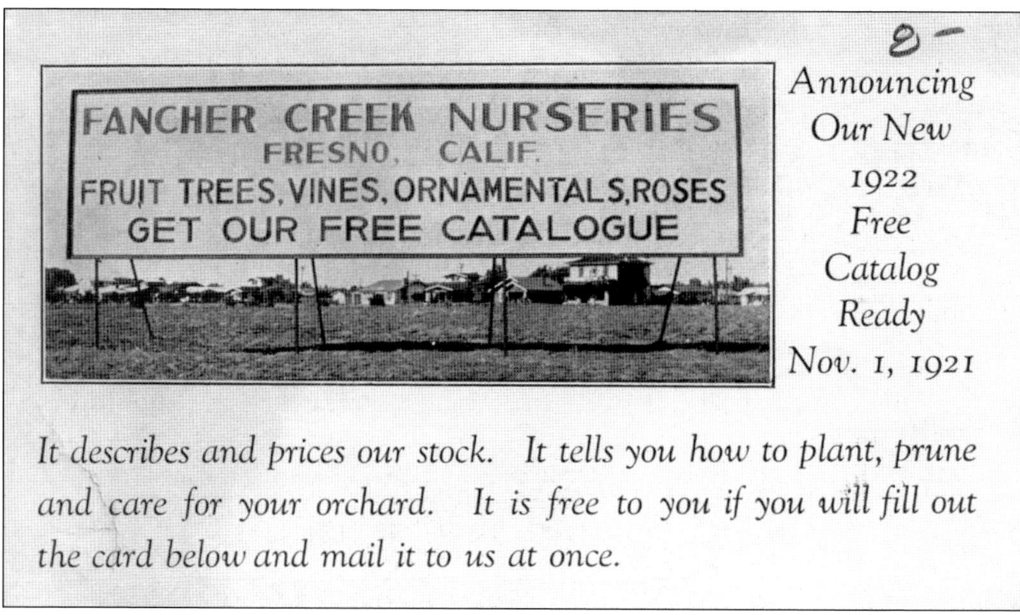

Fancher Creek was one of the nurseries that supplied farmers with the latest varieties of fruit trees, grape stock, and seeds for all kinds of plants. This postcard announces that the new 1922 catalog would be ready November 1, 1921.

Andrew Mattei, a Swiss vintner, came to Fresno in 1887. By 1902, his winery, located south of Fresno, was producing 3,000 gallons of wine and brandy annually. Between 1910 and 1919, he was considered to be the nation's largest vintner and wine maker. During Prohibition, the company continued to use the same business envelopes, but rubber-stamped with the words "non-beverage."

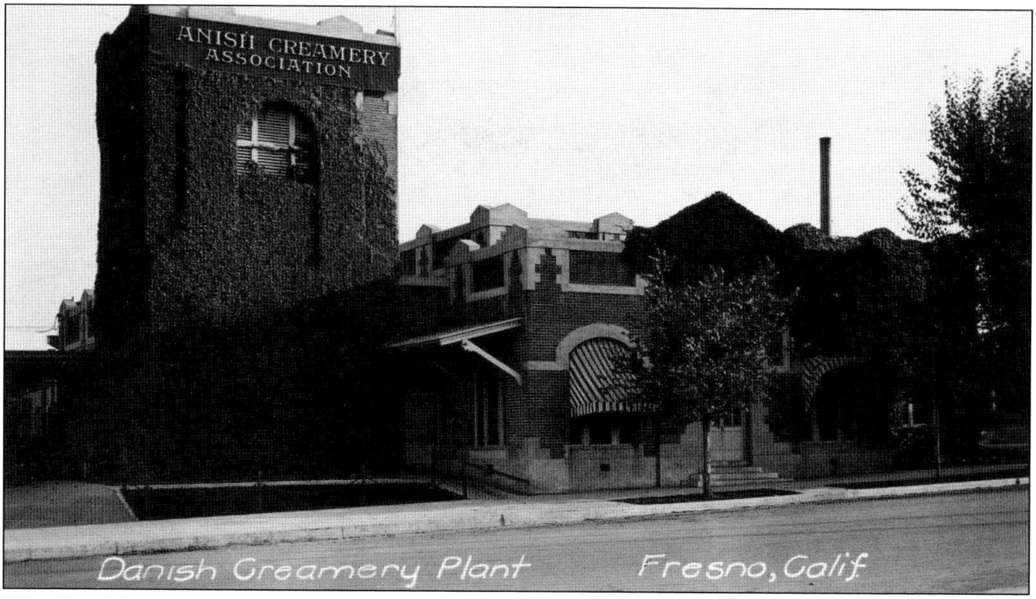

The Danish Creamery Association was formed in 1895 and is still located at 755 F Street. Shown here is the facility that was built in 1910. The creamery processes butter, dried skim milk, and dried buttermilk. It has become the nation's oldest milk processing dairy products cooperative.

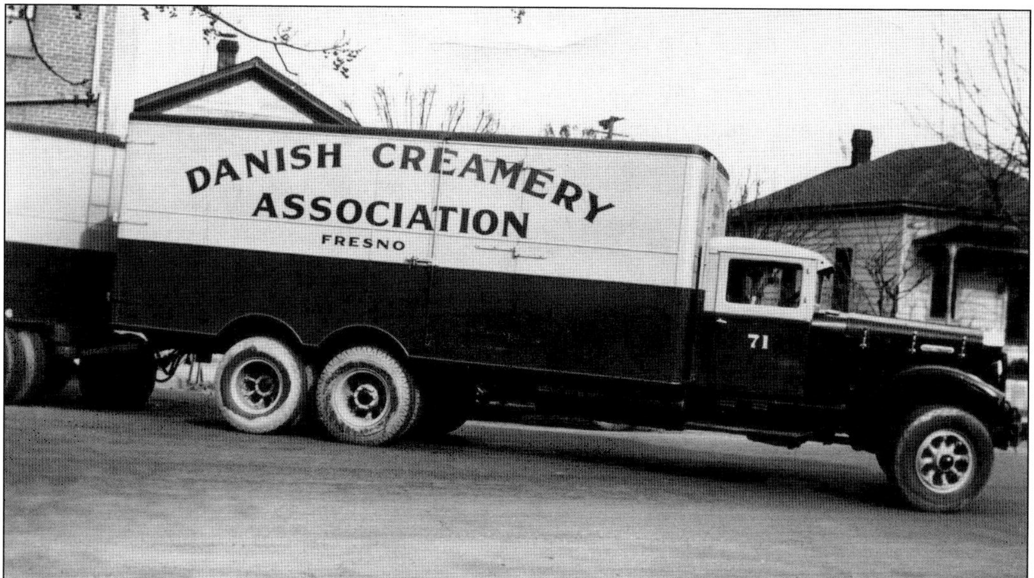

Here is a Danish Creamery Association truck and trailer loading at the creamery warehouse. By the 1930s Danish Creamery had become the district creamery, replacing the many small individual community creameries throughout the county.

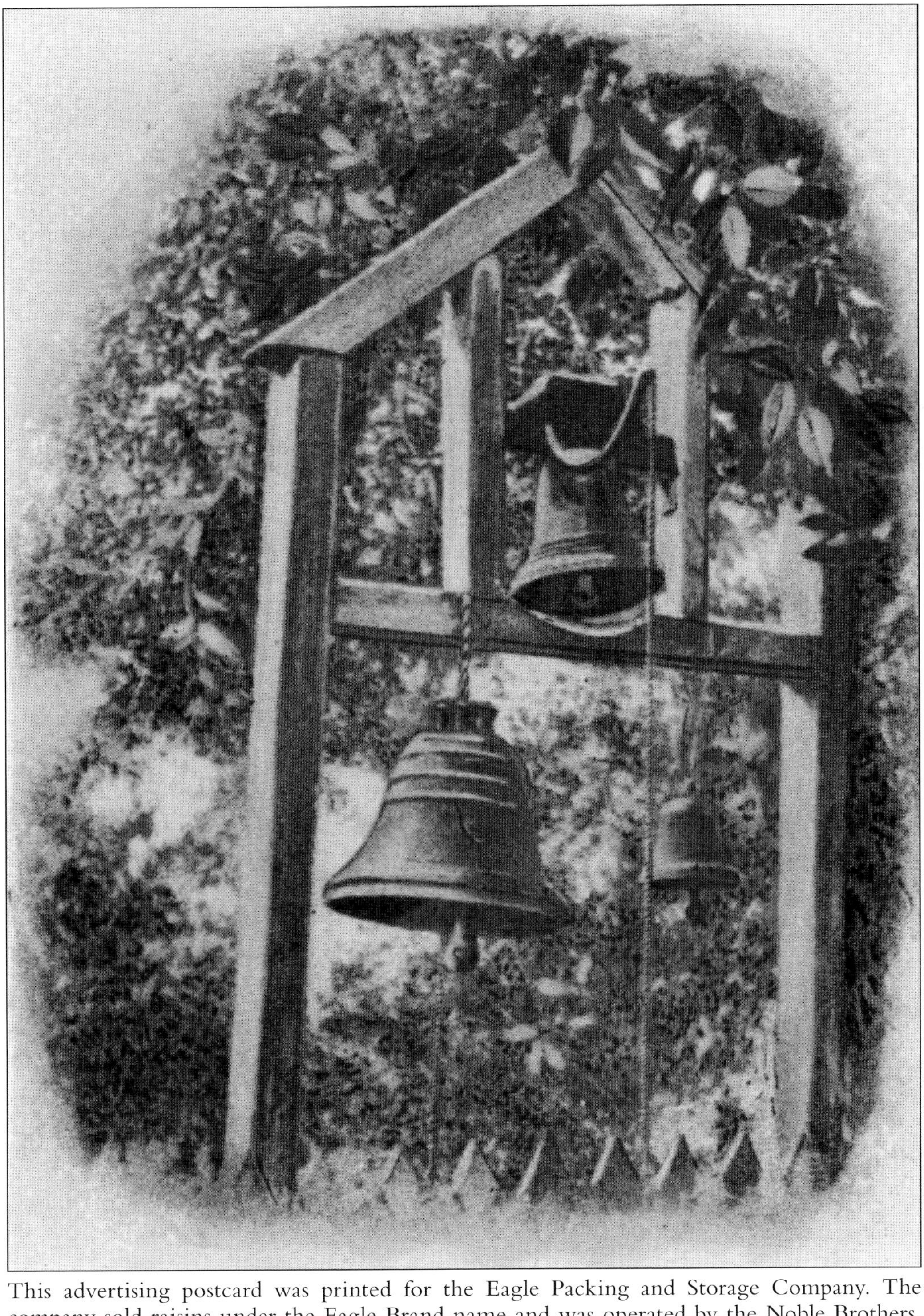

This advertising postcard was printed for the Eagle Packing and Storage Company. The company sold raisins under the Eagle Brand name and was operated by the Noble Brothers, shippers of raisins and other dried fruits.

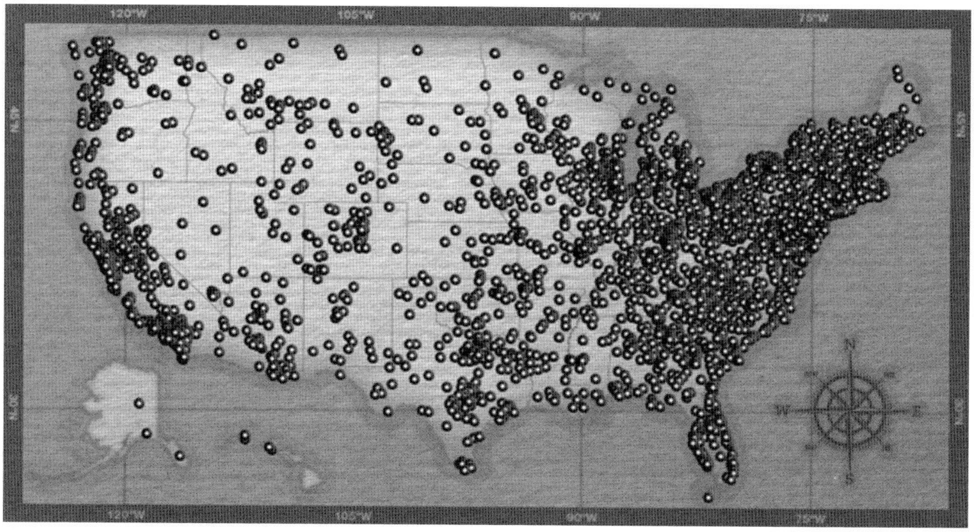